# FANTASTIC FORM

'it is a definite social relationship between men that assumes ...
the fantastic form of a relation between things ... This I call the
Fetishism which attaches itself to the products of labour so soon
as they are produced as commodities'

Karl Marx, *Capital*, vol. 1

BILL RISEBERO

# FANTASTIC FORM

## ARCHITECTURE AND PLANNING TODAY

NEW AMSTERDAM, NEW YORK

First published in the United States of America, 1992, by
New Amsterdam Books by arrangement with The Herbert Press
Limited, London.

House editor: Julia MacKenzie
Designed by Pauline Harrison

Set in Aldus
Printed and bound in Great Britain.

New Amsterdam Books
New York

The Library of Congress Cataloging in Publication Data is
available.

ISBN 1–56131–057–3

# Contents

# To Matthew

## Acknowledgements

Many of the themes in this book have been discussed with colleagues and students at the Polytechnic of East London and Strathclyde University. I am grateful to them all, particularly to Gillian Elinor for arranging a research seminar and to Jane Riches and Jonathan Charley for their generosity with ideas.

I am grateful too for the long-standing support of Mike Edwards and his colleagues at BISS, and of the *A3 Times* editorial team, especially Nasser Golzari, Rex Henry and Nicholas Hobbs, with their wide knowledge of modern architecture.

The book itself has been much improved by the perceptive, often sceptical, criticism of Pat Daunt, Julia MacKenzie's helpful editorship, and Diana LeCore's indexing.

David and Brenda Herbert have once again been both patient and tolerant, and my wife Christine has been enormously supportive, as always.

# 1 Production and Ideology – the role of modernism

In Le Corbusier's Villa Savoye, the Domnarkomfin apartments by Ginsburg or Mendelsohn's De La Warr Pavilion we see a clear, consistent theory at work: sheer plain walls, large areas of glass, flat roofs and the fluid arrangement of three-dimensional space express the designers' excitement at the scope of the twentieth-century building process – an excitement not only in a new aesthetic but also at the prospect of real social progress. Physical form and social content are brought together. These buildings would probably be most people's idea of modern architecture. On the other hand, they are far from contemporary; all were built over half a century ago, before most people alive today were born.

By contrast, John Outram's pumping station in the Isle of Dogs or Robert Venturi's extension to the National Gallery in London are contemporary buildings, but their superficially Classical or even pre-Classical architectural imagery is a deliberate denial of what we think of as modernism, both aesthetically and socially. We use the term 'post-modern' to make the distinction.

Richard Rogers's buildings, such as the Pompidou Centre or Lloyd's, offer a third image. They are at once contemporary and modern, though their modernity, with its spectacular use of complex forms and glossy, 'high-tech' materials, differs considerably from the calm elegance of the early examples cited above. More importantly, today's buildings, separated by such a historical gulf from the heroic buildings of the early modern period, do not represent a similar concern with social change.

It is an explicable paradox therefore that there can be modern architecture which is not contemporary, contemporary architecture which is not modern, and new architecture which may be called modern but in such a different sense from the 'old' modern that the terms are barely synonymous.

For some critics of modernism, recent architecture has thankfully become more pluralist and varied; to some modernists, it has simply become directionless and confused. In place of the early modernists' ideological conviction that they were changing the world for the better is the feeling that the task of changing anything is too great even to attempt. In place of an architecture informed by a more or less consistent

1

body of theory, there are now various theories and various practices with little or no discernible relationship with each other.

Since the Prince of Wales's Hampton Court speech in 1984, in which he criticized architects and the proposals for the National Gallery extension and for Mansion House Square, media coverage of architecture has become more usual. However, familiarity through the colour supplements with the bewildering variety of current architectural styles does not necessarily help people to understand what is going on.

I shall try to make sense out of this pluralist – or confusing – picture. To do this it will be necessary to go much further than a merely stylistic debate between modernism and post-modernism. This is not simply because architecture is much more than a matter of style – though it obviously is that. More importantly, it is because architecture, like all branches of human culture, can be understood only if one first recognizes and understands the fundamental forces at work in society, of which culture is merely a manifestation. We must begin not with architectural theory but with real life. As Marx said in one of his most famous formulations:

> The mode of production of material life conditions the social, political and intellectual life process in general. It is not the consciousness of men that determines their being but, on the contrary, their social being that determines their consciousness.[1]

The 'social being' of Britain in the early nineties is one of great contrasts. A 1989 report for the Salvation Army[2] estimated that around 75,000 people were homeless in London. Almost no new public housing is being built in London, but twelve million square feet of high-tech offices are under construction at Canary Wharf and more are planned for Kings Cross and Spitalfields. The eighties saw the construction of some of Britain's most spectacular postwar buildings, but also the deterioration of the general urban environment to a worse state than at any time since the forties.

Ironically, at a time when the aesthetic aspects of architecture have attracted a lot of attention in the press, there appears to be very little serious architectural debate on more fundamental questions – homelessness, the collapse of the housing system, the commercial exploitation of our cities. It seems to me important to look at our recent architectural and planning history and to try and understand the current situation. Architecture should be seen not only in aesthetic terms but also as an important aspect of our social life, affected by and in some ways affecting our economic system and the changes which take place within it. Nothing, says Hegel, can be understood in isolation; cause and effect are not simplistic and linear but are part of a complex, interlinking system: the world is in a constant state of change and development; everything produces its own negation, and there is a tendency towards negation of

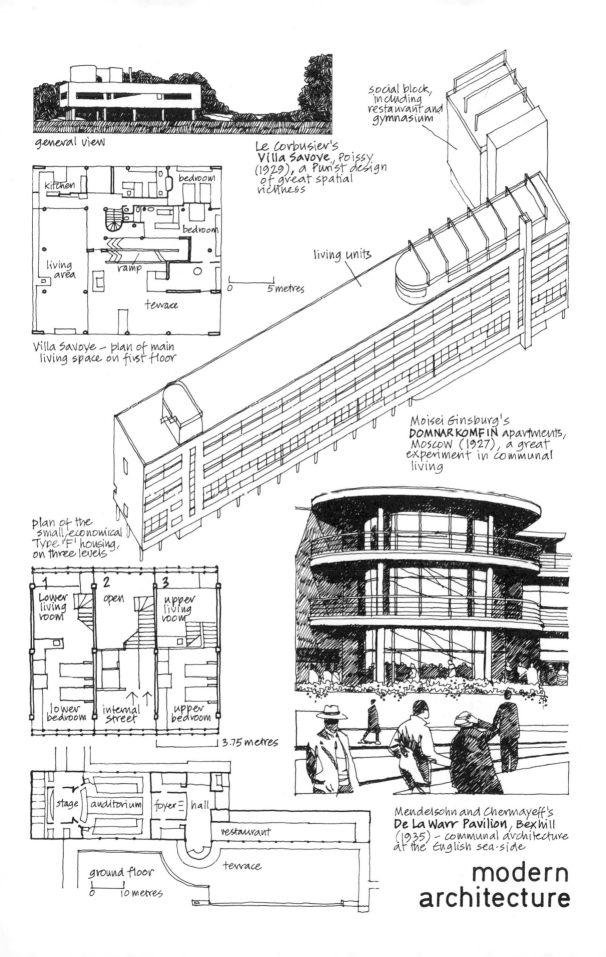

general view

Le Corbusier's **Villa Savoye**, Poissy (1929), a Purist design of great spatial richness

kitchen

bedroom

bedroom

living area

ramp

terrace

Villa Savoye – plan of main living space on first floor

0    5 metres

social block, including restaurant and gymnasium

living units

Moisei Ginsburg's **DOMNARKOMFIN** apartments, Moscow (1927), a great experiment in communal living

Plan of the small, economical Type 'F' housing, on three levels

| 1 | 2 | 3 |
|---|---|---|
| Lower living room | open | upper living room |
| lower bedroom | internal street | upper bedroom |

3.75 metres

stage    auditorium    foyer    hall

restaurant

ground floor

terrace

0    10 metres

Mendelsohn and Chermayeff's **De La Warr Pavilion**, Bexhill (1935) – communal architecture at the English sea-side

# modern architecture

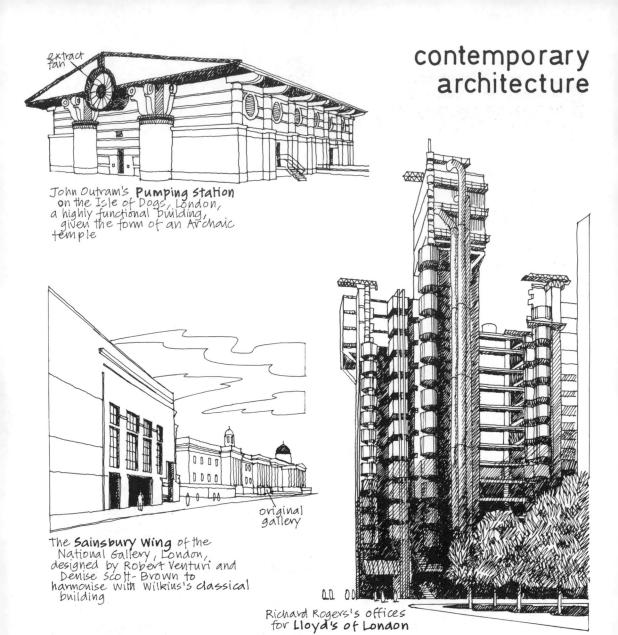

John Outram's **Pumping Station** on the Isle of Dogs, London, a highly functional building, given the form of an Archaic temple

extract fan

The **Sainsbury Wing** of the National Gallery, London, designed by Robert Venturi and Denise Scott-Brown to harmonise with Wilkins's classical building

original gallery

Richard Rogers's offices for **Lloyd's of London**

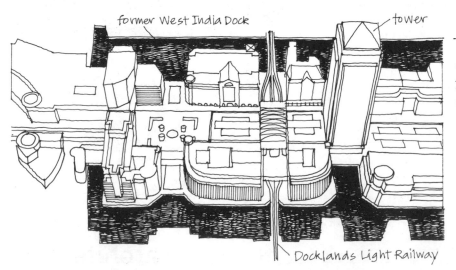

former West India Dock

tower

the **Canary Wharf** development on London's Isle of Dogs – the tower block designed by Cesar Pelli

Docklands Light Railway

the negation itself. A dialectical approach, then, by seeking to recognize and understand the forces at work in society, can help to make sense of architectural history as it happens and can lead, what is more, towards a dynamic and creative outcome.

This book deals mainly with Britain, though not exclusively. It is difficult to confine architectural ideas and techniques – more so the economic forces which determine them – within national boundaries. It will be necessary to refer not only to the traditional sources of influence on British architecture, such as Germany and France, and to the more universal and current influence of the United States, but also, for example, to what has happened in eastern Europe.

However, the British experience in the eighties does demonstrate with great force the workings of international capital and its effects on architecture. In some respects Britain is an exemplar of an overall situation, in others it is extreme and untypical. The extent to which the British state has strengthened its political control over society while allowing the private sector to dominate economic life is more marked than in most of the rest of Europe. This of course has much to do with the phenomenon of Thatcherism, but although Thatcherism did have an undoubted political influence, it was still much more an effect than it was a cause. The political circumstances of 1979 were created by the contradictions of our modern economic system; these rather than the politics of this or that party will continue to be the principal determinants of the way society works and architecture is produced.

This first chapter will look at 'modern' architecture and all that it represents, because the establishment of modernism, its successes and failures, and the reactions against it, form the background from which current architectural ideas and practice have emerged. We must begin by recognizing modernism as more than a style, a merely visual expression. It needs to be defined in a wider and deeper way, one which does justice to its historic economic and social significance, as well as its aesthetic role. Modernism strives for a unity of theory and practice; its ideology demonstrates a very particular view of the contemporary world, and its forms seek to express this as clearly as possible. Neither ideology nor forms would be possible outside the context of an advanced industrial society, for it is from the dynamism of capitalism that both the ideas and the techniques have emerged. At the same time, modernism emerged to challenge capitalist society: rejection; confrontation; the possibility of some dramatic – even violent – change from the status quo. This is where we see the dialectical significance of modernism: industrial capitalism has created it, but it strives to become the negation of capitalist society. And in its turn capitalism strives, in its various ways, to achieve the negation of modernism.

5

The work of Marshall Berman[3] identifies a number of philosophic strands in the complex web of modernism. Some modernists advocate detachment from the contemporary world, and Berman points to the insistence of Barthes and the structuralists that the artist 'turns his back on society and confronts the world of objects without going through any of the forms of History or social life'.[4]

To others, modernism is a permanent revolt, a confrontation with today's world and its morality. It should establish, in the words of Harold Rosenberg, 'a tradition of overthrowing tradition'.

Berman also identifies a third approach, what he calls 'the affirmative vision of modernism'. This is the positive approach, whereby 'the great romance of construction' has been pursued over the years by a number of modernists 'from Carlyle and Marx to Tatlin and Calder, Le Corbusier and Frank Lloyd Wright, Mark di Suvero and Robert Smithson'.

These positions can be seen as part of the same interlinked process. The most dialectical modernist programmes tend to encompass all three, beginning with the rejection of the bourgeois world and its values, followed by its destruction, and its replacement by a new revolutionary agenda.

Nowhere has modernism been more innovative, more spectacular and more committed to change than in the work of the Russian avant-garde immediately before and for a few years after the October Revolution of 1917. This short-lived movement, in the words of John Berger, 'for its creativity, confidence, engagement in life and synthesising power has so far remained unique in the history of modern art',[5] and presents us with imagery so expressive of what we think modernism to be that it still seems 'to refer to the future, now'.

The avant-garde had a far-reaching programme: aesthetic, political, social and economic; this is expressed dramatically in Mayakovsky's epic propaganda poem *150 million*, whose title celebrates the whole population of the Soviet Union in the year 1920:

> We will smash the old world
> wildly
> we will thunder
> a new myth over the world.
> We will trample the fence
> of time beneath our feet.
> We will make a musical scale
> of the rainbow.[6]

It is not difficult to see where the inspiration for this comes from: Lenin's *The State and Revolution*, published in the early months of 1917 and very quickly a major influence on the programme of the Bolshevik party, contains just such a scheme. It begins by dissociating the reader from the bourgeois state, which exists for the specific purpose of oppressing the underprivileged; it then describes the revolutionary process through which the state can be opposed and overthrown; it concludes with an outline of the commune, the new society which will replace the old.

The Russian avant-garde followed this scheme closely. In the years before the Revolution, avant-garde experiment had pushed the boundaries of art as far as they could go; under this terminally declining old regime, abstract art was the ultimate expression of alienation; art under capitalism could go no further than, for example, Malevich's *Black Square* of 1913.

But the Bolshevik uprising provided the opportunity for the avant-garde to move into a genuinely revolutionary phase, as it attempted to sustain and spread the infant revolution through the Agit-Prop programme. Lissitzky's *Beat the Whites with the Red Wedge*, of 1920, was abstract art which had suddenly found a political purpose. With the new regime established, a third phase, one of reconstruction, began in earnest. The Constructivist designers offered new ideas for harnessing technology, for establishing and fostering new social relationships: a whole new vision of society. Mass-production techniques were applied to clothing and furniture; new building types, such as workers' clubs or communal flats, were invented; the new residential developments took unprecedented forms, reflecting the rediscovery of community life. The relationship between modernism and revolutionary socialism was established. From 1922 onwards, the ideas spread widely through Europe, and the western world also began to associate modernism with social change.

In one way, Lenin was this century's most significant modernist; through his particular combination of theory and practice modernism would have been capable of attaining its ultimate goals. The fact that it did not is a matter of history, beginning with the subversion of the Revolution under Stalin and the transformation of the nascent socialist economy into state capitalism. Under capitalism – eastern or western – modernism was and is incapable of living up to its promise. A movement which comes to express only alienation, or actively to oppose the society in which it exists, or to express social alternatives, cannot fully develop until that society is superseded. Any form of modernism that exists under capitalism is inevitably flawed: constrained by the logic of the capitalist mode of production and compromised by bourgeois ideology.

Modern architecture arrived in Britain from continental Europe in the late twenties. This does not deny the fact that contemporary writers were able to trace a long line of British antecedents of modernism. J. M. Richards, for example,[7] cited the 'noble engineer's' architecture of

7

# overthrowing tradition 1

Moisei Ginsburg's entry for the **Orgametals** building competition (1926)

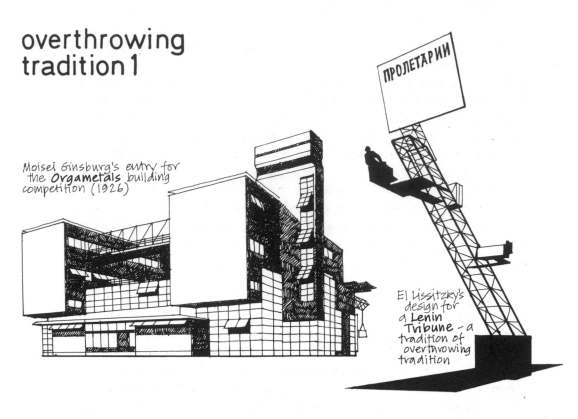

El Lissitzky's design for a **Lenin Tribune** - a tradition of overthrowing tradition

ПРОЛЕТАРИИ

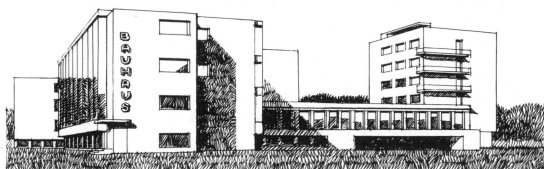

Walter Gropius's **Bauhaus** at Dessau (1925-6)

BAUHAUS

one of the low-rent houses on the suburban estate at **Frankfurt am Main** (1925-9) designed by the City Architect's Department under Ernst May

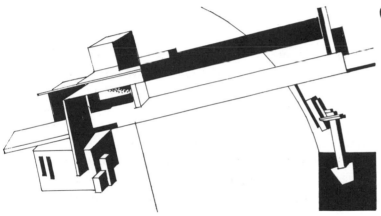

one of Lissitzky's **PROUNS** ('for the New Art') designed to bridge between sculpture and architecture (1919)

plan of the Dessau **Bauhaus** building

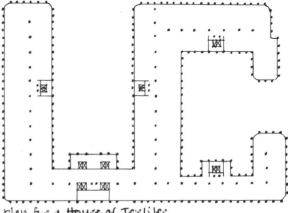

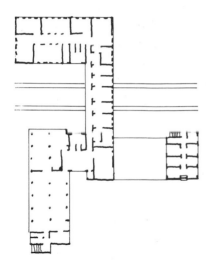

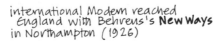

plan for a **House of Textiles** building, by Ginsburg (1925) – the organized, yet informal plan-form was essentially modern

international Modern reached England with Behrens's **New Ways** in Northampton (1926)

Le Corbusier and Mies van der Rohe at the Weissenhof in Stuttgart in 1927 – western Europe had inherited Constructivism

Thomas Telford and the 'startling' Red House designed by Philip Webb for William Morris. Nikolaus Pevsner indeed, in his own investigation of international modernism,[8] made Morris the starting point of the whole process. Nevertheless, it was in mainland Europe that all the various contributory theories and practices began to crystallize into a new and radically different form of architecture, and this came to Britain in 1926 when the German architect Peter Behrens built a house called 'New Ways' for Bassett-Lowke, the Northampton inventor. The connection is typical, since Germany was the main channel of modern architectural ideas into Britain.

Behrens was a major contributor to the design-for-industry tradition which culminated in the Bauhaus system and took physical form in the Bauhaus building itself. As the Nazis took over, numerous emigrés, including the key Bauhaus figures Walter Gropius and Marcel Breuer, worked briefly in Britain before moving on, producing influential buildings like the Fry and Gropius house in Chelsea, and this may be one of a number of reasons why British critics have always tended to emphasize the role of the Bauhaus in the development of modern architecture. This has remained the conventional wisdom for fifty years or more. It has helped to obscure the revolutionary role devised for the modern movement by the Russian avant-garde – in particular the clarity with which it defined the social purpose of modern architecture.

By the time the socialist theory and practice of the Constructivists had been filtered through the liberalism of the Weimar Republic, the clear association between revolutionary politics and modern architecture had already been lost. In the west, modernism gradually established itself under bourgeois-democratic regimes whose fear of Bolshevik revolution was even greater than their fear of fascism. Even in 1940, J. M. Richards felt it necessary to point out that modernists were not Bolsheviks,[9] while Le Corbusier concluded his most famous written work[10] with 'Architecture or Revolution. Revolution can be avoided.'

This did not prevent, then or since, those opposed to modernism or Marxism or both from deliberately associating the two; the best-known example was Hitler, to whom the modernist – and distinctly social-democratic – Weissenhofsiedlung at Stuttgart was 'cultural Bolshevism'. Nor did it stop social-democratic advocates of modernism, while yet fighting shy of revolutionary politics, from claiming modern architecture as the architecture of social progress, political change and human justice. And there was often a much greater appetite for social change than most social-democrats display today. This is shown, for example, by J. M. Richards, whose ideas for social reform would be considered extraordinarily far-reaching now. His *Introduction to Modern Architecture* includes the statement that 'the private ownership of land, for example, is one of the things that makes the orderly development of our towns – which constitutes the whole background for architecture – so difficult to achieve.' Not only land nationalization but also the proper planning of cities, of farmland and forests, the provision of a national transport system, and the overhaul of the building industry were all seen as an integral part of the architectural problem.

Ideas of this kind were being rehearsed throughout World War II. The destruction created the need to rebuild; the wartime imperatives – control of the economy, organized factory production, subsidized agriculture, rapidly developing technology – seemed to open up the opportunity of creating a new world and of banishing forever the inequalities and stagnation of the twenties and thirties.

Plans for the rebuilding of Coventry were begun the day after the Luftwaffe destroyed it. Other plans were being produced to guide the rebuilding of London: a green belt; garden cities; the devastated East End rising like a phoenix. In 1941 a special issue of the popular magazine *Picture Post*[11] outlined the Britain of the future: work for all, an education system, a health service, social security, planned towns, decent housing, modern architecture. Schemes like the Quarry Hill flats in Leeds, built in 1935 and themselves derivative of examples in social-democratic Germany, were illustrated to indicate the shape of things to come.

In 1942 the Beveridge report was published, with its 'security plan' which aimed 'to put things first, so as to ensure the abolition of want before the enjoyment of comfort'. Nine-tenths of the population supported the Beveridge proposals. Throughout the war, public opinion moved steadily to the left. Following the Soviet Union's entry into the war in 1941 there was a popular if superficial upsurge of interest in socialist ideas, and even Conservative MPs found no incongruity in singing the 'Internationale' at 'Aid to Russia' weeks. It was widely considered to be appropriate for the government to intervene in all aspects of life. When the Uthwatt committee reported in 1942, for instance, they proposed a tax on 'betterment', whereby a property developer would return to the public a sum equal to the increased land value accruing from his development.

The political right, including Churchill, felt uneasy but it is clear that there was a strong and serious sense of purpose about all this utopian thinking which reflected the aspirations of most of the people. B. L. Coombes, a Welsh miner, summed it all up:

> Between the dear coal and the cheap cutting, the scarce apples and those that rot, I think I can see the peace aim I would like to achieve. It is security – security against war and exploitation, by man or country. And what I ask for ourselves should be granted to the whole world.[12]

The reformist socialist theories on which the welfare state was to be founded took it as a matter of faith that such a world could be created. In an attempt to stabilize the volatile market system, it seemed appropriate to apply the principles outlined in 1936 in J. M. Keynes's General Theory. An enlarged public sector would create a demand for goods and services and thus prevent crises of overproduction and falling profits. The traditional industrial areas would be saved from decline by subsidy and nationalization. The market system, thus regenerated, would solve the problem of production, and would be managed benignly, through government controls, so that its benefits could be more equitably distributed.

In 1945 the newly-elected Labour government began what Colin Buchanan later called 'a burst of noble legislation', intended to turn Beveridge's ideas of social equity into reality. Four main initiatives would achieve this: state control of the economy; the extension of public ownership; legislation to control the behaviour of both the private and the public sectors; public subsidies channelled where they were needed. As a result, development finance could be offered, schools, hospitals and houses built, and payments or subsidies directed towards needy groups and individuals, classes and regions.

Keynesianism did succeed in bolstering up the capitalist system; after a few years of postwar austerity, industry entered a period of unprecedented growth, based essentially on the rapidly expanding 'permanent arms economy'. On the other hand, the social programme in practice fell far short of the high aspirations expressed during the war. State control of the economy was deliberately limited in its scope; long-term economic planning was rejected in favour of short-term monetary control. The nationalization programme fell short of dealing with the land ownership question. The new health and education systems permitted private medicine and private schools to continue. And the Conservative government returned in 1951 began quickly to repeal the measures least palatable to private enterprise; the tax on developers' profits was among the first to go.

It is too easy to treat the arguments as party-political ones: that the welfare state had been given too few powers or far too many. The fact is, however, that welfare capitalism could never have brought the peaceful socialist millennium its supporters hoped for, nor the incipient Marxism its detractors feared, because the imperatives of the productive process, which provided its whole context, dictated otherwise. Capitalism undoubtedly provided the dynamic for the welfare state: not only the need but also, through the buoyancy of the postwar economy, the financial means. However, it is not possible for any social system to obtain the benefits of capitalism without also experiencing its contradictions. The social programme could exist only by respecting the logic of the mode of production.

Capitalism is based on commodity production. Marx's analysis[13] identifies two kinds of commodity: 'use-values' which are physically useful in themselves, and 'exchange-values' which the capitalist system uses as the basis of production and trade. Buildings, like most commodities, fall into both categories, but it is with exchange-values that Marxist theory is mainly concerned, and with the extent to which, under capitalism, they constrain and define the nature of all social relationships. They determine, for example, the relationship between capital and labour, turning labour itself and those who perform it into commodities. The 'cash nexus' thus established between capital and labour makes the relative position of each of them a contentious issue; class conflict, oppression and inequality thus become essential aspects of the economic system.

Through 'the fetish character of the commodity', not only economic life but also social life is affected; relationships between individuals as well as between classes are distorted and objectified. Just as ownership of the means of production confers power, and denial of it brings subjection, so does the ownership of commodities bring status, and the lack of them ensure insignificance.

The welfare state, set up within this context, displayed all the contradictions of capitalist society. A booming postwar economy allowed considerable sums to be channelled into the improvement of the built environment. Postwar reconstruction demanded a widespread renewal of Britain's physical fabric. A massive housing programme was begun, with a target of 300,000 new dwellings a year which was met and surpassed. A new town-planning system was set up to control the redevelopment of the cities; green belts and rings of new towns became a feature of the biggest conurbations. Transport services were nationalized and a big road-building programme was begun. Efforts were made to reform and rationalize the unwieldy building industry.

However, buildings, roads, bridges and vehicles are all commodities. They meet people's everyday needs as use-values but, more significantly, they play a crucial part in the economy as exchange-values. All those new houses clearly met a need but economically this was secondary in importance to their performance as exchange-values; the growth of industrialized building was one result of this, as system-builders like Camus, Coignet, Larsen and Nielsen, Bison and Reema competed for the lucrative public-housing market. The Rachmanism of the inner-city private landlords was another. The much-praised planning system had its successes, but nonetheless failed to control the profit-led office boom of the sixties and in some respects stimulated it. New towns, too, had their negative side, becoming channels through which manpower and investment were encouraged to flow from the inner cities. Transport planning

soon became dominated by the motor industry and its growth requirements, and was particularly affected by the emergence of the powerful
'road lobby' whose political supporters ensured that disproportionate
investment went into road building. And the building industry, though
far from immune from financial crisis, was nevertheless successful in
fighting off nationalization.

Commodity fetishism also played a significant part in the way the
environment was shaped. New housing was often designed to look
dramatic and conspicuous, architectural fashions conveniently coinciding
with the electoral ambitions of the politicians; the brief but disastrous
fashion for high-rise flats is the most obvious example of this. Office
towers too were often statements of conspicuous luxury reflecting the
prestige of their developers or owners. And of course in postwar
automobiles the fetish character of the commodity is displayed to a degree
unmatched elsewhere. Barthes likens them to Gothic cathedrals in that
they are 'the supreme creation of an era, conceived with passion by
unknown artists, and consumed in image if not in usage by a whole
population which appropriates them as a purely magical object.'[14]

This rather extravagant and approving description somehow typifies
the attitudes of the fifties and early sixties. There was a general
consensus, firstly that capitalism was here to stay and secondly that
economic growth should – and would – continue. This was the conventional wisdom of the social-democratic left as much as of the right, since
the very existence of the welfare state depended on the surplus thrown up
by the prosperous conditions; politically as well as economically it was
easier to defend welfare if the wealthy did not have to tighten their belts
too far.

And this uncritical attitude to capitalism encouraged an equally
uncritical attitude to modern design. Modernism expressed the wonders
of modern technology; it represented society's progress towards a new
world. Ed Bacon and Louis Kahn's modernist plan for the reconstruction
of Philadelphia was praised for its 'powerful design ideas', strong enough
to survive the compromises of the implementation process.[15] The utopian
theories of the thirties – about design for factory production, about
communal living, about dramatic multi-level cities – could be pressed into
service. For ideas originally conceived to express the emerging socialist
revolution, and then adapted by liberal theorists between the wars,
postwar capitalism could find new relevances. And in the interests of
progress and growth few doubts were expressed.

By the mid sixties the situation had changed. There had always been
lone voices to challenge society's assumptions. In 1947 Paul and Percival
Goodman's *Communitas* had put forward a libertarian alternative to
the repressive city. In 1958 Galbraith's *The Affluent Society* criticized

14

'private opulence and public squalor', and argued that economic growth should be handled in a more egalitarian way. In 1961 Jane Jacobs's *The Death and Life of Great American Cities* critically examined the failures of the town-planning system.

By about 1964 these isolated voices had been augmented into a chorus of disapproval of contemporary society and its priorities. There had been a qualitative as well as a quantitative change; political theorists on the left, like Marcuse and Sartre, and maverick economists, like Edward Mishan or E. F. Schumacher, were now joined in their criticisms of state policies by establishment organizations: UNICEF, the World Health Organization, the Club of Rome.

The reason is not hard to find. Rapid production and consumption had produced an unprecedented period of worldwide capitalist expansion, the contradictions of which had led to a series of struggles, from the anti-war movement to the Paris 'events' of 1968. The material conditions existed for change, and the readiness with which the workers and students were prepared to respond to them gave confidence to social critics – including radical young architects – and shook the establishment, for whom it became a matter of priority that in the interests of the survival of the system its contradictions should be resolved.

It was this which provided the context for a growing campaign of criticism of modern architecture. Here too, the criticism was rooted in the real, material contradictions and the struggles they gave rise to: the disastrous fire at the Summerland leisure complex in the Isle of Man in 1973, the collapse of the system-built flats at Ronan Point in Canning Town in 1968, protests over motorway proposals, tenants' campaigns, rent strikes and the squatters. Suddenly the architectural press was full of instant solutions. Few architectural critics – in strong contrast to their counterparts of the forties – spoke of any structural change in society, but there was no lack of short-term proposals to make the present system more workable: low-rise instead of high-rise; traditional instead of industrialized building; brick rather than concrete.

A typical reaction came from the *Architectural Review* which published a special edition in November 1967 called 'Housing and the Environment'. The magazine criticized a number of quite celebrated public-housing schemes, from Avenham Street in Preston to Park Hill in Sheffield, stating baldly that 'housing since the war has been a failure. It has failed chiefly because it has been isolated from the other aspects of community building; administratively, financially and technically it has become divorced from its true context – the real community.'

Suddenly the technocracy of the sixties was out and 'the community' was in. Much pseudo-sociology was being talked and written, and the terminology, if not the substance, of Marxist politics was much in

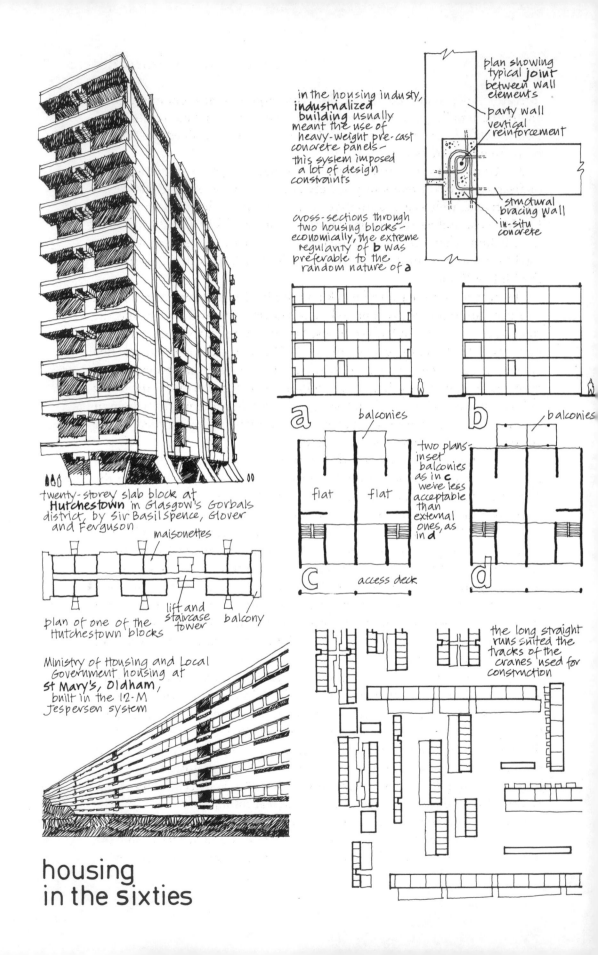

in the housing industry, **industrialized building** usually meant the use of heavy-weight pre-cast concrete panels — this system imposed a lot of design constraints

plan showing typical **joint** between wall elements

party wall

vertical reinforcement

structural bracing wall

in-situ concrete

cross-sections through two housing blocks — economically, the extreme regularity of **b** was preferable to the random nature of **a**

a

b

balconies

balconies

two plans — inset balconies as in **c** were less acceptable than external ones, as in **d**

flat   flat

c

access deck

d

twenty-storey slab block at **Hutchestown** in Glasgow's Gorbals district, by Sir Basil Spence, Glover and Ferguson

maisonettes

lift and staircase tower

balcony

plan of one of the Hutchestown blocks

Ministry of Housing and Local Government housing at **St Mary's, Oldham,** built in the 12-M Jespersen system

the long straight runs suited the tracks of the cranes used for construction

# housing in the sixties

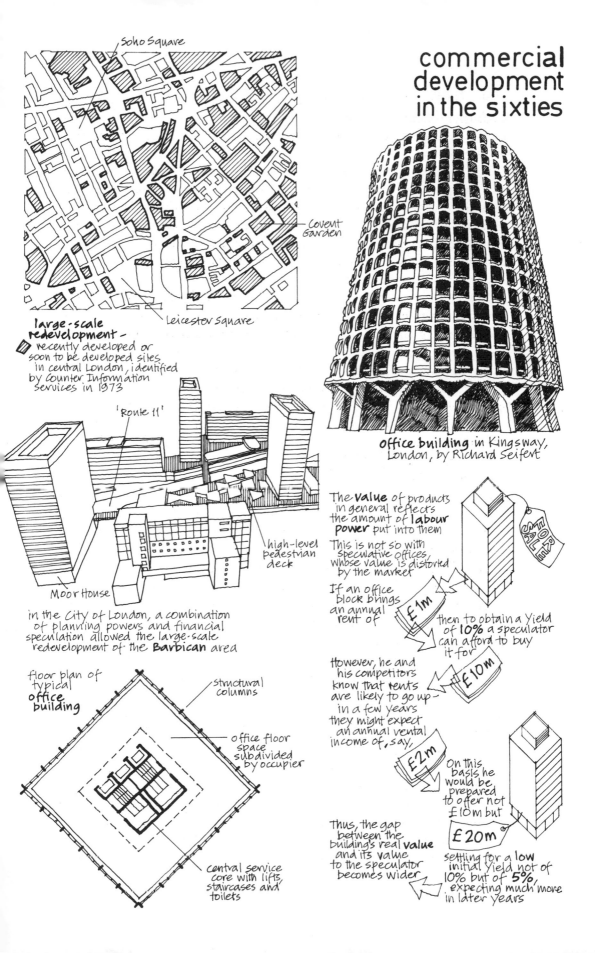

Soho Square

Covent Garden

Leicester Square

## commercial development in the sixties

**large-scale redevelopment –**
recently developed or soon to be developed sites in central London, identified by Counter Information Services in 1973

'Route 11'

high-level pedestrian deck

Moor House

in the City of London, a combination of planning powers and financial speculation allowed the large-scale redevelopment of the **Barbican** area

**office building** in Kingsway, London, by Richard Seifert

floor plan of typical **office building**

structural columns

office floor space subdivided by occupier

central service core with lifts, staircases and toilets

The **value** of products in general reflects the amount of **labour power** put into them

This is not so with speculative offices, whose value is distorted by the market

FOR SALE

If an office block brings an annual rent of £1m then to obtain a yield of **10%** a speculator can afford to buy it for £10m

However, he and his competitors know that rents are likely to go up – in a few years they might expect an annual rental income of, say, £2m

On this basis he would be prepared to offer not £10m but £20m

Thus, the gap between the building's real **value** and its value to the speculator becomes wider

settling for a low initial yield not of 10% but of **5%**, expecting much more in later years

evidence. The American critic Charles Jencks felt able to revise Le Corbusier's famous dictum; he ended *Modern Movements in Architecture* with a political postscript, concluding with a call for 'Architecture *and* Revolution'.[16]

But if Marx's politics were a live issue, his economics were much less so. The sustained growth of the postwar period led almost everyone, including many Marxists, to believe that it would continue. The Marxist philosopher Ernst Fischer felt compelled to write: 'Marx assumed that economic crises would become increasingly acute, and in his time the assumption was well founded. Despite the world economic crisis of 1929, history does not seem to have fulfilled his prediction.'[17]

Not so. Crises of capitalism continue to recur and Marx alone seems to have a coherent explanation for their inevitability. The capitalist mode of production is qualitatively different from all preceding economic systems. Historically, crises had been crises of scarcity, which of course had brought want and privation, but which could be solved by improved productivity. Capitalism was unique; here was a system in which productivity itself created not peace and prosperity but crisis and conflict.

Marx identified in capitalism a long-term tendency, as production expanded, for total profits to go up but for the rate of profit to fall. One reason for this was mechanization: as more and more money was spent on buildings and machinery relative to wages, it became more difficult for the capitalist to extract profit from the process. With his fixed capital costing him more and more, all he could do to compensate was to squeeze wages, and these in any case formed a decreasing proportion of his total commitments.

Then there was the problem of under-consumption, which had two features. One of these was 'disproportionality', the fact that the anarchic, unplanned nature of capitalism made it impossible to judge the right level of production for the available market; the constant fluctuations and adjustments created economic instability. The other was overproduction, the fact that the general tendency to produce more and more led inevitably to too many goods being produced and too few sales made.

Marx made it clear that all these factors were interlinked. A falling rate of profit, for example, 'promotes overproduction, speculation, crises, surplus capital along with surplus population ... the barrier of the capitalist mode of production becomes apparent'.[18]

Some of these factors, especially the falling rate of profit, might occur gradually over time and be susceptible to short-term remedies. But more than one factor operating simultaneously might on the other hand produce an unusually deep recession. Falling sales or declining rates of profit would result in layoffs of workers, with all the social problems this implied; employers unable to sell goods would cut their capital investment in future production – and on buildings – with further effects on employment both in their own and their suppliers' workforces – including the building industry; unemployment would reduce society's buying power and with it the demand for goods; further cutbacks, further unemployment, further contractions in the market would result.

In Britain it became apparent in the early seventies that such a crisis had begun. It was stimulated by the Arab-Israeli war and the related oil crisis of 1973, but it was in fact the culmination of a number of factors present throughout the sixties. During the postwar period, the profits of British companies were steadily increasing, from around £3 billion a year in the early sixties to £9 billion or more by the early seventies, but over the same period the profit rate was falling, from around 14 per cent to 9 per cent, and continuing downward.

Smaller industries foundered, though multinationals kept afloat and the financial sector prospered as never before; interest rates rose from around 2 per cent at the end of the forties to 12.5 per cent in 1974. And the products of Britain's industry were increasingly failing to find markets; growth in productivity averaged about 3 per cent per year over the postwar period, but buying power at home was limited by inflation, and Britain's share of markets abroad was declining in the face of foreign competition, entry into the EEC in 1973 having curtailed Britain's preferential trade agreements with the Commonwealth. All this created a stagnant, inflationary economy, a rising level of unemployment and the problem of an increasingly unequal society which the Labour governments of the seventies, respectful of the City of London and pressed by the IMF, could do little to resolve.

In history, almost nothing is inevitable; there were a number of different scenarios for the resolution of this situation. In view of Britain's recent history however, and the extent to which Keynesianism, high employment and the welfare state were still part of the national consciousness, few people can have expected the actual outcome, no matter how much it complied with the logic of the market system.

The crisis demanded that some areas of capital be destroyed to protect the remainder. In the event, priority was given to protecting the financial sector and to ensuring the future of the City of London as an international market. All else could be sacrificed to this end, including areas of capital which under welfare capitalism had themselves been protected. The poor and disadvantaged and other beneficiaries of the welfare state would be badly affected, and so would other areas of private capital, including the building and manufacturing industries. To achieve this, there were two further necessities, complementary to each other. The first was the election of a government prepared to pursue a class struggle and to take on the unions. The second was a radical shift in the dominant ideology, sufficient to turn public opinion away from the welfare state. The first came in May 1979 when the general election was won by the Conservative party under Mrs Thatcher; the second began soon after.

These economic imperatives, this new political regime and this new ideology had a profound effect on the way people led their lives, on the environment, on planning, transport and housing, on the building industry and on architecture, both how it is practised and how it is theorized about. What these effects were, how and why they happened, and what problems we now face as a result, provide the themes for the rest of this book.

# 2 Unkindest Cuts – the decline of welfare capitalism

Ten years into the life of the Thatcher government, the Salvation Army sponsored a survey of London's homeless people.[1] A pilot survey in 1988 was followed by a major survey one night in April 1989 in which teams of volunteers attempted to uncover the nature and scale of homelessness in London. It was a cold night but 753 people were found sleeping in the open; this figure was thought to have been an underestimate. The survey figures also indicated about 18,000 people in homeless persons' hostels, about 25,000 in bed-and-breakfast hotels and, a rougher estimate, around 30,000 people squatting in empty houses. The overall conclusion was that 75,000 Londoners were 'overtly homeless' and many more were housed but, because they were sharing cramped accommodation or for other reasons, needed rehousing.

The survey had generally been expected to show a significant problem but few expected this to be quite as big as it proved to be. The introduction to the report concluded that

> London has a shanty town as large as might be expected in a Latin American city, but it is hidden. People live illegally in squats, or in cramped, badly equipped hotels and crowded hostels. If they do not fall into a group that the government recognises as having a special need, or they cannot locate in one of the very few spare spaces indoors, they find that they have no choice but to survive on the streets.

The report compared its own survey results with relevant figures from past surveys. Comparison with one carried out by the National Assistance Board in 1965 seemed to suggest that the number of people sleeping rough, for example, is much higher now than it was then.

1965 is a good reference point for any discussion of London's housing situation, since it was then that the last major report on the subject was produced. The Milner Holland committee had been set up by the Conservative government in 1963 following the emergence of 'Rachmanism' – exploitation and harrassment of tenants – in the private rented sector of the inner city. It seems likely that the exploiting landlords, of whom Perec Rachman was just one example, had been encouraged by the Conservatives own Rent Act of 1957, which had decontrolled rents and reduced security of tenure, with the stated aim of encouraging market forces to provide more housing. It was public outrage at the unprincipled landlords' activities that pushed the government into setting up the investigation.

In fact, the Milner Holland committee reported to a newly elected Labour government, which was already taking steps to establish 'fair' rents and to restore security of tenure. However, the most significant lesson of Milner Holland lay not in its recommendations for rent control and security but in the overall picture it painted of housing in London. The committee revealed that, despite the enormous effort made since the end of the war, there was an acute shortage of rented housing of any kind in London. The stock of privately rented housing was diminishing fast and would not be stabilized until a balance was struck between the conflicting needs and demands of the landlord and the tenant. Even if the private rented sector did become stable and productive there would still remain 'many thousands' of families unable to afford market rents. For them, and others with special needs, 'a very great addition to the stock of assisted housing' was needed; local authority provision and the output of the housing associations 'must be accelerated as far as possible'.[2]

The Milner Holland report stimulated renewed efforts to confront the problem of output; in both 1967 and 1968 more than 400,000 new dwellings were completed, half of them in the public sector. North Kensington in London, identified by Milner Holland as a special problem area, soon became a focus of activity. Public housing developments by the GLC (Greater London Council) and by local housing associations, such as Kensington Housing Trust, Notting Hill Housing Trust and Golborne Housing Trust, and initiatives by the North Kensington Amenity Trust, began to change the face of the area.

There was a qualitative difference between these new schemes and the cruder solutions put forward in the early sixties; tenants themselves were making their voices heard. The political organization of tenants – around issues like re-housing, rent levels and the environment – took its inspiration from the wider political struggles of the late sixties. For a short time community action in North Kensington, Liverpool 8, St Ann's in Nottingham, Handsworth in Birmingham and elsewhere achieved many positive results and elicited some support from the authorities. Housing was built or refurbished and environmental projects carried out in accordance with local people's own wishes. Greater emphasis was placed on keeping existing communities intact. In North Kensington the Kensington Housing Trust carried out a housing redevelopment in phases, to allow existing residents to be re-housed on the site rather than 'decanted' elsewhere. In the same area the GLC designed new housing with the help of the local people. In Liverpool the Shelter Neighbourhood

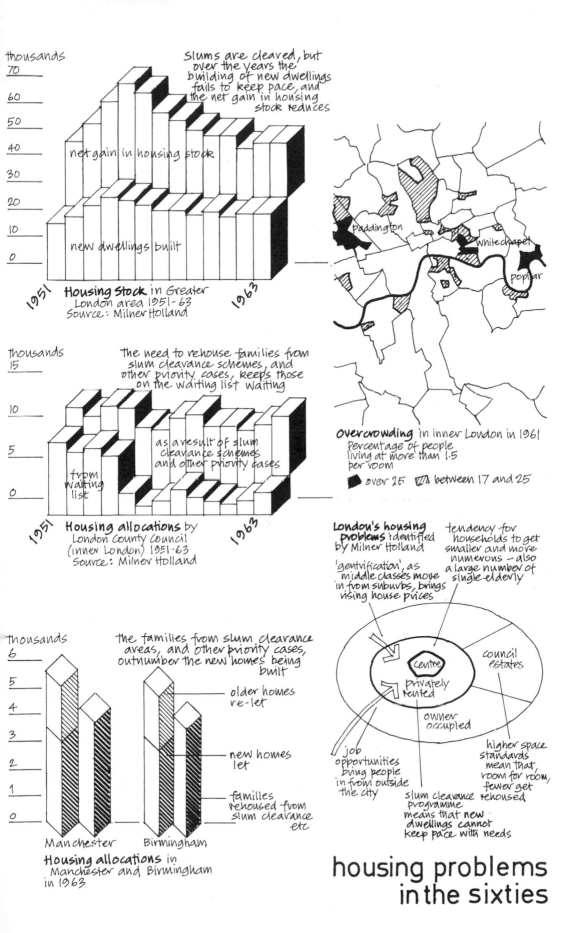

thousands

70
60
50
40
30
20
10
0

Slums are cleared, but over the years the building of new dwellings fails to keep pace, and the net gain in housing stock reduces

net gain in housing stock

new dwellings built

1951    1963

**Housing Stock** in Greater London area 1951-63
Source: Milner Holland

paddington
whitechapel
poplar

**overcrowding** in inner London in 1961
Percentage of people living at more than 1.5 per room
■ over 25   ▨ between 17 and 25

thousands

15
10
5
0

The need to rehouse families from slum clearance schemes, and other priority cases, keeps those on the waiting list waiting

from waiting list

as a result of slum clearance schemes and other priority cases

1951    1963

**Housing allocations** by London County Council (inner London) 1951-63
Source: Milner Holland

**London's housing problems** identified by Milner Holland

'gentrification', as middle classes move in from suburbs, brings rising house prices

tendency for households to get smaller and more numerous — also a large number of single-elderly

centre
privately rented
council estates
owner occupied

job opportunities bring people in from outside the city

slum clearance programme means that new dwellings cannot keep pace with needs

higher space standards mean that, room for room, fewer get rehoused

thousands

6
5
4
3
2
1
0

The families from slum clearance areas, and other priority cases, outnumber the new homes being built

older homes re-let

new homes let

families rehoused from slum clearance etc

Manchester    Birmingham

**Housing allocations** in Manchester and Birmingham in 1963

# housing problems in the sixties

Action Project set up a local office to consult local people on the improvement of the area. In St Ann's the local people organized a campaign against the city corporation's proposals for redevelopment. In Handsworth, the setting up of an adventure playground by local people became the catalyst for further community action. Almost everywhere the gains were social as well as physical; the more control ordinary people were able to achieve, the more effective they felt.

The late sixties had been a period of political dissent, across all strata of society. The whole concept of redevelopment, for example, was being challenged. The objectors included working-class groups, like those of Tolmers Square or Covent Garden, who objected to the destructive social and economic effects on their communities; they included middle-class home owners whose property values were to be affected by road proposals or by the construction of London's third airport; they also included pressure-groups of aesthetes, fearful of the erosion of historic towns or the loss of old buildings.

But the activities of squatters who took over empty houses, or of tenants' groups who organized rent strikes, not to mention reports like that of the Milner Holland committee itself, might have been taken as indications that environmental problems were more than a matter of design. They were also a matter of supply, of management, of social priorities, of class politics – in short, of the control of economic power.

But it was natural that the politicians and professionals should be reluctant to surrender too much power to local people. Architects on the whole still sought to be arbiters of what was right for the people, rather than agents of community-led projects. In the previous chapter I quoted the *Architectural Review* of November 1967 on the reasons for the failure of postwar housing. Though it was felt that concern for 'the community' was the key to better housing, it was nevertheless clear that to the professional mind, continued professional control was essential. The *Architectural Review* pointed approvingly to new schemes in which 'Professional teams have first investigated the social, economic, visual, functional and constructional needs, have evolved design criteria based on these investigations and have then designed schemes to meet them.' Schemes by Tayler and Green, Peter Phippen and Michael Neylan, among others, mainly in new towns, were singled out for praise.

So politicians and professionals embarked on revisionist programmes, in which the community played only a slightly more important part than before. A new set of architectural theories took over. High-density low-rise became fashionable as an alternative to high-rise; traditional building methods began to take over from system-building; the rustic brickwork of 'neo-vernacular' building replaced reinforced concrete. But the municipal system remained intact, together with its methods and management structures. Participation might have improved – at least in the public sector – but the landlord-tenant relationship remained. The buildings on the whole continued to be designed for an anonymous public, and their quality was still subject to the dictates of politics and profitability. In the public as well as the private sector tenants continued to experience the pressures of life within the system: the inadequacies of health care, education and employment which intensified the problems of poor housing. Thus it was that before long the new generation of housing schemes began to exhibit their own problems, not only, or even mainly, because of their design, but more because of the unsatisfactory way they were administered, controlled, funded or maintained. The London Borough of Camden's highly-praised high-density low-rise estate at Alexandra Road had heating problems, as did the City of Westminster's prize-winning neo-vernacular Mozart estate. Camden's Maiden Lane, another highly-regarded low-rise scheme needed extensive rehabilitation, there was controversy over the demolition of the celebrated Southgate estate in Runcorn New Town, while the London Borough of Haringey's critically acclaimed Broadwater Farm estate was the scene of much social unrest.

Once again it had been thought that social goals could be achieved through architectural design. This kind of argument bears little examination but it is remarkable how much time it is still given in architectural writing and how seriously it was taken at the time. Thirty years of economic growth had failed to create a postwar utopia. Architects and critics had no real answers, and were only too willing to simplify the issues. How much more straightforward it would be if social progress could be held to depend on something the architect had under his control, rather than something he did not. At least he could offer 'stylistic multivalence', to use a phrase of the time.

It remains true, of course, that ordinary people's everyday problems can be alleviated to some extent by greater sensitivity of design. As long as the housing system, at both central and local government levels, continued to function, and there was enough money to pay for adequate space standards, and there were subsidies to offset the extra costs of building on difficult inner-city sites, and local groups continued to press for their rights, then gradual improvements could be made here and there. But when the economic crisis of the early seventies began to take effect, even this was jeopardized.

Keynesians believed in the welfare state, though not only – or even principally – for the benefits it offered its recipients. Of greater importance was the strength it gave the economic system and, by implication, the class structure on which it was based. In the crisis-laden period between the wars there had not of course been a lack of manpower, nor even a

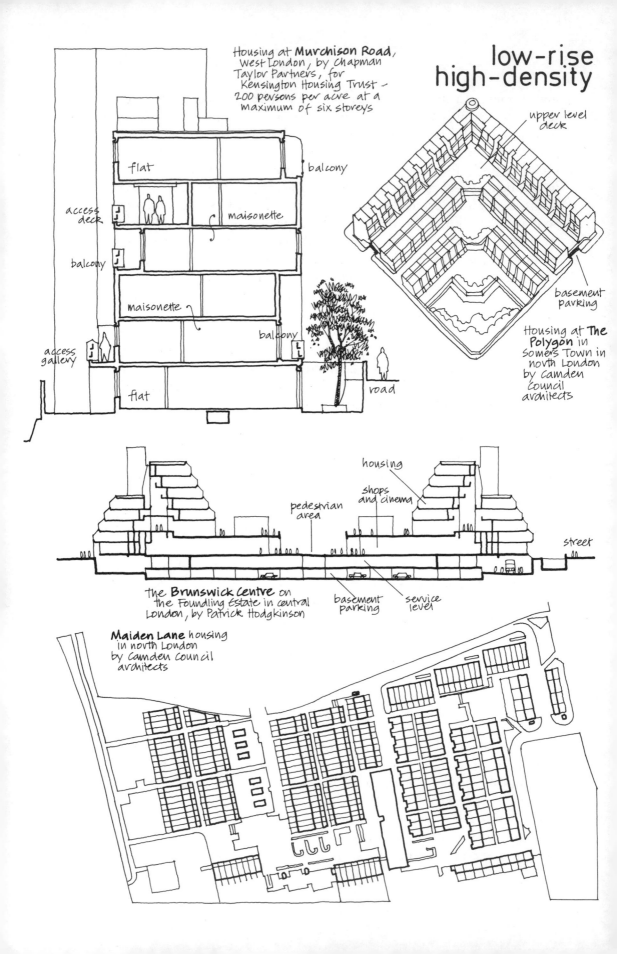

# low-rise high-density

Housing at **Murchison Road**, West London, by Chapman Taylor Partners, for Kensington Housing Trust - 200 persons per acre at a maximum of six storeys

flat

balcony

access deck

maisonette

balcony

maisonette

balcony

access gallery

flat

road

upper level deck

basement parking

Housing at **The Polygon** in Somers Town in north London by Camden Council architects

housing

shops and cinema

pedestrian area

street

The **Brunswick Centre** on the Foundling Estate in central London, by Patrick Hodgkinson

basement parking

service level

**Maiden Lane** housing in north London by Camden Council architects

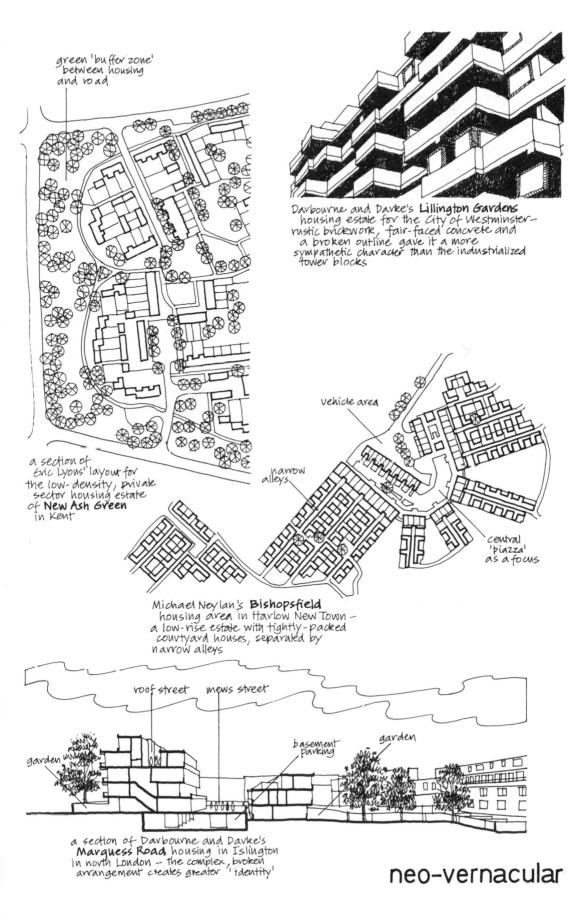

green 'buffer zone' between housing and road

Darbourne and Darke's **Lillington Gardens** housing estate for the City of Westminster- rustic brickwork, fair-faced concrete and a broken outline gave it a more sympathetic character than the industrialized tower blocks

a section of Eric Lyons' layout for the low-density, private sector housing estate of **New Ash Green** in Kent

vehicle area

narrow alleys

central 'piazza' as a focus

Michael Neylan's **Bishopsfield** housing area in Harlow New Town - a low-rise estate with tightly-packed courtyard houses, separated by narrow alleys

roof street    mews street

basement parking    garden

garden

a section of Darbourne and Darke's **Marquess Road** housing in Islington in north London - the complex, broken arrangement creates greater 'identity'

# neo-vernacular

lack of capital; the main problem had been unemployment, which had reduced spending power and with it the demand for goods. It is no accident that despite the existence of modern technology so few modern buildings had been built before 1945, nor that most of these were for private clients and in the wealthy southeast of England. The public sector had been in embryo only, and the economy as a whole had in any case generated insufficient wealth to finance a big building programme.

To Keynes, the solution had been clear: stimulate the economy by spending on public works; this would provide employment, the earnings from which would create a demand for goods and thus encourage growth. It was a feature of Keynesianism that a strong public sector could balance the economy in a way the private sector alone could not. Keynes, as I have said, was thought to have solved the interlinked problems of unemployment and crisis. The view persisted till the early seventies: 'The basic fact is that with the acceptance of the General Theory, the days of uncontrollable mass unemployment in advanced countries are over. Other economic problems may threaten; this one, at least, has passed into history.'[3]

Shortly after this was written, the situation changed. As the crisis of the early seventies intensified the falling rate of profit, the Labour government itself began to strengthen its support for finance capital and in the process to withdraw from the welfare state. As yet the problems were not dramatically apparent, but were significant enough to demand a reduction of housing subsidies and cuts in public-sector housing investment. Of course the rhetoric did not change; the government still declared its support for the public sector, for public consultation and local democracy. But the only way the system as a whole was able to deal with a crisis was to allow large amounts of capital to be destroyed. The weaker industries or companies collapsed and eventually the overall rate of profit began to match the lowered level of productivity.

In such circumstances, the public sector as a whole and the building industry in particular are vulnerable; subsidized housing, being a product of both, is especially at risk. Government subsidies and loan sanction were now offered only for cheap 'green field' sites. Those which presented problems – and this included many inner-city sites where development costs were high – remained undeveloped, or were sold to the private sector to finance many a local authority's growing budget deficit.

The London Borough of Camden's experience was typical of the new circumstances. At the beginning of the seventies Camden was building housing on a number of unused railway yards, the last remaining large sites in a congested borough. With some 14,000 families on the waiting list, this work was given priority, and large areas of land were being acquired. The biggest of these, Elm Village in Camden Town, was to become a high-density low-rise development, housing 3,000 people around a four-acre park and a district shopping centre. The land was bought in 1975 when, under the prevailing conditions, the borough might have expected to receive generous help from the government to defray the heavy costs of a high-density scheme and of building it on an expensive, badly-serviced site. By 1977, when, following widespread consultation, the scheme was designed, it became impossible. High-density developments were now unacceptable, no government money was available to help with the extra costs, and Camden itself was in financial difficulties. Overnight the scheme was changed. Part of the site was sold to the Post Office, another became an area of commercial development. The reduced housing area was also sold, half to a housing association and half to a design-and-build private developer. The revenue helped defray the Council's running expenses for a while.

From 1979 onward the cutbacks continued under a Conservative government but the need for political equivocation was less. Strong policies were supported by strong ideology. An economic theory was devised – or rather resurrected from the pre-Keynesian past – which contradicted the conventional wisdom on public speaking. This was Monetarism, associated originally with Friedrich von Hayek but latterly with the 'Chicago School' of Milton Friedman. Monetary controls of one kind or another had of course been a feature of British economic policy for many years but to Keynesians they had been part of a package designed to stimulate output and create employment. Friedman argued that the main enemy was not unemployment but inflation. Strict control of the money supply was the only measure needed to control inflation and run a sound economy, all other aspects of which could be left to the 'free market'.

At one point, Friedman himself complained that the government invoked Monetarism 'to cover anything that Mrs Thatcher at any time expressed as a desirable object of policy'.[4] She seemed to be less interested in economic theory than in political fact. To define inflation as the main problem and money control as the main solution gave authenticity to a whole political programme. High interest rates benefited the City's financial institutions; so did the offering of shares in public assets such as telephones, gas and water; so did the public money being ploughed into ailing City firms like Johnson Matthey; and so did the government's continued attempts to maintain the strength of sterling – to the detriment of many of the country's exporting industries. In these areas at least, capital was being protected.

While the banks announced record profits, domestic industry, for whom high interest rates meant an end to investment and whose ability to sell goods abroad was compromised by a relatively strong pound, went into decline. Multinational firms – including to some extent the biggest building contractors – could of course protect themselves by switching capital from one place to another; monetary controls were not for them. In domestic industry and in large areas of the public sector, however, capital was being destroyed.

Those who had least suffered most. Trade-union protection was legislatively reduced, amid allegations of undemocratic procedures and unjustified wildcat action. While press reports of scrounging increased, welfare rights were steadily eroded. The concept of 'over-spending' inner-city councils was promoted, and helped to justify rate-capping, the surcharging of councillors, the privatization of public services and the abolition of the Metropolitan Counties and the GLC. The privatization of public housing and the reduction of tenants' rights in the private sector hit low-income families hard. The virtual cessation of new-build council housing hit them even harder. The characteristic housing development of the early eighties was no longer the council estate but the private sector estate built by companies such as Barratt or Fairview.

The introduction of a poll tax was a further imposition; one major effect was to take money from the poor and give it to the rich. And all this came at a time when the lack of capital investment in domestic industry pushed unemployment – particularly in the building industry – to unprecedented levels.

Since the emergence of industrial capitalism in the nineteenth century, and the political policies which go with it, the building industry has always been vulnerable to crisis. Of a building workforce of nearly two million representing some 8 per cent of the economically active population, about 250,000 were out of work by 1977 – a figure representing some 14 per cent of those in the industry and about 15 per cent of the total unemployed. Total unemployment at that time stood at a million and a half; since then, both this figure and the contribution made to it by unemployed building workers have increased considerably. Despite the so-called mini-boom of the early and mid eighties – one created essentially by the large number of bankrupted enterprises leaving more profit for those that survived – the registered unemployed in 1984 numbered over three million and of these about half a million were building workers.

The decline in construction employment was matched by a decline in house building. In 1987 the total number of houses started was about 221,000, only two-thirds of the total begun in 1975. During this period the number of houses built by the private sector had slightly increased but the public sector by contrast had almost completely collapsed. About 174,000 public-sector houses were begun in 1975; by 1987 the number was only 29,500 and was continuing to decline year by year. The lack of investment in new-build put greater pressure on the existing stock, but the lack of money for estate modernization or maintenance was creating a crisis here too. The stock was falling rapidly into disrepair and more

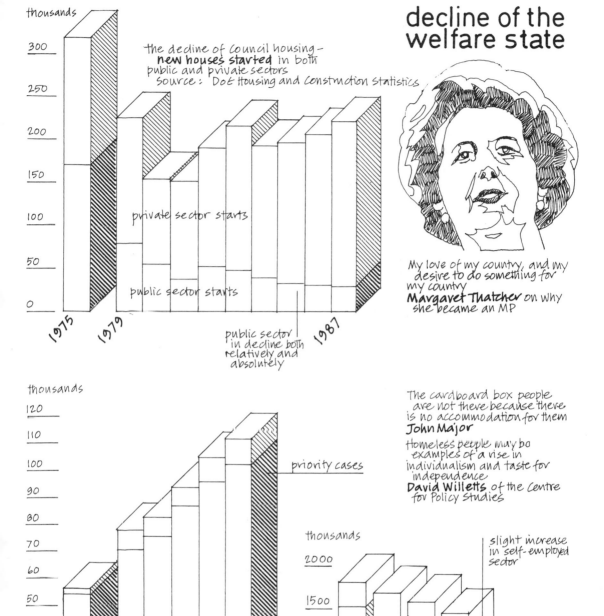

# decline of the welfare state

**thousands**

300
250
200
150
100
50
0

the decline of Council housing — **new houses started** in both public and private sectors
Source: DoE Housing and Construction Statistics

private sector starts

public sector starts

1975  1979  1987

public sector in decline both relatively and absolutely

My love of my country, and my desire to do something for my country
**Margaret Thatcher** on why she became an MP

The cardboard box people are not there because there is no accommodation for them
**John Major**

Homeless people may be examples of a rise in individualism and taste for independence
**David Willetts** of the Centre for Policy Studies

**thousands**

120
110
100
90
80
70
60
50
40
30
20
10
0

priority cases

1979  1983  1987

the corresponding growth of homelessness — **families accepted as homeless** by local authorities in England alone
Source: Hansard

**thousands**

2000
1500
1000
500
0

slight increase in self-employed sector

decline in both public sector and

main contracting

1970  1975  1980  1985

simultaneous **decline of employment in the construction industry**
Source: DoE Housing and Construction Statistics

houses were remaining empty as council improvement schemes failed to proceed.

A spate of housing, planning and local-government legislation was enacted between 1986 and 1990. Ostensibly this was to bring home ownership and choice to a wider range of people and to stimulate the provision of more private-sector rented accommodation by giving incentives to the landlords. But the effect was to transfer dwellings out of the public sector into the hands of speculators, as well as to reduce the security and rights of tenants. Public-sector tenants might find their estates privatized against the wishes of the majority, while private tenants might be evicted to allow their landlords to improve and sell their homes.

Political advantage could derive from the break-up of large council estates, the traditional areas of working-class organization. Much was to be gained therefore by tempting council tenants into home ownership, though the products they were buying were often inferior in both quality and space standards to those of the public sector. There were risks, too. In 1990 there was a much publicized case of a private-housing developer in London's Docklands going out of business. Rising interest rates and prohibitive mortgage payments resulted in the foreclosure of many loans, forcing many of those whose expectations had been raised by government publicity into literal homelessness or the hidden homelessness of having to share. And to the problems experienced by families struggling on low incomes to keep up rent payments were added the cutting of housing benefits, a provision on which no less than two-thirds of all public-sector tenants were estimated to rely.

The objectives were essentially economic but the means were political. One example of this was the electoral system devised by the government to decide whether a council estate should be put into the hands of a private landlord. The decision was to be based on a simple majority vote by the tenants, 'yes' or 'no'. However, abstentions and absentees were also to be counted as 'yes' votes. Despite this loading – or perhaps because of it – numerous inner-city estates began to record very high turnouts and almost unanimous votes in favour of staying in the public sector.

In October 1989 large advertisements appeared in the national press headed 'Solving the housing shortage – the hard facts, not the soft soap'. Produced by a campaign called 'More Land for Homes', the advertisements stated that two million new homes were needed by the end of the century and that the way to achieve this lay mainly through the lifting of planning restrictions. 'Planning policies', rather than the economic situation, were preventing new homes being built. More houses should be built outside the cities, and fewer restrictions should apply to Green Belt and agricultural land.

The campaign was sponsored by various federations of builders, building materials producers and building societies, so it was not surprising that the unfettering of the private sector should be their solution to a 'crisis'. The crisis perceived by the campaigners did not appear to be one of homelessness, or of the decline of public-sector housing, or of inner-urban decay. Houses for sale on green belt land do nothing to relieve the problems of the poor of the inner city. If anything, the crisis was one of profitability for the campaign's members. The campaign represented the efforts of one branch of capital, the building industry, to share the benefits that another branch of capital, the financial sector, was gaining from the break-up of the welfare state. Aversion of the housing crisis, if it means anything at all, must mean an emphasis on housing provision for the most disadvantaged, within the context of a coherent and humane strategy for the country as a whole, in which a balance is struck between policies for energy, employment, transport, conservation and housing. For almost twenty years the general drift of policy has been in the opposite direction.

During World War II and in the immediate postwar years progressive architects saw the need to confront the central problem of inequality in housing. What is more, they realized the necessity of doing this within the context of a national planning strategy, as the thinking of J. M. Richards[5] and many others makes clear.

But a major difference between the Milner Holland report and the various reports on housing need which appear today is one of context. In 1965, a concerted if inadequate attempt could be made to match the need; economic and political circumstances both permitted and demanded it. Now, however, the prospects of improving the housing of all those in need are much more remote. Even when the right economic and political circumstances do emerge, an entire system of housing provision will have to be recreated.

# 3 Down with Modernism — the New Right ideology

If we consider any modern building, from a single house to a big commercial development, we can see that it comes into being by means of a complex web of economic choices and decisions. Architecture, like all other elements of the social superstructure, rests on our society's economic base, that is, the capitalist mode of production, which determines its essential nature. However, it is also affected by other elements within the superstructure, by the state, for example, its politics, bureaucracy and laws. The various parts of the superstructure are related, not only because of their common base, but also because of the way they are used, in our society, to maintain and support each other. Most architectural commentators will allow, for example — even if they do not investigate the question very deeply — that architecture, like all our culture, is strongly affected by politics.

Conversely, politics depend on culture. What Antonio Gramsci calls 'hegemony', that is, the ability of a bourgeois-democratic state like that of Britain to obtain and exercise power, depends not only on the coercive machinery of the state itself but also on the participation of most of the people. Gramsci describes this process clearly:

> The 'normal' exercise of hegemony in the area which has become classical, that of the parliamentary regime, is characterised by the combination of force and consensus which vary in their balance with each other, without force exceeding consensus too much. Thus it tries to achieve that force should appear to be supported by the agreement of the majority, expressed by the so-called organs of public opinion — newspapers and associations.[1]

Our entire cultural apparatus — education, literature, entertainment, the press and television, art and architecture — tends to send out messages of support for the state, so that the consent of ordinary people to their own manipulation is secured. 'The ruling ideas of any age', as Marx and Engels have said, 'have ever been the ideas of the ruling class'[2] — and these ideas include architectural ones.

For the last ten years and more, the cultural thinking most closely associated with Britain's ruling group has been that of the 'New Right'. There is, of course, very little that is 'new' about the Right, but the term does express something of the extra confidence with which right-wing views have been expressed since 1979. To some, Thatcherism represented a qualitative change from the consensus politics that were said to have existed since 1945. The difference, if any, lay in the rapidly worsening crisis, which gave Thatcherism both its urgent economic task and the political will with which to address it.

The latter depended partly on establishing a climate of opinion in which narrow class-objectives could be represented as national ones and in which the 'caring' ethos of the welfare state could be replaced by a more individualistic one. These two apparently opposing aims – a broad nationalism and a narrow individualism – were fostered by two basic components of New Right thinking.[3] One of these, 'economic libertarianism', with its references to pre-Keynesian economics, its opposition to the public sector and its reliance on no more than monetary controls, has already been mentioned above (see p. 29). The other, 'social authoritarianism', has several recurring themes. These include support for the concept of 'the nation' and its 'culture', promotion of the idea of 'the family', and the rediscovery of 'Victorian values' and 'traditional morality'.

The reconciliation of libertarian and authoritarian views is clearly effected in the following comment from Roger Scruton: 'the main tasks for conservative rhetoric are to establish in the public mind the inseparability of market freedom and economic leadership, and to integrate the philosophy of the market into the underlying principle of order.'[4]

The *Salisbury Review*, edited by Scruton, is one of a number of conservative projects which have emerged or developed in the last few years, from the economic – such as the Adam Smith Institute or the Institute of Economic Affairs – to the more obviously social – such as the Family Policy Group or the Salisbury Group itself. The concerns range widely, from political, economic and racial themes to history, philosophy, aesthetics and architecture. These last four are brought together by Scruton, David Watkin and other historians into a politically conservative, anti-modernist view of architectural history.

The New Right's historical philosophy seems to be built on two main foundations. One of these is the historical tradition of Peterhouse College, Cambridge, with which a number of the writers are associated. This relies mainly on the work of Herbert Butterfield, particularly his analysis of what he called the 'whig interpretation' of history.[5] Butterfield was critical of 'certain fallacies' offered by progressivist British historians who in his view distorted history by abstracting events from their historical context. From a position of hindsight, 'whig' historians had invested the past with a false sense of progress towards the present. Butterfield criticized in historians 'the tendency ... to praise revolutions ... to emphasise certain principles of progress in the past and to produce a story which is the ratification if not the glorification of the present.'

Butterfield's critique of whig history was extended by others to Marxism which, its critics felt, was also concerned with questions of historical inevitability. Some key works of Karl Popper, for example,[6] which seem to form the other main intellectual base of New Right thought, attack the 'Marxist' view of history. Popper took issue not only with the idea of inevitability but also with the 'social engineering' which he said Marx advocated; society should be allowed to develop in a gradual and 'piecemeal' way. For Popper, 'our western civilization is an essentially pluralistic one ... monolithic social ends would mean the death of freedom; of the freedom of thought, of the free search for truth, and with it, of the rationality and dignity of man.'[7]

As a criticism of Stalinism, this has much substance, and of course it was written in the forties when western interpretations of Marx were strongly influenced by Stalinist reality. As an attack on Marx, it is unnecessary and unjust, since Marx's work itself makes clear that freedom, scientific truth and human dignity are the starting points of his entire philosophy.

Both Popper and Butterfield, however undeservedly, seem to have been useful in the development of a conservative theory of cultural history which says in effect that tradition is important and social change is both undesirable and avoidable, that the bourgeois-democratic world is one of freedom and that enemies of capitalism are enemies of liberty.

A good example of New Right cultural theory is Roger Scruton's analysis of architectural aesthetics.[8] Architecture, he says, is an 'everyday' process. It is concerned with craftsmanship, with 'getting things right', that is, with the 'aesthetics of everyday life' rather than with rhetorical, abstract theories. Modern architecture, with its so-called 'rationalism', is wrong because it deliberately separates aesthetics and architecture, because it subordinates architecture to other things it considers more important, and because it confines architecture to nothing more than 'problem-solving'. If beauty occurs at all in modern architecture, which is doubtful, its proponents say that this is the result of something else. So 'rationalism' is not really rational at all, since it leaves out the most important part of an architect's endeavours, namely aesthetic experience and the values which go with it.

Scruton goes on to examine aesthetic experience, which is made up of two things: sense and intellect. The two are brought together by the architect's imagination, exercised on the basis of his aesthetic discrimination, that is, on a set of judgements based on certain underlying values, which indicate the right or wrong way to build. As to the basis of these values, Scruton examines a number of alternative criteria – Freudian, Marxist, semiological and so on – and concludes that none of these is appropriate. Instead he suggests that rightness in architecture depends on two criteria: 'a sense of style' and 'a sense of appropriate detail'. In Scruton's view, the only architecture to satisfy these criteria is the classical, a term he intends to be used less in a narrow stylistic sense than in a more general one.

Classicism is a common interest among New Right historians. David Watkin has written books on Henry Holland, who designed Carlton House in London, C. R. Cockerell, architect to the Bank of England, and Quinlan Terry, the present-day 'classicist'. He has also produced two highly regarded works of historiography,[9] which have set the standard for a type of architectural criticism in which individualism, personal inspiration and elitism are emphasized and modernism is deplored. *Morality and Architecture* was described by Roger Scruton, in an echo of Butterfield, as 'a diagnosis of certain fallacies in architectural theory associated with the Modern Movement'.[10]

In *The Rise of Architectural History* Watkin describes the English great country house.

> As the uniquely rich product of a society which saw the family as the stimulus to achievement and the channel of its transmission, country houses have been amongst the chief victims of the ultimately Marxist policies of successive Liberal and Labour governments throughout the twentieth century in persistently and deliberately eroding the concept of the family and private property as the basis of society.

The great country house is of much interest to conservative architectural writers and a useful focus for their endeavours. The perceived threat to country houses, as they pass out of family ownership, or as the workings of the market economy make their maintenance increasingly difficult, can be used as a vehicle for a variety of political and social as well as architectural comment.

A major contribution to the scholarship of country houses has been made by the magazine *Country Life* and its various celebrated writers including Mark Girouard and Marcus Binney. The former has produced a number of books describing the great house as both an architectural and a social institution; the latter, with Roy Strong, was responsible for a major exhibition at the Victoria and Albert Museum in London in 1975, which expressed concern at the physical destruction of a number of country houses, out of which in 1977 emerged a preservation society called SAVE Britain's Heritage. A major campaign the same year to save the contents of one country house from dispersal was described by David Watkin as 'the great sale at Mentmore, to which Marcus Binney and others drew the attention of the nation'.

It is common to represent comparatively narrow class interests as the concern of 'the nation'. It often occurs in discussions on the conservation of historic buildings. Conservation in the modern sense began in 1877

# the great country house

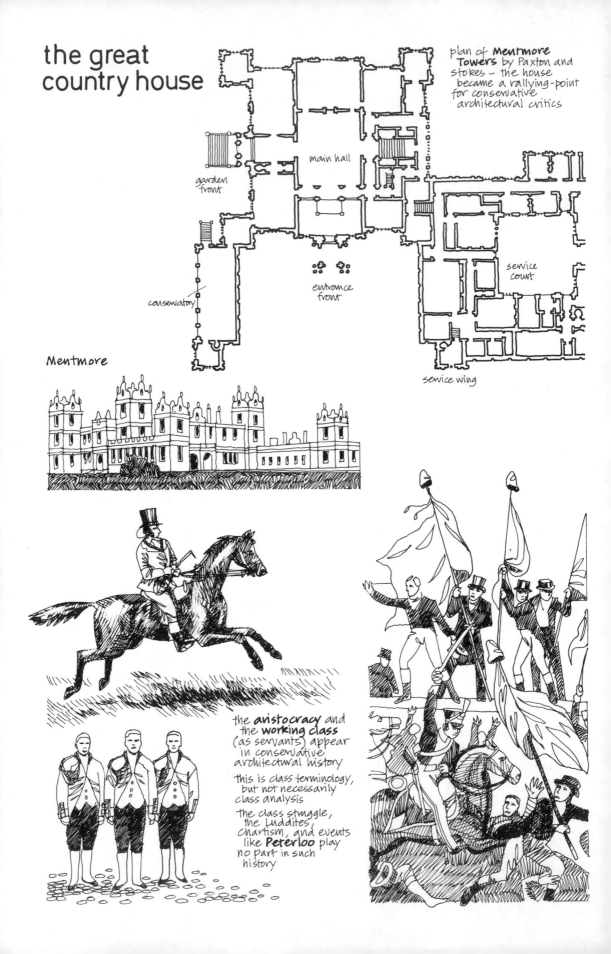

plan of **Mentmore Towers** by Paxton and Stokes – the house became a rallying-point for conservative architectural critics

garden front

main hall

conservatory

entrance front

service court

service wing

Mentmore

the **aristocracy** and the **working class** (as servants) appear in conservative architectural history

this is class terminology, but not necessarily class analysis

the class struggle, the Luddites, Chartism, and events like **Peterloo** play no part in such history

with the founding of the Society for the Protection of Ancient Buildings; legislation followed. Protection was given not only to scheduled Ancient Monuments but also to buildings listed as being of special architectural or historic interest. Till the late sixties the powers were used sparingly and selectively but in 1967 the situation was changed by the Civic Amenities Act. Local authorities were given power to designate 'areas, the character and appearance of which' it is desirable to 'preserve and enhance'. Protection was given now not only to single buildings, but also to large areas of Mayfair or Belgravia, to historic town centres from Durham to Devizes, to Cotswold villages and garden suburbs.

The Act marked the beginning of a period of strong conservationist feeling. Alan Dobby describes it thus:

> Clearly just as the postwar phase of redevelopment in Britain reflected the notion of a better future which had been put up as a major benefit of victory, so the conservationist era we are now in reflects the uncertainties and disillusionment of the age in which we live ... our country grapples somewhat pathetically with decline. Add to this the scepticism with which the unprecedentedly rapid redevelopment of our buildings and cities has been received and one has a thorough condemnation of the environmental consequences of progress ... Thus there is a retrospection to the days before so much was changed and to the past as a whole rather than to the future and its perhaps violent uncertainties. Conservation therefore seeks to retain the symbols of the past.[11]

'Conservation' is of course a term used in two separate contexts: not only in the narrower sense of the built environment but also in the much wider sense of the earth's finite resources. Theoretically the two concerns are compatible and complementary but in practice they seldom are. Conservation in the ecological sense is on the whole progressive, concerned with the future and therefore with political change; conservation of the built environment is almost always about the past and, more immediately, about the preservation not only of a physical but also of a social and political tradition which is seen to be under threat. This elegiac view of the past is expressed by Gavin Stamp in his introduction to a book of photographs of Victorian London.[12] 'Sadly [the photographs] suggest, in meticulous detail and with haunting clarity, that almost every change that has taken place in London since those pioneering days of photography has been a change for the worse.'

Conservation Areas have become familiar features of modern urban life. In them, all buildings and most trees are protected, and money is spent on improvements. They tend to be areas where change is resisted, where modern architecture is frowned on and where property values are high. There can be no denying that, intentionally or not, they are usually privileged places to live. The terminology of conservation includes the

# conservation

ancient monuments like Stonehenge have
been protected since the Act of 1882

by definition, Conservation Areas are
'areas of architectural or historic
interest', so they tend to be comparatively
wealthy areas

Within them, buildings are protected from
unauthorized demolition...

Eltham House,
Kent, mid-
17th century

buildings of architectural or historic
interest have been protected since 1944

... and most trees are
protected

the Civic Amenities Act of 1967 brought
protection to entire areas 'the
character or appearance of which it
is desirable to preserve or enhance!
these were termed **Conservation
Areas**

planning applications affecting
Conservation Areas are publicly
advertised, and carefully
scrutinized by experts

design guidelines are often prepared
to help control the appearance of
details, like roof extensions and
shop-fronts

money can be made available in the
form of grants to improve the
appearance of buildings, and in the
form of environmental improvement
schemes, like pedestrianization

Hampstead, London

Queen Sq., London

concept of 'heritage', often preceded by the word 'our', something it is thought desirable to protect but which is seldom defined. Just as 'nationhood' begs the question as to who constitutes the nation, 'our heritage' is used to create a general feeling of community where none necessarily exists, and makes one ask whose heritage is being preserved and for whose benefit. Resistance to change is not in everyone's interest, either environmentally or politically.

Clearly it is worth preserving many old buildings and environments for their own sake: for their architectural or historic interest and for the light such things shed on our present condition. However, the market adds another dimension. Historic buildings are use-values, but 'heritage' becomes an exchange-value and takes on the fetish character of the commodity. To ideologists, country houses are worth more than their value as mere architecture; as we have seen, they can be symbols of a threatened social system. Conservation Areas can be areas of middle-class privilege. 'Heritage centres' devoted, as they often are, to Britain's industrial past can commercialize and trivialize the history of the working class. And through the architecture of Britain's aristocratic past – that of the classical eighteenth century – new owners can inherit a noble tradition.

Classical architecture, of course, can be reproduced. Throughout the twentieth century there have always been some architects willing to design in a classical style. At times the style has been used creatively, as a point of departure for the imagination. Though Lutyens's classically-inspired buildings tend also to be his most pompous ones, some of them, for example the *Country Life* building in Covent Garden or the Midland Bank in Piccadilly, display the informality and even humour associated with his house designs. John Belcher's free, inventive Edwardian Baroque is seen at its best in the Institute of Chartered Accountants in the City of London. John Burnet's simplified classicism, as in Kodak House in London's Kingsway, formed a link with the early Modern Movement. Albert Richardson's Bracken House in the City, designed originally for the *Financial Times*, continued the inventive classical tradition into the fifties. The principles of classicism even informed the early Modern Movement; Behrens's AEG Turbine Hall in Berlin and Mies van der Rohe's Farnsworth House at Plano, Illinois, being two celebrated examples.

But the crisis of confidence that has affected architecture in the last two decades has affected classicism too. Much recent classicism, by architects such as Raymond Erith, Quinlan Terry and Robert Adam, attempts a literal replication of the Georgian style. Substitute modern materials are often used – precast concrete for stone, or plastic for cast iron – in ways which mimic the originals. In Terry's Richmond Riverside in Surrey, the classical façades hide a modern office interior, raising the question of how

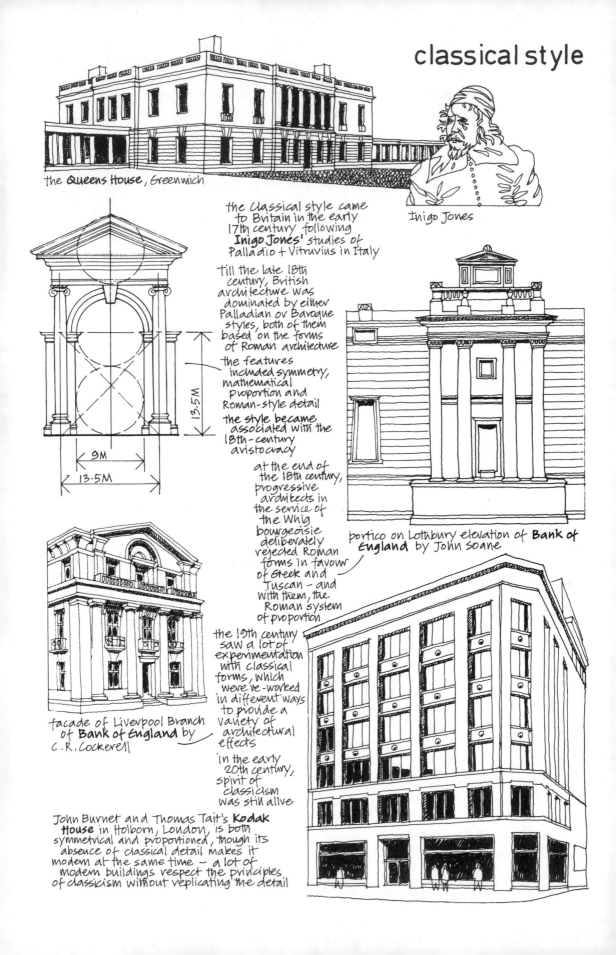

the **Queens House**, Greenwich

Inigo Jones

the classical style came to Britain in the early 17th century following **Inigo Jones'** studies of Palladio + Vitruvius in Italy

till the late 18th century, British architecture was dominated by either Palladian or Baroque styles, both of them based on the forms of Roman architecture

the features included symmetry, mathematical proportion and Roman-style detail

the style became associated with the 18th-century aristocracy

13.5M

9M

13.5M

at the end of the 18th century, progressive architects in the service of the Whig bourgeoisie deliberately rejected Roman forms in favour of Greek and Tuscan — and with them, the Roman system of proportion

portico on Lothbury elevation of **Bank of England** by John Soane

facade of Liverpool Branch of **Bank of England** by C.R. Cockerell

the 19th century saw a lot of experimentation with classical forms, which were re-worked in different ways to provide a variety of architectural effects

in the early 20th century, spirit of classicism was still alive

John Burnet and Thomas Tait's **Kodak House** in Holborn, London, is both symmetrical and proportioned, though its absence of classical detail makes it modern at the same time — a lot of modern buildings respect the principles of classicism without replicating the detail

appropriate they are to the internal functional needs. There is often a gap between the buildings' mundane purpose and the grand and fanciful messages their exteriors seek to convey. 'The Classical Orders were given at the Dawn of History; to me they are Divinely inspired ... Classicism ... is the only alternative; it can and must replace Modernism.'[13]

The 'Dawn of History' argument is common among enthusiasts for classicism. The implication is that classicism is 'our' style, part of 'our heritage', never really far from us at any time in history, but occasionally displaced by foreign imports like modernism. David Watkin points to the arrival of Pevsner in England in the thirties and his 'propaganda' on behalf of the 'refugee architect Gropius' through such books as *Pioneers of the Modern Movement* 'in which "modern", i.e. Bauhaus-inspired, design and socialism were projected as part of a single package'.[14]

Such views of the indigenous nature of classicism and the foreignness of modernism ignore the fact that classicism was introduced into Britain by Inigo Jones early in the seventeenth century and that modernism in Britain has roots which go back to the early Industrial Revolution in the eighteenth century. And Pevsner's supposed socialism fits uneasily with his strongly expressed view that modernism reached its apotheosis in its association with AEG, Siemens and the rest of the industrial capitalist system.

The connection between modernism and socialism was reiterated in 1988 by Quinlan Terry when, rather prematurely, he sounded the death knell of positivism. He said that 'our minds have been so conditioned by the theories of Darwin and Marx that we expect everything to progress ... Now these ideas have been refuted.'[15] 'All through the sixties,' he said, 'the world seemed to have gone mad,' citing as evidence 'buildings which we now recognize as terrible mistakes.' But buildings are created by society itself. As John Lyly wrote in the sixteenth century, an earlier capitalist age, 'If we present a mingle-mangle, our fault is to be excused, because the whole world is become an Hodge-Podge.'

The modern buildings of the sixties were not the result of some great socialist revolution but of the high noon of the capitalist mode of production. And here lies an essential contradiction of conservative architectural theorists. They are supporters not only of traditional values but also of the capitalist system, yet are clearly unhappy with the buildings and environment produced by that system. Unable to recognize or admit this however, they lay the blame elsewhere, as their political conditioning dictates: on Darwin, Marx, Lloyd George, semiotics, modernism, foreign architects, the decline of the family, or simply on the very idea of social progress.

Of course it could be argued that a small number of eccentrics on the periphery of architecture do no harm. At best, their activities can be

# new classicism

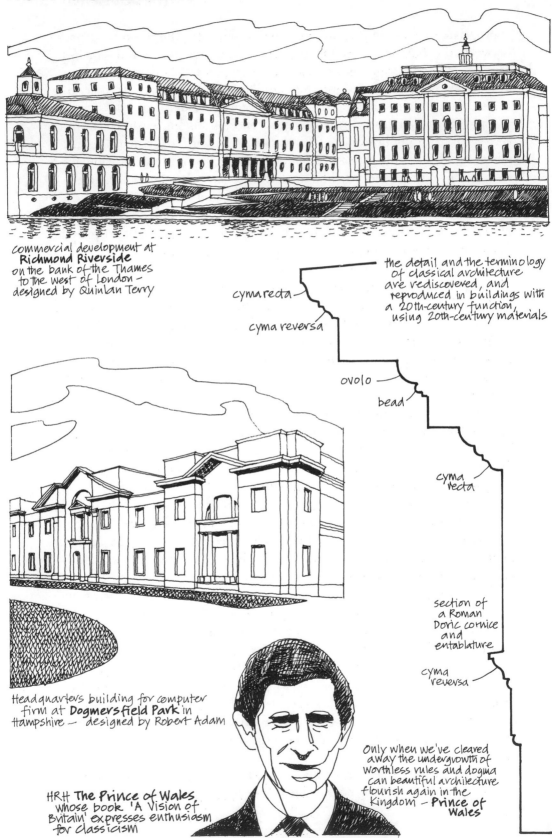

commercial development at **Richmond Riverside** on the bank of the Thames to the west of London – designed by Quinlan Terry

the detail and the terminology of classical architecture are rediscovered, and reproduced in buildings with a 20th-century function, using 20th-century materials

cyma recta

cyma reversa

ovolo

bead

cyma recta

section of a Roman Doric cornice and entablature

cyma reversa

Headquarters building for computer firm at **Dogmersfield Park** in Hampshire — designed by Robert Adam

HRH **The Prince of Wales,** whose book 'A Vision of Britain' expresses enthusiasm for classicism

Only when we've cleared away the undergrowth of worthless rules and dogma can beautiful architecture flourish again in the Kingdom – **Prince of Wales'**

stimulating, and at worst inconsequential; surely a lot is to be gained from cultural variety. In Bolshevik Russia, after all, Constructivism, classicism, Formalism and much else, all coexisted, making their contribution to what Lenin called 'the chaotic ferment, the feverish search for new solutions and new watchwords'. But in revolutionary Russia artistic variety, wide though it was, promoted a single task, that of social reconstruction. For us, artistic variety may result not only from a need to experiment but also from the alienation and conflict of a class society.

If the purpose of ideology is to underpin a political programme, then that of the New Right is to promote class hegemony. Its arguments do not have to be overt, or clear, or coherent; it is enough that they create a generalized feeling of support for tradition, elitism, law and order and market forces, and an equally generalized hostility to immigration, welfare and social progress. In 1991 Mrs Thatcher, with donations from some of the richest capitalists and ruling families of the world, set up a foundation to promote right-wing ideas on an international scale. As long as such ideas persist, there is little hope of bringing about a fairer society by democratic means. And nor is there any hope of creating a sane, balanced city environment, whether it be in the classical, modern or any other architectural style.

# 4 The Surreal City – post-modern architecture and urbanism

In the two previous chapters I have tried to show how architecture is shaped by economic forces and influenced by ruling-class ideas. I shall now look in more detail at the effects of these two factors on architecture and urban design in the late seventies and the eighties. Central to the debate is the question of post-modernism.

This term covers a complex body of ideas affecting all of the contemporary arts and meaning something different in each case. The unifying idea is that post-modernism represents a break from the theory and practice of modernism itself. Sometimes this break is made in a positive sense, in order to develop modernism further. Other times it amounts to a rejection of all that modernism stands for. Most structuralists, for example, would probably see their critical theory as a development rather than a rejection. Post-modernism in architecture, on the other hand, was defined from the start as a negation of the Modern Movement, and destined to rise from the ruins of modern architecture.

Architecture became 'post-modern' in 1977, when an issue of *Architectural Design*, edited by Charles Jencks, popularized the term.[1] The contributors included Charles Moore, a practitioner, Paul Goldberger, a critic, and Geoffrey Broadbent, an academic. However, Jenck's own views dominated the issue since four of the articles focused on his new book *The Language of Post-Modern Architecture*.

The centrepiece of the argument was a genealogical table which sought to classify the architecture of post-modernism. Seven categories were identified. Vernacular-Popular included Portmeirion, Port Grimaud and Disneyland; Metaphorical included Le Corbusier's chapel at Ronchamp, the Sydney Opera House and Saarinen's TWA air terminal in New York; while Adhocist included the work of Bruce Goff, Herb Greene, Ralph Erskine and Lucien Kroll. A category called Historicist-Regionalist-Pluralist appeared to be the key group and included a number of Japanese designers from Maekawa and Tange to Isozaki and Tayekama, various regional movements such as the Barcelona School and Italian neo-Liberty, and a number of rising American designers such as Robert Venturi and Charles Moore. There were three rather more peripheral categories:

Quasi post-modern, which included Philip Johnson, Michael Graves and Peter Eisenman; Urbanist-Activist, which included the writers Jane Jacobs and Robert Goodman and the theorists O. M. Ungers and Robert and Leon Krier; and a category called Straight Revivalist, which included historicists such as Erith and Terry.

It was a *tour de force* of compilation which raised the immediate question of how such a varied group of designers and movements could possibly be united under a single banner. This was a point the editor seemed to have anticipated by saying that the term post-modern

> does not specifically nominate the characteristics of this new architecture. And this ... is as it should be, because ... the architecture of the modern movement was too specific, too exclusivist in style to fulfil the myriad needs of complex modern society – whereas 'post-modernism' sets no limits other than to advocate opposition to the modern movement.

This raised further questions: how modernism should be defined, and whether all these designers really did consider themselves opponents of it. I have already tried to emphasize modernism as a social as well as a technical and stylistic project. Precisely because the modernists tried to confront a variety of human problems, they had actually produced an enormous variety of solutions. Jencks, however, chose to define modernism narrowly, in terms of style alone. Furthermore, by implicitly equating modernism with crude Functionalism, he was able to claim that it lacked stylistic variety, ignoring the fact that it had always been regionalist, pluralist, adhocist and many other things besides. Many modernist architects were themselves deeply dissatisfied with the postwar environment and were continuing to humanize their architecture, improving user-participation, raising technical standards and allowing local or regional variations to create ever greater variety.

Much of the work categorized by Jencks as post-modern actually belongs in this group. Ronchamp, for example, is a modernist building, and has been praised, in the words of Dennis Sharp, 'for its spatial organization, its originality and the way, as a design, it enriched rational architecture'.[2] Its 'metaphorical' content was inherent in its programme and not something to be separated out in order to be able to say it was not a modern building. Erskine's Byker Wall too was highly functional: its *raison d'être* was that it was designed to meet the specific needs of its tenants. To say that its unorthodox appearance made it something other than modern was to disregard how that appearance was arrived at. And Kenzo Tange's masterpiece, the Tokyo Olympic sports-hall complex, with its dynamic and unprecedented roof structures, was one of the key works of modern architecture.

To apply the label 'post-modern' to such works was perhaps unexceptionable in itself. What was more dangerous was the implication that lay

47

# post-modernism 1

Charles Jencks's category of **Vernacular-Popular** included Disneyland, together with Clough Williams-Ellis's **Portmeirion** (left) and François Spoerry's **Port Grimaud** (above)

the **Metaphorical** category included Le Corbusier's chapel at Ronchamp, Eero Saarinen's TWA air terminal at Kennedy Airport, and Jorn Utzon's **Sydney Opera House** (above)

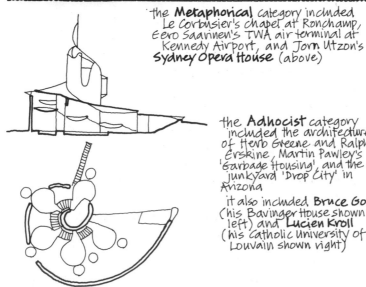

the **Adhocist** category included the architecture of Herb Greene and Ralph Erskine, Martin Pawley's 'Garbage Housing', and the junkyard 'Drop City' in Arizona

it also included **Bruce Goff** (his Bavinger House shown left) and **Lucien Kroll** (his Catholic University of Louvain shown right)

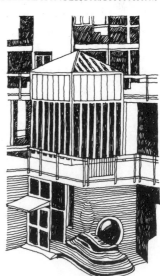

Venturi's **Guild House** apartments

Charles Jencks's category of **Historicist-Regionalist-Pluralist** included the work of Robert Stern, Charles Moore, and **Robert Venturi**

the category of **Quasi-post-Modernism** included the work of Saannen, Philip Johnson and Michael Graves, and of **Peter Eisenman**

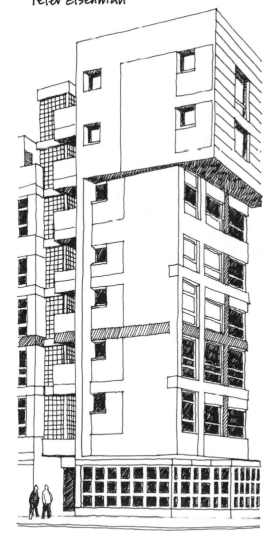

apartment block by Eisenman at the **IBA** in Berlin

the category of **Urbanist-Activist** included Robert Goodman, Oscar Newman and **Jane Jacobs**, author of 'The Death and Life of Great American Cities'

a final category of **Straight Revivalist** included the work of classicists like Erith and Terry

behind it: that society and its architecture were now entering a new age, and that problems and solutions were qualitatively different from before. By breaking with modernism, post-modernists could conveniently lose sight of some of its most difficult, challenging and valuable concepts: the social role of architecture, the strong link between theory and practice, the close integration of design and technology, the sense of dynamism, progress and revolutionary change. In their place would come flimsy, stylistic theorizing which, like that of the New Right, would obscure the issues and make social criticism more difficult.

Jencks's symbol of the death of modern architecture was the much-publicized demolition in 1972 of the Pruitt-Igoe flats in St Louis, Missouri, designed by Minoru Yamasaki only twenty years before. The high level of vandalism on the estate was said by the authorities to have demonstrated the unsuitability of its design. From this, Jencks inferred the unsuitability of modern architecture for public housing. This argument appears to have been based not on the examination of the social or economic issues, on questions of ownership, management, income or employment, but on aesthetic criteria. The supposed 'univalence' of the modern style was said to be limited compared with the 'multivalence' of the stylistic pluralism offered by the post-modernists. Post-modernism used the architectural equivalent of language – words, syntax, metaphor – to project its 'meaning'. The aim was to supplant the simple language of modern architecture with one of greater subtlety, a metaphorical language full of overlaid meanings.

This thinking owed a lot to structuralism, especially to the terminology – if not always the method – of semiotics. Semiological analysis deals with language as a system, rather than with what individual languages say about reality. There had been parallels between modern architecture, with its search for truth and honesty, and what one might call early modern literary theory which, from the nineteenth century onwards had required the novelist and poet to express his or her true self and had expected the written work to tell some kind of truth about real life. Neither semiotics nor, in its turn, post-modern architectural theory were primarily concerned with the expression of truth about the author or the world.

To Barthes language was a pre-existing system from which the author drew ready-made constructs. Barthes rejected the view that words refer to actual things in the world; his idea of the inseparability of the mark on the page, the 'signifier', and the concept it conveyed, the 'signified', gave signs and sign-systems a life of their own, independent of the everyday world of objects. Thus language became relative, complex and indeterminate; it was no longer a simple expression of truth-to-life, but a kind of negotiated contract between the word and the person reading it. Words evoked different concepts for different people, so the reader was as much part of the literary process as the words he or she read.

Into this complex world of literary methodology stepped the post-modern architectural theorists, Jencks, Venturi and others, concerned to divorce architectural theory from the mundane world of tower blocks, industrialized building and vandalism, and to create a subtle architectural language with different levels of meaning, to which onlookers would respond differently, according to their level of sophistication: 'I like complexity and contradiction in architecture . . . I like elements which are hybrid rather than pure . . . I am for messy vitality over obvious unity . . . I prefer "both-and" to "either-or".'[3]

Most of the modernists had thought they could change society by architectural means alone. The post-modernists expected to achieve more positive results merely by substituting one style for another. Paul Goldberger described post-modernism as

a reaction against everything that modern architecture has come to represent – although not, curiously, against all that the modernists said. Their rhetoric, oriented more to social concerns than formal ones, retains a certain appeal. But its underlying belief that better architecture would bring about the good life for us all seems, today, hopelessly naive at best, destructively wrong-headed at worst . . . Some of the roots of Post-Modernism are thus philosophical: they emerge from the modest, anti-utopian impulse, from a belief in incremental movement rather than cataclysmic change.[4]

This is a fair criticism of some of the underlying attitudes of the modernists. It also suggests that the post-modern programme was seen as making some kind of social contribution, if not through radical change then at least through gradual improvement. But a predilection for visual pluralism and a liking for architecture overlaid with 'meanings' were inadequate means with which to confront the manifold inner-city problems that lay behind the failure of Pruitt-Igoe.

Already in 1977 in Britain the worsening economic situation was forcing a withdrawal from social commitment in architecture. With finance capital determined to save itself from the recession, the idea of social progress would have needed much more support than that offered by the vague theories of the post-modernists. On the other hand, post-modernism seemed highly appropriate to Britain's increasingly market-based society. One by one, the various strands of post-modernism ceased to represent the way forward and became part of conventional bourgeois wisdom.

Jencks described his first category as Vernacular-Popular, though his examples were not so much traditional vernacular design as they were Pop. When Pop Art emerged in the late fifties it came in the wake of a period of postwar angst in western culture. The existentialism of Sartre, for instance, or the abstract expressionism of Jackson Pollock represented a disengagement from ordinary life which Pop Art seemed about to rectify. Pop was fresh and uncomplicated, accessible and seemingly democratic. It appeared to have hit on a genuinely popular artistic language, and promotion in the media brought it to a wider audience than usual for an artistic movement.

Richard Hamilton's collage for the 'This is Tomorrow' exhibition in London in 1956 was an extraordinary compilation of popular images, which both celebrated and made an ironic comment on the consumer society. The paintings of Andy Warhol, showing Marilyn Monroe, Jackie Kennedy or such subjects as automobile accidents or the electric chair, offered poignant or horrific views of the modern world. Warhol disclaimed any social significance for his work, but there is no doubt that Pop Art was well placed to express not only the excitement but also the degradation of life under capitalism.

Pop also challenged the concept of what art was. The repetition of photographic images, as in *Marilyn Monroe*, flew in the face of centuries of painterly tradition. Lichtenstein's use of comic-book material raised similar questions of technique, and also of subject matter. Oldenburg's giant household objects – ice-cream cones, hamburgers, typewriters – some of them designed as public monuments, challenged the traditional concept of civic dignity. But it is not really surprising that Pop Art, so saleable, and so close in mood to the world of show business and popular music, should end up commercialized. It was unable to sustain its critical commentary on the commercial world because that world assimilated it.

Pop architecture had never been so challenging. Portmeirion in north Wales was a poetic and very personal piece of escapism, while Port Grimaud, a luxurious Riviera holiday resort, and Disneyland, an entertainment centre in California, were unashamed essays in commercialism. 'Popular' here means commercially successful rather than democratic, and 'vernacular' means not the unselfconscious use of indigenous architectural forms but the conscious exploitation of nostalgia for all it is worth.

Another of Jencks's categories was Metaphorical. It is true that, like Ronchamp, both Sydney Opera House and the TWA terminal at Kennedy airport have a strong metaphorical content. However this is not superimposed from some external source but derives essentially from the way the functional problems are solved in each case. In none of these buildings is there a reliance on prefigured forms; instead they are invented anew, as modernism demanded but as post-modernism, increasingly, did not.

During the eighties, architectural metaphor took on forms which, far from being invented anew, derived from some pre-existing stylistic tradition. Metaphorical expression in architecture became dominated by a school of 'free-style Classicists', some of them former modernists, to whom language was more important than function. In the United States there were Charles Moore, Robert Stern, and the firm of Venturi, Rauch and Scott-Brown; in Japan there were Arata Isozaki and Takefumi Aida, and the Europeans included James Stirling, John Outram, Aldo Rossi, Hans Hollein and Ricardo Bofill. Classical elements tended to be applied, whatever the function or status of the building. The justification for this was often the same as that on which Quinlan Terry's more literal classicism relied: that classical architecture is a common inheritance for the west, which goes back to the dawn of history. John Outram's quest for these architectural roots, for example, has been described as 'a highly romantic, almost Jungian urge towards the primeval, as he searches for architectural origins in Greek and Egyptian antiquity, in the creation of the Earth and its elements, and in the subconscious fantasies of the mind'.[5] The building in question is a water-authority pumping station in London's Isle of Dogs.

Outram describes another of his buildings thus:

Each of the five pediments ... shelters a similar being: a cylinder of bricks. This ideal [Platonic] form stands in the position of the statue in its aedicule, that is, centralized on the axis of the fastigium. Yet the cylinder also mimics the role of the guardians of the aedicule, that is, the columns, those transformations of person into pillar which became the orders.[6]

This building is a row of five light-industrial workshops in Kensal Rise, London. The question obviously arises why a pumping station or a workshop should be designed as an ancient religious building. Again there is a gap between the buildings' humble but worthy purpose and the grandiose architectural rhetoric with which they are presented.

Many current 'free-style classical' projects are private houses, such as Hollein's Haus Molag in Vienna, Aida's 'Toy Block' house in Tokyo, Robert Stern's Silvera House in New Jersey and Charles Jencks's own house in Cape Cod, Massachusetts.

It might be argued that the style of a private house, grandiloquent or not, is nobody's business but the owner's. The application of such stylistic virtuosity to mass housing is more questionable. Jencks approvingly describes the Palace of Abraxas, Theatre and Arch, a high-density housing scheme in Marne-la-Vallée, designed by the Spanish post-modernist Ricardo Bofill, as follows: 'Previous constructional elements – column, entablature, capital – are now amplified in scale ... The result is surreal, as one would expect, and frightening, due to the Piranesian scale.'[7] Surrealism was the art of Freudian nightmare, and Piranesi drew imaginary prisons. The Pruitt-Igoe flats and many other modernist blocks were rightly condemned for the inhuman environments they offered.

53

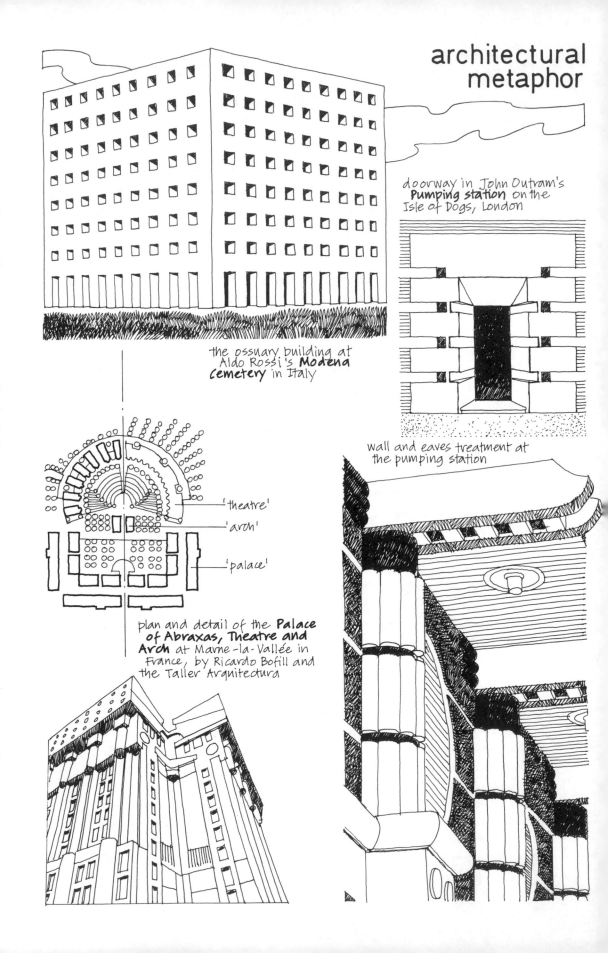

doorway in John Outram's
**Pumping station** on the
Isle of Dogs, London

the ossuary building at
Aldo Rossi's **Modena
cemetery** in Italy

wall and eaves treatment at
the pumping station

'theatre'

'arch'

'palace'

plan and detail of the **Palace
of Abraxas, Theatre and
Arch** at Marne-la-Vallée in
France, by Ricardo Bofill and
the Taller Arquitectura

Their failures were due partly to external circumstances and partly to architectural miscalculation or ineptitude; the inhumanity was arguably unwitting. The post-modernists had claimed to offer something better. However, the uncompromising environment of Bofill's Palace, Theatre and Arch seems to have been the *raison d'être* of the project, effectively turning the tenants into no more than walk-on players in the architect's 'surreal . . . and frightening' theatrical conception.

Classicism is claimed to be universal, part of everyone's 'heritage'. As Stalin said, 'The people deserve columns'. But in reality, the classical tradition is one of privilege. It became so in Renaissance Italy, when the architect ceased to be an artisan, and learned his art from books, becoming, in the words of William Morris, 'the great architect, carefully kept for the purpose, and guarded from the common troubles of common men'. From then on, classicism was an arcane cultural language, dependent on a privileged education and understood only by initiates, the language of the aristocracy and their successors. Versailles, St Petersburg, Washington, DC, New Delhi, Mussolini's EUR and Speer's Berlin were all in their different ways expressions of hegemony, of the superiority of one class over another. When the people are given classicism as 'their' architecture, democracy and equality are often the last things on offer.

This is the cultural context of 'free-style classicism'. In O. M. Ungers' project for an architectural museum in Frankfurt one must apparently read references to Schinkel. Isozaki's Tsukuba civic centre has elements of Ledoux and Michelangelo. Aldo Rossi's Modena cemetery evokes an image of the Nazi death camps, while Rob Krier's 'White House' apartments in Berlin-Kreuzberg resemble the work of Heinrich Tessenow, the tutor of Speer. Metaphorical post-modernism, as defined by Jencks in 1977, seemed to offer a lively pluralism which distinguished it from the monotony of which he accused modernism. 'Metaphor' as now practised means something much less pluralistic: the application of a set of arcane rules with disturbing overtones of repression.

One of the more positive approaches defined by Jencks was the one he called Adhocism. The prairie architecture of Bruce Goff and Herb Greene – for example the former's Bavinger House and the latter's Greene House, both at Norman, Oklahoma – had long been famous for its creative use of local materials and its sensitivity to the needs of individual clients. Then Ralph Erskine in the late sixties and Lucien Kroll in the seventies developed the same tailor-made approach to the design of buildings for whole communities, the former for council tenants at Byker on Tyneside and the latter for university students at Louvain in Belgium. Kroll acted as what he called an 'orchestrator' of other participants' ideas: the clients and the building workers were enabled to improvise parts of the buildings themselves. The benefits were both architectural and social.

# ad hoc architecture

Bruce Goff's **Bavinger House** at Norman, Oklahoma, built in 1950-55

a 'junk-yard' geodesic dome house at **Drop City**, Arizona, in the mid-1960s

Herb Greene's **Greene House**, also at Norman, Oklahoma, built in 1960-61

0   5 metres

car port

gallery + lounge

kitchen dining

bed room

outdoor living space

bed room

Bruce Goff's **Ford House** at Aurora, Illinois, built in 1950, out of 'Quonset' prefabricated frames

the Medical Faculty Buildings 'orchestrated' by Lucien Kroll and designed with the help of students and workers, at the **Catholic University of Louvain**, near Brussels, in 1969-74

In 1968 Erskine was asked to help in the redevelopment of the depressed area of Byker, near the centre of Newcastle-upon-Tyne. Around 8,000 people were to be rehoused, many from the existing inner-city housing of Byker itself. Erskine was therefore able to enter a dialogue with the people who would occupy the new homes. He set up an office on the site to study local people's needs and preferences; it became a drop-in centre to which both complaints and suggestions were directed, and had a crucial effect on the form of the housing. Many positive features emerged from the consultation: the retention of some of the buildings proposed for demolition but which the people wanted to keep; a rolling programme of demolition and rehousing which helped to keep old social ties intact; the inclusion of more ground-level family homes than had been previously proposed; the disposition of workshops and community spaces throughout the development to provide a richer mix of activities. One would have to insist on a very narrow definition of modernism to conclude that such a progressive social programme was not modernist. However, labels are less important than the concept itself which was that architecture was and should be moving in a more democratic direction.

There were two main aspects to the housing crisis of the sixties and seventies. One was a problem of quantity: that an increasing number of people in both industrialized and industrializing countries were badly housed, if at all. This was a problem to be solved only by greater productivity, to which the architect could make a major contribution through his or her technical skill, but which depended ultimately on the treatment of housing production as a matter of public priority. Clearly, this could be addressed better in some societies than others, where it would demand structural social change.

The other problem was one of quality; it was recognized that even in – or perhaps especially in – advanced capitalist societies, high levels of housing production did not in themselves produce good housing. In most kinds of housing, much greater sensitivity to people's needs was required. Here again, architects could make a major contribution – though here too it would ultimately be necessary to confront issues which derived from the organization of capitalist society itself.

In the work of the Adhocist designers, the problem of quality was addressed more than that of quantity. By promoting participation in the design and management of public housing they could compensate people to some extent for the alienation of the housing production process. Through the innovative and imaginative use of cheap and unconventional building methods, a direct response to the literally ad hoc methods of Third World shantytown dwellers forced to rely on their own resources, they could offer prototypes for a more democratic and sensitive environment.

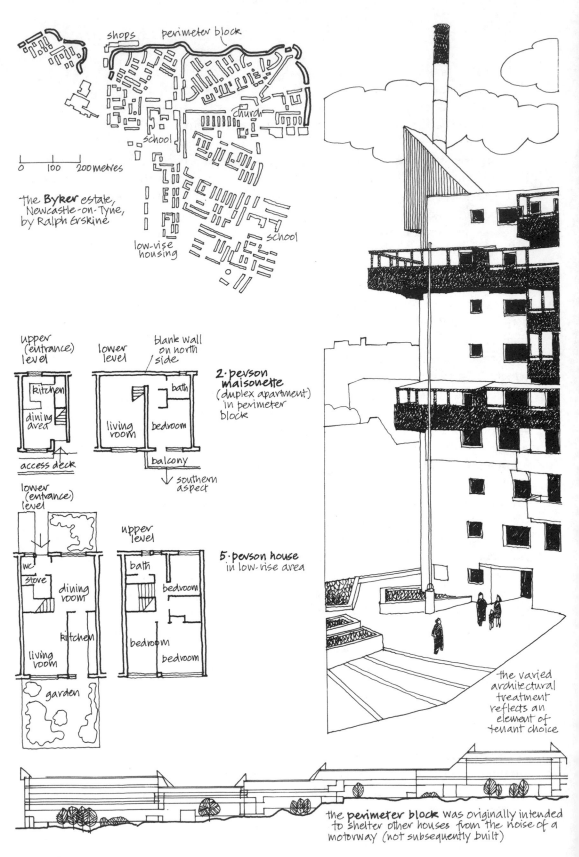

shops　perimeter block

the **Byker** estate,
Newcastle-on-Tyne,
by Ralph Erskine

0    100    200 metres

church

school

low-rise
housing

school

upper
(entrance)
level

lower
level

blank wall
on north
side

kitchen

dining
area

access deck

bath

living
room

bedroom

balcony

southern
aspect

**2-person
maisonette**
(duplex apartment)
in perimeter
block

lower
(entrance)
level

upper
level

wc

store

dining
room

kitchen

living
room

garden

bath

bedroom

bedroom

bedroom

**5-person house**
in low-rise area

the varied
architectural
treatment
reflects an
element of
tenant choice

the **perimeter block** was originally intended
to shelter other houses from the noise of a
motorway (not subsequently built)

# Byker

But architects working as individuals to make gradual improvements in their own attitudes or methods have only a marginal effect on such large-scale problems. Since the seventies, Third World urbanization has continued to grow, creating an ever more desperate housing shortage. The environment of the industrialized cities has also deteriorated, and shantytowns in their various forms have spread through the western world. In 1977 Jencks went so far as to categorize the bidonvilles – the oil-drum cities – as post-modern Adhocism. This romanticism was questionable at the time; it would be even less appropriate now that world poverty has greatly increased and even in London hundreds of people live in cardboard boxes.

The fourth category cited by Jencks was the most mainstream post-modern group of all: what he called, in a turn of phrase worthy of Polonius, Historicist-Regionalist-Pluralist. Here were the key figures of early post-modernism – Venturi and Rauch, Moore and Stern – around whose ideas, I suspect, the whole post-modern edifice had been raised. They were the most dedicated anti-modernists, deliberately setting out to refute the principles of modernism and to ensure that their buildings consciously offended modernist canons of taste and correctness. Mies van der Rohe's doctrine of 'less is more' was contradicted by Robert Venturi's half-serious, half-flippant, 'less is a bore'. Le Corbusier had aspired to the qualities he saw in Greek temples and gothic cathedrals. The inspiration for post-modern Historicist-Regionalist-Pluralist architecture was often consciously banal, ranging from Californian Spanish-colonial to the dour brick style of twenties apartment blocks, from the commercial buildings of the Los Angeles boulevard to the illuminated advertisements of the Las Vegas strip. Or alternatively, high architectural styles would be used, but in a spirit of light-hearted mimicry. Either way, the serious purposes of modernism would be made to seem over-sophisticated; at the same time post-modernism would achieve its own kind of sophistication for initiates, who would recognize the amusing stylistic cross-references.

Robert Venturi's house for his mother at Chestnut Hill, Pennsylvania, was deliberately simple, like a child's drawing of a house, and his Brant House at Greenwich, Connecticut, derived both from the eighteenth-century tradition and from Art Deco. One of Charles Moore's best-known works was the Piazza d'Italia in New Orleans, an external space surrounded by a studied composition of neo-classical facades, in bright colours and picked out in neon strip lighting; the initiated would read in it light-hearted references both to ancient Rome and to the architecture of Schinkel. Perhaps the best-known post-modern building was the office block in Portland, Oregon, designed by Michael Graves almost as a gigantic gift-box with classical-style wrapping. The classicism, Jencks commented, was to 'communicate with the public'.[7]

# historicism

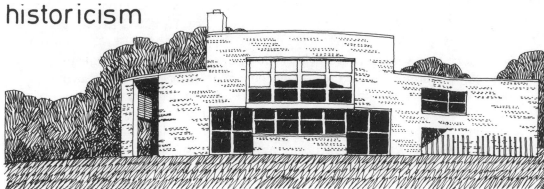

Robert Venturi's **Brant House**, Greenwich, Connecticut, whose bay-windowed form is reminiscent of the 18th C house, and whose Jazz-Modern brickwork recalls Art Deco

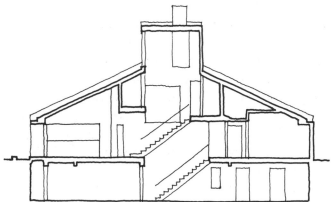

the **Vanna Venturi** house, by Robert Venturi for his mother, at Chestnut Hill, Pennsylvania

Michael Graves's 'gift-wrapped' **Portland building**, in Portland, Oregon

light-hearted classical imagery at Piazza d'Italia

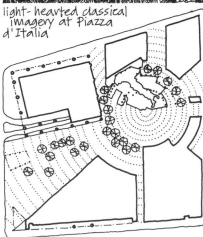

Charles Moore's **Piazza d'Italia**, classical buildings, piazza and fountain with a map of Italy, in New Orleans, Louisiana

This quintessential post-modernism was as American as the Modern Movement itself had been European. The universal influence of American culture has often met with European disapproval, criticized by the left for its perceived neocolonialism and by the right for the way its more popular aspects erode 'traditional values'. This was less true of Britain, perhaps, where a political 'special relationship' had existed at least since the forties. During the eighties, the economic crisis had brought Reagan's right-wing administration to power, and it discovered many common interests with the Thatcher government: hostility to eastern and suspicion of western Europe, an interventionist foreign policy, a distaste for domestic welfare spending. A broad cultural unanimity emerged, which the sympathetic British media were ready to help foster. A consensus of support for the USA developed in the press. It became possible to say, for example, that the United States was 'the most successful experiment in human living that has been achieved on this planet so far ... The debt of civilization to the United States in the twentieth century is incalculable ... it is only thanks to the United States that free institutions have survived anywhere in the world.'[8]

Post-modernism was part of this ideological tendency. It indicated the end of modern utopianism, the rejection of welfare capitalism. In their place had come the 'free market', of which post-modernism, in theory and practice, was a clear expression. In Britain, an all-purpose post-modern style appeared, applicable equally to housing, superstores, studio work-shops and office blocks. It was recognizable by its rudimentary pediments, cylindrical columns and semi-circular arches, polychrome brickwork, low-pitched roofs with overhanging eaves, colour-coated window frames and glazed, barrel-vaulted 'atria'. The architecture of Chassay Wright, for example the houses in St Alban's Road in north London, or of Campbell, Zogolovitch, Wilkinson and Gough, best known for their 'Cascades' housing in London's Docklands, displayed a certain confident elegance; that of scores of others offered only ostentation. Typified perhaps by Richard Seifert's *Daily Telegraph* building in Docklands, this post-modernism was the style of Thatcherism: inappropriate and indifferent to the urgent tasks of the inner city.

Of Jencks's three remaining categories – Quasi post-modern, Straight Revivalist and Urbanist-Activist – it was the last which had the most relevance to contemporary urban problems. In compiling his catalogue, he had included some distinguished theorists: Jane Jacobs, whose *The Death and Life of Great American Cities* criticized planners for their lack of awareness of the way urban life was really lived; Robert Goodman, who in *After the Planners* emphasized the political strength of community action; and Oscar Newman, whose work on 'defensible space' was a strong but positive criticism of conventional housing design. Which of these, if any, are post-modern, is debatable. All were critics of the way modernism had been applied, and all advocated humanization of the system which had created it. On the other hand, there is clearly a big gap between their essential social-mindedness and the stylistic escapism and hard commercialism of much post-modern thinking.

There were other urbanists on Jencks's list, however, to whom style was quite important. These included the German professor Oswald Ungers and two brothers, Robert and Leon Krier, from Luxembourg. All three were practitioners – with some buildings to their credit – lecturers, and writers, much of whose reputation rested on their theories of urban design as embodied in various hypothetical schemes for the reconstruction of major cities. These theories depended principally on classical traditions of urban design, and made reference to Hadrian's Villa, to the Renaissance city, to neo-classicists like Piranesi and Schinkel, and to more recent examples of neo-classicism, like Speer's Berlin. Their schemes, like Ungers' design for student housing in Berlin, Leon Krier's Triangular Civic Building project, designed for Rome, and Robert Krier's Ritterstrasse housing in Berlin, were strongly utopian. In them they attempted to challenge the values of the modern city by referring to some lost or mythical world of civic-mindedness and communality, a kind of syndicalist society in which individual self-development takes place within an overall framework of benign public order. The latter is expressed through a rather authoritarian combination of neo-classical architecture and grand civic spaces. 'Architecture must avoid the ever-changing whim of the market place. It doesn't need innovation. Classical architecture has no innovation. No style except one – immutable. The buildings of classical architecture are not objects of consumption.'[9]

The unreality of this world is underlined by the surreal nature of many of the drawings in which it is depicted; the dream-like townscapes of Giorgio de Chirico, for example, seem to have had a particular effect on Leon Krier. There is a more fundamental unreality too; all these theories look towards a changed future society, yet there is no indication of the kind of critical political and economic practice that would be necessary to accomplish such a change. Quite the reverse.

This can be seen in the big neo-classical scheme proposed by the Prince of Wales and his collaborators for the Paternoster area near St Paul's Cathedral in London. Here the Prince used his influence to secure the rejection of a modernist redevelopment proposal and to replace it with one in which all the major post-modernists and neo-classicists – from Terry Farrell to John Simpson, from Robert Adam to Demetri Porphyrios – have collaborated. The way privilege has been used to override the planning process and to prescribe a particular solution is neither democratic nor progressive.

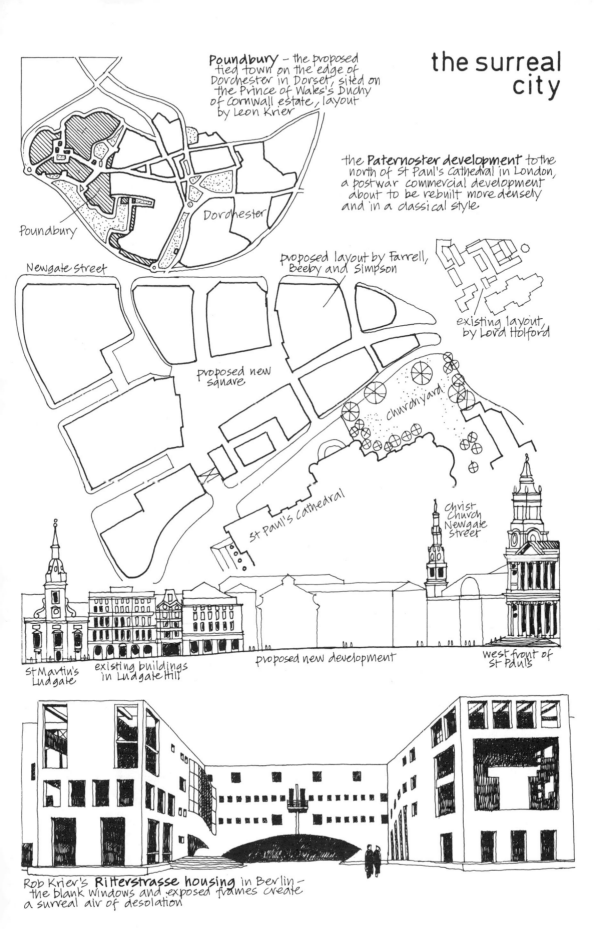

**Poundbury** – the proposed tied town on the edge of Dorchester in Dorset, sited on the Prince of Wales's Duchy of Cornwall estate, layout by Leon Krier

Poundbury

Dorchester

the **Paternoster development** to the north of St Paul's Cathedral in London, a postwar commercial development about to be rebuilt more densely and in a classical style.

Newgate Street

proposed layout by Farrell, Beeby and Simpson

existing layout, by Lord Holford

proposed new square

churchyard

St Paul's Cathedral

Christ Church Newgate Street

St Martin's Ludgate

existing buildings in Ludgate Hill

proposed new development

west front of St Paul's

Rob Krier's **Ritterstrasse housing** in Berlin – the blank windows and exposed frames create a surreal air of desolation

This is also seen in Leon Krier's collaboration with the Prince in the development of part of the Duchy of Cornwall estates on the edge of Dorchester in Dorset. An area now known as Poundbury has been designed by Krier as an ideal suburb, which, it is suggested, will reverse the twentieth-century trend towards alienation by providing family accommodation focused round a 'public realm' in which people can meet. Its centralized land-ownership, its neo-classical design, its cottage industries and its emphasis on neighbourhood values make it a present-day version of the utopian tied towns of the nineteenth century. In Bournville and Port Sunlight the well-intentioned paternalism was demeaning and restrictive; prescriptive theories imposed from above do not bring freedom; authoritarianism, however well disguised, does not create a new society, merely a strengthening of the old one.

When the term 'post-modernism' was first coined, the architecture it described seemed to hold out hope for the future.

> It's an architecture of strong forms, sometimes overtly literary or symbolic, deliberately eliciting interpretations. It denies ultra-simplicity, bald functionalism, plain machine technology. It's often eclectic – it harks back to historical forms, and uses them richly . . . Imagination is back . . . it has the vitality and interest of a new direction, the first really new one in architecture in over fifty years.[10]

But during the eighties, social theory had become more retrogressive. It was not necessary to subscribe to the ideas of the New Right; a number of revisionist neo-Marxist theories were meanwhile offering a falsely progressive and newly 'realistic' view of the world. The British Communist Party said that we now lived in 'new times'. The old class-struggles, which had so characterized the thinking of the early modern period, were now said to be dead. In the seventies, Daniel Bell had noted 'the coming of post-industrial society', and now André Gorz bid 'farewell to the working class'. Post-modernism was part of this general retreat from reality into a so-called 'New Age' which in fact was rather conservative.

Modernism, with its 'bald functionalism', had many faults, but one of its strengths was the way it attempted to unite theory and practice into a coherent programme for social renewal. There is a wide gap between post-modern theory and practice. The theories are broadly utopian but the practice is at best marginal and inconsequential, at worst aggressively commercial – in effect, an obscurantist theory disguising an exploitative practice. Over the last few years the surreal city has flourished, but the real one has fallen further into decline.

# 5 Going to the Dogs – enterprise culture today

So far this book has been concerned mainly with what one might call qualitative issues: how the capitalist mode of production determines the architectural process; how bourgeois ideology influences architectural theory; and how these two factors together affect architectural design. But it is also important to look at the quantitative aspects of architecture: at how our resources are being allocated, to see what and how much is being built, and where, by whom and for whose benefit.

The first thing to remark is the continued decline of public-sector building in relation to private. Throughout the sixties and up to 1977 the public sector fairly consistently attracted comparable resources; since 1977, however, it has shrunk rapidly and continues to do so, while the private sector grows not only in relative but also in absolute terms.[1]

A second point is that this private-sector growth is not due to any increase in private-sector house building, which in fact has tended to decline, but to a remarkable expansion of the commercial sector. In 1985 alone, commercial work to the value of £1.8 billion was commissioned in Britain, three times as much, in real terms, as in 1975. This increase could be verified empirically by any observer of the urban scene in the mid eighties. At no time, it seemed, had so much building been going on in or near the city centres: the construction of big new shopping malls, superstores and retail warehouses, of luxurious leisure complexes, of high-tech studio workshops and large office developments, to which the dilapidated schools, shabby hospitals and poor inner-city housing formed a poignant contrast.

Glasgow's city centre, with commercial redevelopments such as the St Enoch's Centre and a newly pedestrianized Sauchiehall Street, earned it the title of European 'City of Culture' for 1990, but Glasgow also contains the decaying 'peripheral' estates of Red Road and Drumchapel, and the inner-city area of Hutchestown. A member of the Grieve Inquiry into Glasgow's housing[2] commented that 'There is almost unbelievable human misery on our own doorstep. I would not have believed that such misery could exist in this country as a result of bad housing.'

In Liverpool the Albert Docks were refurbished – very well, it is true – to provide private flats, museums and a gallery, gift shops, wine bars and boat moorings, but the unemployment figure for Greater Merseyside in

# enterprise culture 1

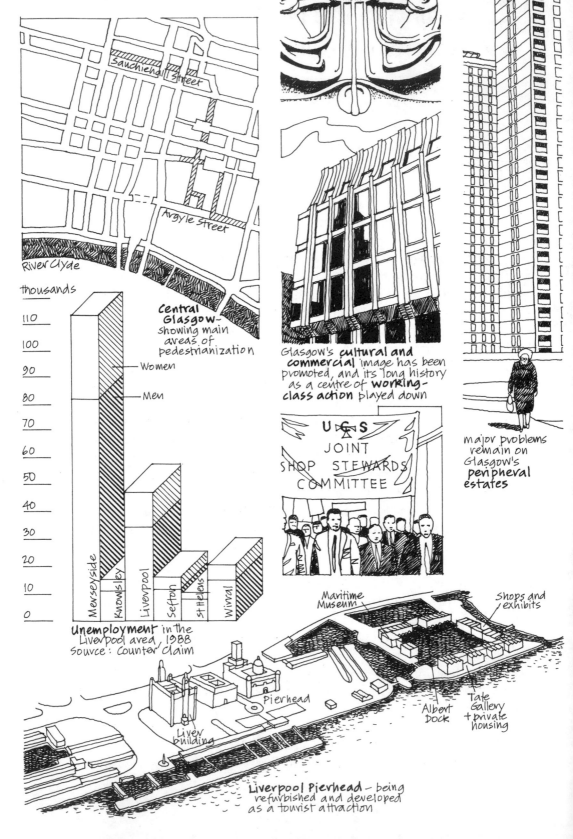

Sauchiehall Street

Argyle Street

River Clyde

**Central Glasgow** – showing main areas of pedestrianization

Glasgow's **cultural and commercial** image has been promoted, and its long history as a centre of **working-class action** played down

U C S
JOINT
SHOP STEWARDS
COMMITTEE

major problems remain on Glasgow's **peripheral estates**

thousands

110
100
90 — Women
80 — Men
70
60
50
40
30
20
10
0

Merseyside
Knowsley
Liverpool
Sefton
St Helens
Wirral

**Unemployment** in the Liverpool area, 1988
Source: Counter Claim

Maritime Museum

shops and exhibits

Pierhead

Liver building

Albert Dock

Tate Gallery + private housing

**Liverpool Pierhead** – being refurbished and developed as a tourist attraction

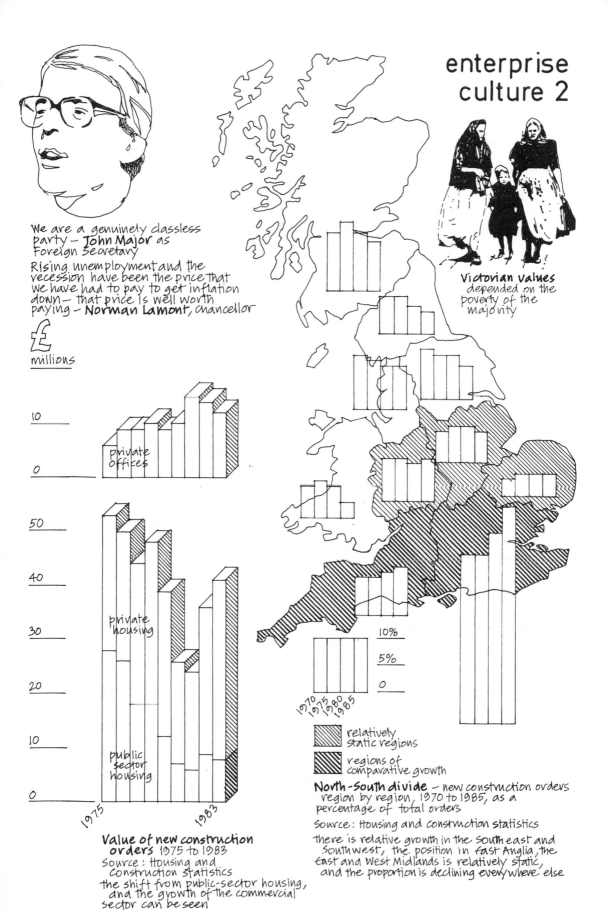

We are a genuinely classless party — **John Major** as Foreign Secretary

Rising unemployment and the recession have been the price that we have had to pay to get inflation down — that price is well worth paying — **Norman Lamont**, Chancellor

£ millions

**Victorian values** depended on the poverty of the majority

private offices

private housing

public sector housing

10%
5%
0

1970
1975
1980
1985

relatively static regions

regions of comparative growth

**North-South divide** — new construction orders region by region, 1970 to 1985, as a percentage of total orders

Source: Housing and construction statistics

there is relative growth in the south east and southwest, the position in East Anglia, the East and West Midlands is relatively static, and the proportion is declining everywhere else

**Value of new construction orders** 1975 to 1983
Source: Housing and Construction statistics
the shift from public-sector housing, and the growth of the commercial sector can be seen

the late eighties stood at something in excess of 100,000. Tyneside, another major area of unemployment, where numerous pits and ship-yards have closed without much alternative employment being created, now has the Gateshead Metro Centre, where consumers who have the money can enjoy the biggest shopping complex in Europe.

And London, where inner-city housing programmes have come almost to a standstill, has the biggest group of office-development proposals in Europe, including those for Spitalfields, Kings Cross, and for the vast area of Docklands, which covers development sites at London Bridge City, the Royal Docks, Canary Wharf and in the Isle of Dogs Enterprise Zone.

It has long been recognized that the advanced industrial city is a place of economic conflict, treating rich and poor very unequally. From time to time, as conditions become intolerable, the conflict becomes physical; in 1981 there were riots in Brixton, Moss Side and Toxteth, described by Mrs Thatcher as 'the worst experience we have yet had in this country'. In 1985 there were riots in Handsworth and Tottenham, the latter preceded by the death of a local resident and involving the death of a policeman. This may have been the incident which finally prompted the government to make 'the inner city' a major issue for the 1987 general election, and the subject of a widely publicized 'action programme' in 1988.

The characteristics of the inner city had been described by sociologists for many years, at least since the twenties, when Park, Burgess and McKenzie had done their pioneering study of Chicago. All big cities are a spatial expression of the forces at work in capitalism as a whole, especially of rapid change and of large-scale concentration. The negative effects of these forces are of course unevenly distributed throughout the city, and it is usually in the inner ring that the pressures are felt most.

In the inner-city areas, such as St Ann's in Nottingham, or St Paul's in Bristol, close to their respective centres, the need to expand the central area forces land values up, putting pressure on rents and on the very existence of low-cost housing. The inner city is also vulnerable environ-mentally, as roads and railways serving the centre are pushed through old residential districts. Unemployment is highest in the inner city, as the traditional industries on which whole local cultures depend – docks and shipyards, railway depots and factory areas – are affected by the drastic shifts of the market system. And it is here too that the dilapidated flats in the private rented sector, and the grim public-sector estates, continue to house the least socially mobile, the lowest wage-earners and the poorest newcomers.

The history of the East End of London bears this out. Lying just downstream of the medieval city, the East End was the most natural place to develop the commercial docks. As trade grew and the docks expanded

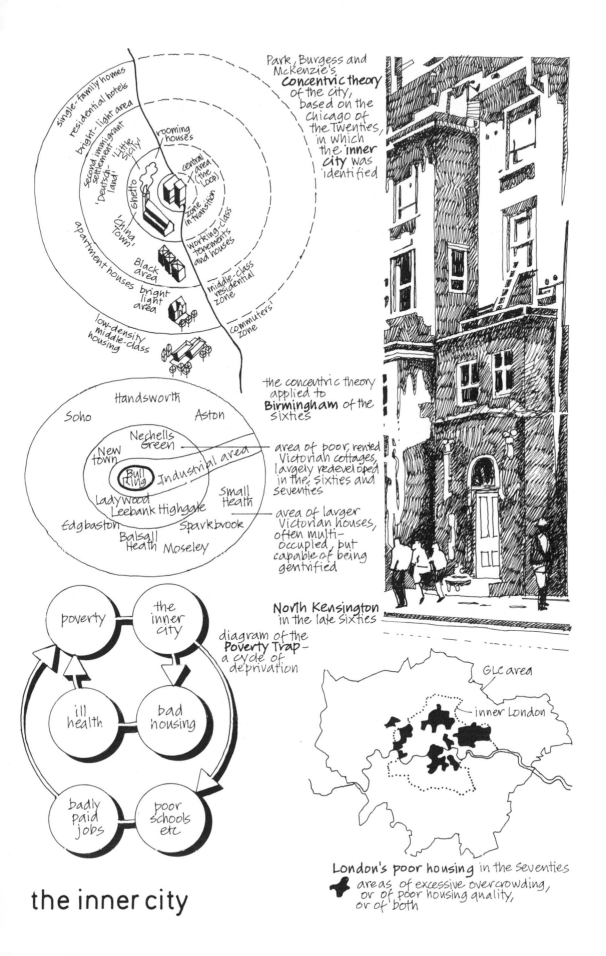

Park, Burgess and McKenzie's **concentric theory** of the city, based on the Chicago of the Twenties, in which the 'inner city' was identified

single-family homes
residential hotels
bright-light area
second immigrant settlement 'Deutschland'
'Little Sicily'
rooming houses
central area (the LOOP)
zone in transition
Ghetto
'China-town'
Black area
working-class tenements and houses
apartment houses bright light area
middle-class residential zone
commuters' zone
low-density middle-class housing

the concentric theory applied to **Birmingham** of the sixties

Handsworth
Soho          Aston
Nechells Green
New town
Bull Ring   Industrial area
Ladywood
Leebank Highgate
Small Heath
Edgbaston   Sparkbrook
Balsall Heath   Moseley

area of poor, rented Victorian cottages, largely redeveloped in the sixties and seventies

area of larger Victorian houses, often multi-occupied, but capable of being gentrified

**North Kensington** in the late sixties

poverty
the inner city
ill health
bad housing
badly paid jobs
poor schools etc

diagram of the **Poverty Trap** - a cycle of deprivation

GLC area
inner London

**London's poor housing** in the seventies
areas of excessive overcrowding, or of poor housing quality, or of both

# the inner city

eastward, an entire working-class culture emerged, enriched by the overseas influences which trade and immigration brought. All kinds of subsidiary industries grew up, based on the import of raw materials and the export of finished goods, such as the clothing industry of Tower Hamlets or the furniture industry of Hackney.

The docks were notoriously prone to fluctuations in workload, and over the last century the dockers have been forced to fight long campaigns to guarantee their pay and working conditions. The furniture and clothing workers too have been badly exploited, suffering sweatshop conditions and low wages enforced by the big West End retailers. Capital accumulation created the docks, dictated the conditions of work while they existed and, in the end, destroyed them again. Changes in relative profitability resulted in the decline of London's docks in favour of other modes of transport, and of the much less labour-intensive container port at Tilbury. Over twenty years, some 20,000 jobs have been lost from the docks alone, and many more from related industries like ship repair and road haulage. Furniture and clothing manufacture have also been badly affected by shifts of capital into other areas.

Even the big East End housing programme of the sixties, initiated with the best intentions, was itself dictated by the market; it was characterized by the industrialized building boom and its scramble for low standards and high profits. The tenants of the Canning Town estate, where Ronan Point collapsed in 1968, had to fight a long campaign for rehousing and for demolition of the tower blocks, which at last came down in 1991.

Ever since the sixties, the inner city has been an urgent social task, one to which no government has paid sufficient attention and which Mrs Thatcher's government had tended to ignore. Their change of heart before the 1987 election was as much a political expedient as an interest in social improvement. For example, the problems of the inner city could be represented as the product of municipal socialism, the ending of which was politically desirable and the dismantling of which had already begun. By focusing on urban unrest, the government could justify further expenditure on law and order, already identified as one of its political priorities. And above all, the failure of both Keynesianism and Labour to create a utopian environment in the inner city could be used to justify a new approach: Victorian values and an enterprise culture.

Early in 1989 the *Guardian* ran a story about the Isle of Dogs in London's Docklands, and the efforts of a small group of mainly working-class residents of Glen Terrace, a row of old houses on the west of the island, to oppose a local development by the London Docklands Development Corporation.[3] The proposals involved the construction of a five-storey mini Town Hall at the end of their gardens, and the loss of a long-promised piece of open space. At first sight, one might think that

# the East End

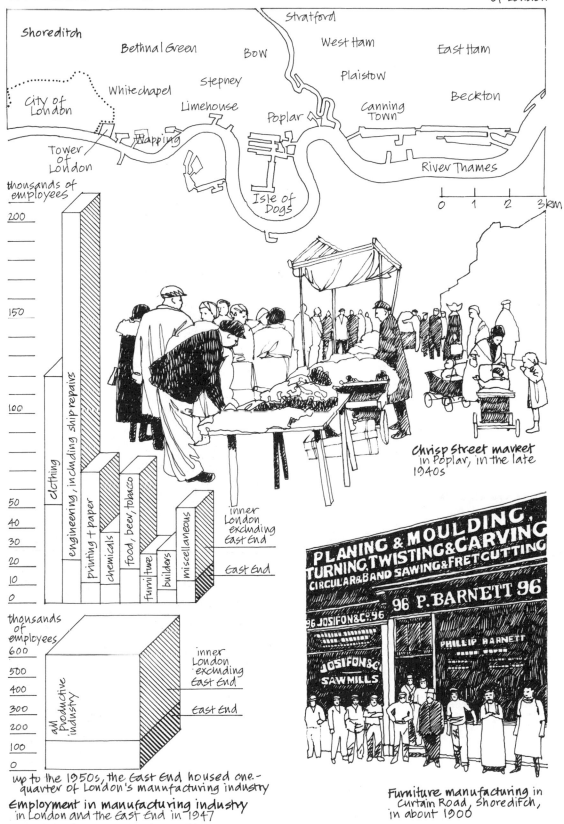

Shoreditch

Bethnal Green

Stratford

West Ham

East Ham

Bow

Plaistow

Stepney

Beckton

Whitechapel

City of London

Limehouse

Canning Town

Poplar

Wapping

Tower of London

River Thames

Isle of Dogs

0 1 2 3km

thousands of employees

200

150

100

50
40
30
20
10
0

clothing

engineering, including ship repairs

printing + paper

chemicals

food, beer, tobacco

furniture

builders

miscellaneous

inner London excluding East End

East End

Chrisp Street market
in Poplar, in the late
1940s

thousands of employees

600

500

400

300

200

100

0

all productive industry

inner London excluding East End

East End

up to the 1950s, the East End housed one-quarter of London's manufacturing industry

**Employment in manufacturing industry**
in London and the East End in 1947

Source: County of London Plan 1951

PLANING & MOULDING,
TURNING, TWISTING & CARVING
CIRCULAR & BAND SAWING & FRETCUTTING

96 P. BARNETT 96

96 JOSIFON & Co. 96

PHILLIP BARNETT

JOSIFON & Co.
SAW MILLS

Furniture manufacturing in
Curtain Road, Shoreditch,
in about 1900

# London Docks 1

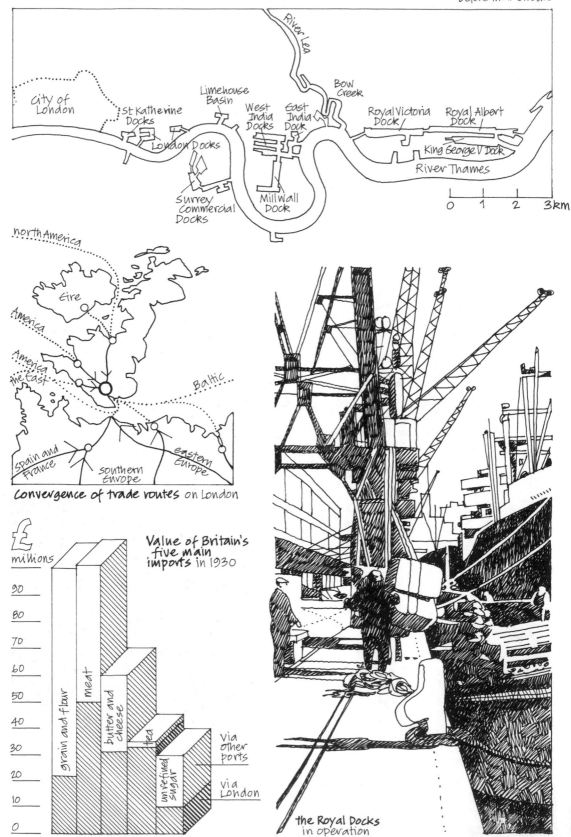

River Lea

Bow Creek

City of London

St Katherine Docks

Limehouse Basin

West India Docks

East India Dock

Royal Victoria Dock

Royal Albert Dock

London Docks

King George V Dock

River Thames

Surrey Commercial Docks

Millwall Dock

0   1   2   3km

north America

Eire

America

America the East

Baltic

Spain and France

southern Europe

eastern Europe

**Convergence of trade routes** on London

**£**
millions

**Value of Britain's five main imports** in 1930

90
80
70
60
50
40
30
20
10
0

grain and flour

meat

butter and cheese

tea

unrefined sugar

Via other ports

via London

the Royal Docks
in operation

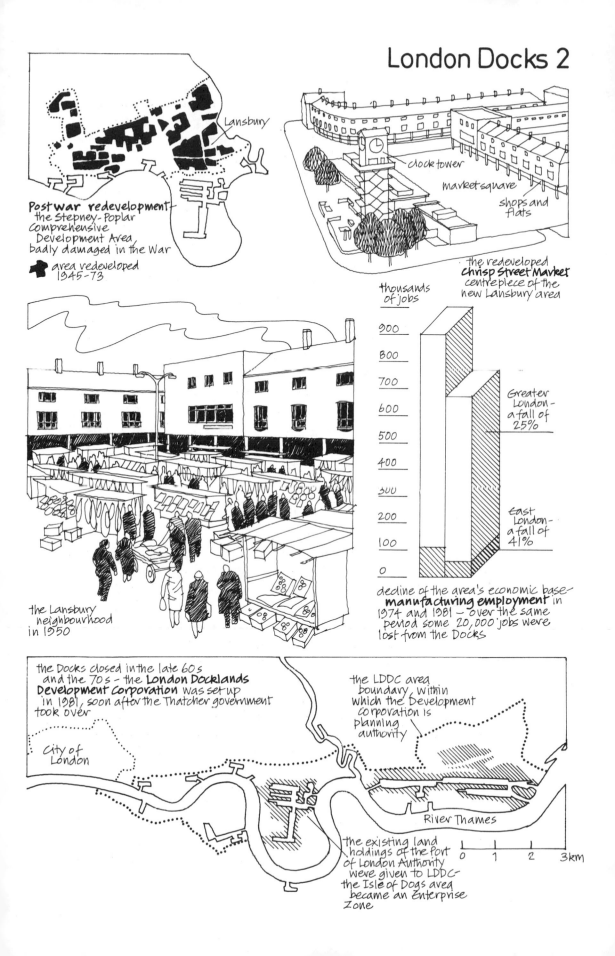

# London Docks 2

**Post war redevelopment**
the Stepney-Poplar Comprehensive Development Area, badly damaged in the War

■ area redeveloped 1945-73

Lansbury

clock tower
market square
shops and flats

the redeveloped **Chrisp Street Market** centrepiece of the new Lansbury area

thousands of jobs

900
800
700
600
500
400
300
200
100
0

Greater London - a fall of 25%

East London - a fall of 41%

the Lansbury neighbourhood in 1950

decline of the area's economic base-
**manufacturing employment** in 1974 and 1981 - over the same period some 20,000 jobs were lost from the Docks

the Docks closed in the late 60s and the 70s - the **London Docklands Development Corporation** was set up in 1981, soon after the Thatcher government took over

the LDDC area boundary, within which the Development Corporation is planning authority

City of London

River Thames

the existing land holdings of the Port of London Authority were given to LDDC- the Isle of Dogs area became an Enterprise Zone

0    1    2    3km

this was a normal planning dilemma: a well-meaning authority obliged to act against the interests of local people in order to provide something of more general benefit. In Docklands however, the situation is not normal. The planning system as a whole may still pursue the old Benthamite philosophy of 'the greatest good for the greatest number', but in Docklands there needs be no such pretence.

When the LDDC (London Docklands Development Corporation) was set up by the government in 1981 as one of the first two Urban Development Corporations – the other being in Liverpool – it was given wide-ranging powers. These included access to government funds, the power to raise money from other sources, the ability to buy land and buildings – and the right to override the local planning system as administered by Tower Hamlets, Newham and Southwark Councils and, in its day, the GLC. On paper the objects of an Urban Development Corporation sound unexceptionable: 'to secure the regeneration of its area'. This is to be achieved by 'bringing land and buildings into effective use, encouraging the development of existing and new industry and commerce, creating an attractive environment and ensuring that housing and social facilities are available to encourage people to live and work in the area'.[4]

In practice the LDDC, with the government's support, has identified these objectives in a partial way, making its first priority the establishment of an enterprise culture. Since 1981 most of its decisions have been to the benefit of speculators and to the detriment of the already disadvantaged working-class community of the area.

Even the mini Town Hall at Glen Terrace was questionable. A scheme for the site had already been devised by Florian Beigel of the Polytechnic of North London's Architecture Research Unit, and Nasser Golzari, one of Tower Hamlets Council's neighbourhood architects, in consultation with local people, which would have provided a hall and meeting place for local use, and workspaces adaptable enough to be converted to housing at a later date if the need arose. The design, by respecting the surrounding buildings and retaining some open space, would have done much to reduce the impact of the building on the local environment. The LDDC, however, decided to reject it in favour of their own more commercial scheme, designed by a private firm of Kensington architects, which omitted the public hall and maximized the office floorspace. This was subsequently built, and put up for sale.

The biggest example of LDDC's enterprise, however, is to be seen in the centre of the island. This is the Enterprise Zone, an area in which virtually no planning controls exist. The *Guardian* report described the Enterprise Zone as a 'tawdry playground' and its inevitably post-modern office townscape as a 'plastic Lego-brick model of a Fritz Lang film set'.

One of the Glen Terrace residents said: 'Not very inspiring is it? ... this is all just bits and pieces really. All different styles. Very messy. The thought of having to look at them until I move out of here in a box doesn't make me very happy.'[5]

The total area controlled by LDDC is over 5,000 acres in extent; it lies mostly on the north side of the Thames, from St Katherine Docks in the west, to the Royal Docks in the east. On the south side of the river it includes an area near London Bridge, together with the old Surrey Docks. The Isle of Dogs is on the north side, in the centre of the area, and contains the old West India and Millwall Docks, around which is clustered the island's working-class housing, dating mostly from the nineteenth and early twentieth centuries. A perimeter road – West Ferry and Manchester Roads – separates this housing from the riverfront, on which are located the emptying wharves and warehouses of London's commercial past. The Enterprise Zone is in the centre of the island, around the dock basins whose derelict quaysides are being turned over to studios, private housing and, most obviously, speculators' offices, the form and style of which have been dictated by developers' architects, and the density and height of which have been determined by the rapidly escalating land-values. The Canary Wharf office development rises in the middle of the Enterprise Zone, its total area of twelve million square feet making it the largest commercial project in Europe. Though it will have a substantial impact on local people's lives, and though its towers – one of them 250 metres high – intrude into views all over London, including the famous views from Greenwich Park, there has been virtually no public consultation.

On the riverfront of the island industrial sites are being closed and the land given over to private housing; some of the schemes are attractive, especially the one designed by Jeremy Dixon, but this is not the point. The Tower Hamlets local plan for the Isle of Dogs had envisaged keeping the industry to provide local employment and providing a public riverside walk. The introduction of private housing frustrates both these objectives. When it was set up, the LDDC became responsible for planning control, but the local authorities retained responsibility for preparing local plans to guide planning decisions. The frequency with which the LDDC reaches decisions contrary to local plan policy, and the number of times such decisions are upheld by the government on appeal, make this arrangement unsatisfactory.

Since the advent of the LDDC, few improvements have been made to the working-class housing of Docklands. The LDDC is not a housing authority; that duty too was retained by the local authorities. But the government's strict control of local authority finance has brought about the collapse of most inner-city public-housing investment programmes.

# the Isle of Dogs

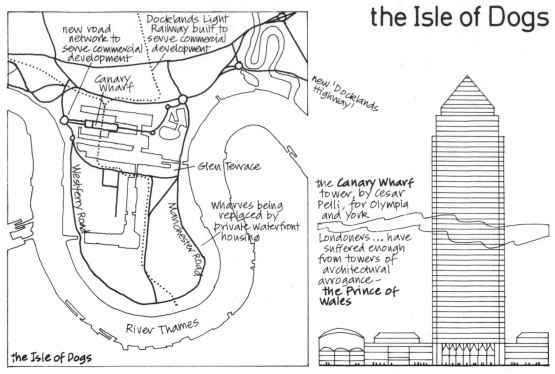

new road network to serve commercial development

Docklands Light Railway built to serve commercial development

Canary Wharf

new 'Docklands Highway'

Glen Terrace

wharves being replaced by private waterfront housing

Western Road

Manchester Road

River Thames

the Isle of Dogs

the **Canary Wharf** tower, by Cesar Pelli, for Olympia and York

Londoners... have suffered enough from towers of architectural arrogance — **the Prince of Wales**

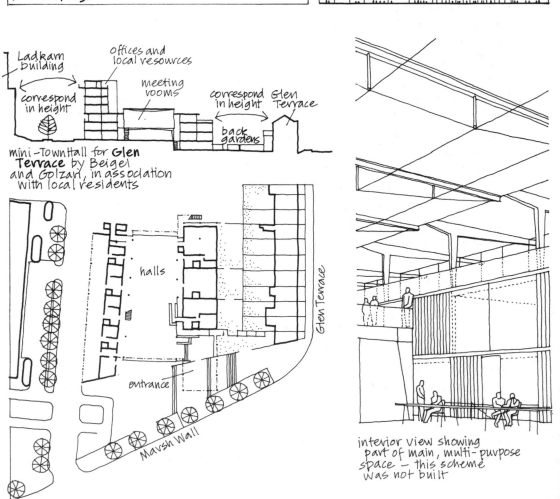

Ladkarn building

offices and local resources

correspond in height

meeting rooms

correspond in height

Glen Terrace

back gardens

mini-Town Hall for **Glen Terrace** by Beigel and Golzari, in association with local residents

halls

entrance

Glen Terrace

Marsh Wall

interior view showing part of main, multi-purpose space — this scheme was not built

For the whole of the eighties no new council housing was built in the Isle of Dogs. Cut off from the waterfront by private housing, surrounded by new employment to which they have no access, and not consulted about planning proposals for their area, a large part of the local community is not being served well by the planning system. As a result, to quote a critical report on the performance of the LDDC, 'two Dockland environments exist side by side, one luxurious enclaves for wealthy incomers, another underfunded estates, parks and community facilities where existing residents live'.[6]

Some improvements have been made, notably the Docklands Light Railway and the Asda superstore, which are of general benefit, but these have been provided mainly to attract the middle classes to the area; they are available to the working-class population only because this does not conflict with the main aim of boosting the confidence of office developers and home buyers.

London's Docklands may be an extreme example of the effects of market forces, but they are not untypical. An area to the immediate north of the City of London has experienced the same sort of decline of its local industries, in this case the fruit and vegetable market at Spitalfields and the railway services at Liverpool Street and Broad Street. The main landowners, British Rail and the City of London Corporation, were willing to enter into agreements with developers, in order to extract the maximum value from their land. Broad Street station has been demolished and Liverpool Street rebuilt to incorporate an office development. The railway land to the immediate north has given way to a new office city known as Broadgate, and further development is proposed at Spitalfields to the immediate east.

Kings Cross is another example. Here too the decline of the railway yards has released land for development. The major corporate landowners – British Rail, National Freight and British Gas – had four consortia competing for the opportunity to develop. Rising costs, and a lack of capital for improving their everyday operations, made the landowners very ready to participate.

The attraction of such sites to developers was stimulated by trading changes in the City of London. The discussions that preceded the 'Big Bang' of October 1986, which was to protect London's trading position in relation to Tokyo and New York, were concerned not only with revising Stock Exchange practice and with the installation of the SEAQ automated system, but also with a perceived shortage of modern office floorspace.

Critics of the laxity of the planning system had long argued that there were too many offices in London. In March 1972 the GLC estimated that nine million square feet of offices were vacant and more still were in the planning 'pipeline'. By the early eighties this situation seemed to have

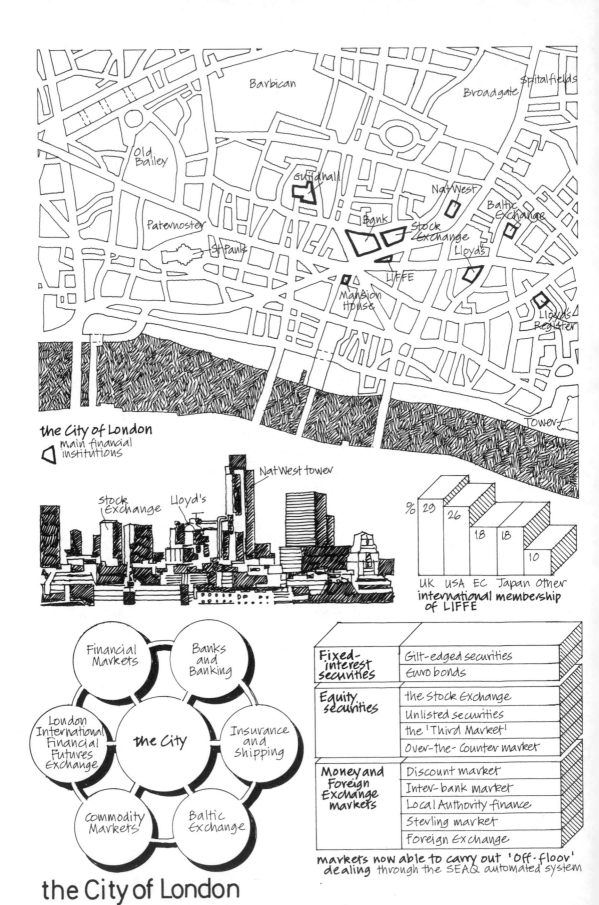

the City of London
◁ main financial institutions

NatWest tower
Stock Exchange
Lloyd's

% 29 26 18 18 10
UK USA EC Japan Other
international membership of LIFFE

Financial Markets
Banks and Banking
London International Financial Futures Exchange
the City
Insurance and Shipping
Commodity Markets
Baltic Exchange

| Fixed-interest securities | Gilt-edged securities |
| | Euro bonds |
| Equity securities | the Stock Exchange |
| | Unlisted securities |
| | the 'Third Market' |
| | Over-the-Counter market |
| Money and Foreign Exchange markets | Discount market |
| | Inter-bank market |
| | Local Authority finance |
| | Sterling market |
| | Foreign Exchange |

markets now able to carry out 'off-floor' dealing through the SEAQ automated system

# the City of London

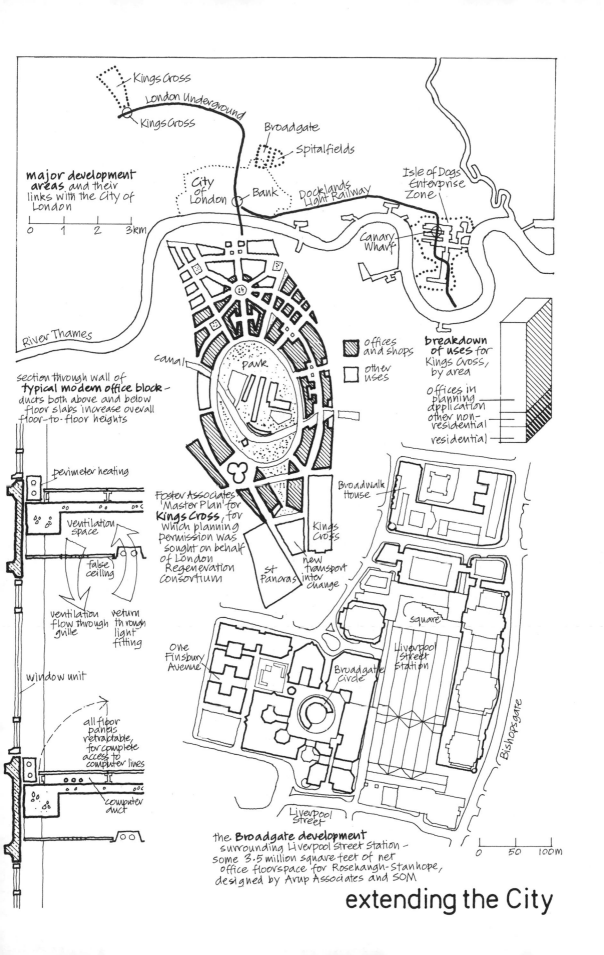

Kings Cross

London Underground

Kings Cross

Broadgate

Spitalfields

Isle of Dogs Enterprise Zone

City of London

Bank

Docklands Light Railway

**major development areas** and their links with the City of London

0 1 2 3km

Canary Wharf

River Thames

canal

park

offices and shops

other uses

**breakdown of uses** for Kings Cross, by area

offices in planning application

other non-residential

residential

section through wall of **typical modern office block** – ducts both above and below floor slabs increase overall floor-to-floor heights

perimeter heating

ventilation space

false ceiling

ventilation flow through grille

return through light fitting

Foster Associates 'Master Plan' for **Kings Cross**, for which planning permission was sought on behalf of London Regeneration Consortium

Broadwalk House

Kings Cross

new transport interchange

St Pancras

window unit

all floor panels retractable, for complete access to computer lines

computer duct

One Finsbury Avenue

Broadgate Circle

square

Liverpool Street Station

Bishopsgate

Liverpool Street

the **Broadgate development** surrounding Liverpool Street Station – some 3.5 million square feet of net office floorspace for Rosehaugh-Stanhope, designed by Arup Associates and SOM

0 50 100m

# extending the City

changed. Not only was floorspace in shorter supply, but much of the space that did exist was outmoded. Today's financial practice requires space for large trading floors, and a high level of servicing for ranks of computers – universal floor ducts, extra air-conditioning, bigger plant-rooms. Many existing office blocks as little as twenty years old could not be adapted.

Docklands, Broadgate and Kings Cross were appropriate for new office developments: large enough to provide many millions of square feet of floorspace, close enough to the City to provide easy access when necessary, yet far enough out to be rather less expensive to acquire than a city-centre site. Docklands was made even more attractive by the high level of government funding; Canary Wharf was only one of many commercial schemes being heavily subsidized by the public.

Like Docklands, neither Broadgate nor Kings Cross can offer much to the local communities. Escalating land values inevitably price out local businesses, local jobs continue to disappear and low-cost housing is lost. The kind of employment and housing that replace them have little relevance to local people's needs. Typically, much is made of developers' willingness to provide community facilities, parks and fair-rent housing as a proportion of the overall profits, but these cannot be substantial enough to make much contribution to local need, and can never offset the disadvantages such developments bring. The roads around Kings Cross are already at capacity, while the inadequacy of the public transport system to cope even with present demands was grimly demonstrated by the underground station disaster of 1987.

One of the biggest social losses will be the opportunity cost incurred by not using these scarce land resources for greater public benefit. The sites are the last remaining inner-city land capable of short-term development. But to use them for office developments for private gain, when they could be providing local employment, low-cost housing and community facilities, is an inevitable part of the process of capital accumulation. Land-owners and developers will make gestures to local need, but only to ensure the acceptance of the projects. Both land-use and building form are determined by profitability. Land and buildings, being use-values, should meet the community's needs; but when exchange-values predominate, urban development will have less social purpose: for a developer, any land-use will do, so long as it is currently profitable.

Commodity production for profit – including the production of buildings – dominates our social life. Human relationships become distorted. They take on, in Marx's words, a 'fantastic form', turning into relationships between objects, defined by exchange-values. The commodity production of buildings is an aggressive, alienating process; decisions are made – about land-use, tenure and ownership, design, management, the allocation of resources – which are based on profitability rather than social justice or human need.

Such conflict has always been part of the capitalist system. In a liberal democracy however, this fact is rarely acknowledged. Instead, an illusion of consensus is created, in which the establishment's interests are presented as being synonymous with those of society as a whole. Under the Conservatives, the illusion of social cohesion has been particularly strained, so apparent has been the promotion of financial interests, and so concentrated the effect on working-class living standards. Many of the measures taken have already been mentioned, but two legislative programmes in particular deserve further comment. The White Paper 'Lifting the Burden' was published in 1985 and 'Action for Cities' in 1988. Together they show both sides of the Thatcherite programme: the former is mainly about the dismantling of welfare capitalism and the latter about opening up the cities to speculators.

'Lifting the Burden' was a major statement of financial policy on a variety of issues, co-ordinated by the Minister without Portfolio and contributed to by the Home Office, the Exchequer and the Departments of Employment, Trade and Industry, Social Security and the Environment. Its proposals included tax and social-security reforms, customs deregulation, and the removal of planning controls. The stated aim was to 'lift the burden' from business by removing as many regulations as possible. In the words of the White Paper: 'It is the cumulative burden of regulation – both major and minor – that saps the energy of business. It is that burden which the Government are determined to reduce – but with care and concern for all in our society.'[7]

The White Paper had a whole section on 'Planning and Enterprise'. This introduced a number of proposals, including Simplified Planning Zones where the need for planning permission would be reduced, changes to the General Development Order and to the Use Classes Order to increase the categories for which planning permission would be unnecessary, cost penalties with which to confront 'unreasonable' planning authorities, quicker appeal procedures and a simplified system of building regulations.

To cut bureaucracy is highly desirable, but these proposals also need to be seen as part of the Thatcher government's longer-term strategy for the planning system. Since 1979 there had been: the abolition of the Centre for Environmental Studies and of the National Building Agency, two important planning and housing research organizations; abolition of the Parker Morris space standards for local-authority housing; withdrawal of Rates Support from many inner-city authorities, and the introduction of rate-capping; abolition of the G L C and the other Metropolitan Councils, the country's main authorities for strategic planning; the introduction of planning fees, bringing market forces into a public service; the gradual privatization of local-authority services, including that of Building Control; and an increased level of support for the developer in appeal decisions. The introduction of the Community Charge (poll tax) in 1989–90 and of charge-capping in 1990 put even more pressure on the planning system, along with all other local services.

'Lifting the Burden' was part of this process. It stated: 'The Town and Country Planning system has not changed in its essentials since it was established in 1947. In many ways it has served the country well, and the Government has no intention of abolishing it.'[8] The main concern was for 'efficiency'. The White Paper stated: 'The Government's policy is to simplify the system and to improve its efficiency ... an efficient and simple system can speed the planning process and facilitate much-needed development which helps to create jobs – in construction, in commerce and industry, and in small firms.'

The 'efficiency' argument is very difficult to sustain. The abolition of the GLC and the assumption of many of its powers by the thirty-two London Boroughs working separately, for example, is seriously questionable, especially in view of the serious underfunding of the Borough Councils. So is the loss of Metropolitan Counties, together with the essential overview they had provided of housing, transport and employment. The privatization of public services, such as buses, street cleaning and refuse collection, has proved to be less an exercise in efficiency than in cost-cutting and worsening levels of service. And the much-publicized 'right to buy' legislation, together with other inducements to home ownership, has proved socially disastrous. In August 1991 the national Council of Mortgage Lenders reported 36,600 repossessions in the first six months of the year, blaming the rise in unemployment.

The White Paper also claimed that a streamlined development process would create jobs. No doubt some jobs are created, but in the absence of any strategic employment policy, market forces predominate; unrestricted office growth is at the expense of industrial employment. Industry has also been hit by high interest rates, and things have been made worse by the lifting of planning controls; the 1987 Use Classes Order, by allowing changes of use from light industry to offices without the need for planning permission, priced a lot of industrial floorspace out of the market. The claim that the White Paper would help small businesses was certainly not true of industrial businesses.

Indeed, the basic claim that the planning system inhibits enterprise was itself questionable. The British planning system, conceived in order to help reconstruct capitalist society, had never been inimical to enterprise; rather it had tried to find a balance between different types of enterprise, between commerce and industry, London and the regions, economic growth and the environment, centres of employment and the housing or

# burdening the cities

Lifting the Burden was produced in 1985 and Action for Cities in 1988

Planning permission is necessary to change from one class to another within the **Town and Country Planning Use Classes Order** – this way, it is possible for planners to protect certain uses – in 1987 the classes were changed

**before 1987**                                                                **after 1987**

| Class II – offices | Estate agents Financial services Professional services | |
|---|---|---|
| | All other types of office | Class B1 – business |
| Class III – light industry | Light industry | |
| till 1987, light industrial floorspace could be protected to some extent | Research and development uses Laboratories 'High-tech' studios | |

after 1987, light industrial floorspace, already in decline, could no longer be protected by planners – it could now be changed, without planning permission, to offices, at 3× the value – office speculators profited, local industry declined further

£ millions

700 — roads programme
— government grant to Docklands Railway
600 — rate allowances in Enterprise Zone
500 — capital allowances in Enterprise Zone
400 — capital grant to LDDC
300
200
100
0

**public money to help private enterprise** – public subsidies for Docklands 1981-87

source: LDDC

the Parker Morris Report **Homes for today and tomorrow** and its accompanying design manual **Space in the Home** might be criticized for the social assumptions they made – but they did ensure a certain standard of housing design

With their abolition, even that minimal standard was lost

space required for 'entertaining visitors' - Space in the Home 1963

£ millions

6000
5000
4000
3000
2000
1000
0

1983-4  1984-5  1985-6  1986-7

—— cost of mortgage-interest tax relief

······ public expenditure on housing

**expanding private house ownership** and decline in public housing 1983-87

source: Labour Research

living
dining kitchen
WC

bed | bed
bed | bath

0      5m

Parker Morris plan for 4-person house by the National Building Agency 1965

transport needed to serve them – in other words to spread the benefits of enterprise as widely as possible. This White Paper, by contrast, was being highly selective; in the name of enterprise in general it was deregulating certain specific areas, creating economic advantages for a few and disadvantages for many.

This approach became clearer with the publication of another proposal in 1988. This was the 'Action for Cities' brochure which represented the fulfilment of the Conservative party's 1987 election promises for the inner city. 'Action for Cities' dealt with six main topics. 'Helping business succeed' was about grants and loans for business; 'Preparing for work' was about training schemes; 'Developing cities' was about lifting planning controls from the development process; 'Safer cities' was mainly about law and order; while 'Better homes and attractive cities' promoted the virtues of home ownership. The regions were acknowledged in a two-page section called 'Wales and Scotland'.

The brochure offered a sidelight on Mrs Thatcher's reported enthusiasm for 'Victorian values' when it said

> The inner cities must also be places where businessmen want to invest. They also want to be able to get on with their business; to press ahead with sensible development without unnecessary red tape; to keep their costs as low as possible, and not be punished by excessive rate demands; to be made welcome. For this to happen, the inner cities need to rediscover the sense of civic pride which once united residents and business.[9]

This statement was accompanied by a photograph of a Victorian city street of offices and shops, though there was no mention of the hidden aspects of Victorian life – the poverty and bad housing – which then, as now, were an essential accompaniment to the process of capital accumulation.

'Action for Cities' received a welcome from the right for its attacks on local government and its promotion of private enterprise. 'A great chance for inner cities', said the *Daily Express*.[10] It was criticized by the Opposition on the basis that it contained no really new proposals nor any big spending programme. Bryan Gould, Labour's spokesperson on the environment, was quoted by the *Guardian* as saying that 'Mrs Thatcher has not got the faintest idea how to tackle inner-city problems' and the paper went on to say: 'He appealed to her to back the consensus that the only way forward was through a partnership of local government, local communities and private capital.'[11]

However, Gould missed the point; in their own terms, these policies did work. Their effect was to exclude local government and the local communities, and to make the inner cities available to the big developers. In the same issue of the *Guardian*, Hugo Young reported: 'As the chairman of Wimpey ... said, they're doing it because they support the

Government and because they want to make a profit . . . No nonsense here about the social fabric and the caring community.'

And by the end of 1988, an executive of the National Westminster Bank was even calling for the preparation of development plans for key inner city areas by 'retailers, housebuilders, industrialists and other interested parties'.[12]

The government, amid growing national unease about the inner city, was promoting speculation, and the speculators were very willing to participate. In economic terms, the approach was successful for a time; the second half of the eighties, while the mini-boom lasted, was a fruitful period for developers. They could expect big planning decisions to be in their favour, either because the government itself was making the decisions, through the appeal process or through the calling-in of applications, or because demoralized local planning authorities, and even local communities, were putting up less resistance. Now that there was so little prospect of building council housing or community facilities with public money, many local authorities turned to 'planning deals' – giving planning permission to large commercial developments so that some part of the profits could be channelled into 'community gain'. Some houses were built, but the destructive effects on the local economy, on employment patterns and on traffic generation was often out of all proportion to the benefits.

The government stressed the virtues of the market, and the need to restrict the 'high-spending' councils. At the same time, it directed a lot of public money towards entrepreneurs. Between 1981 and 1988, for example, the LDDC and the Isle of Dogs Enterprise Zone are said to have received some £700 million in public subsidy; it is estimated[13] that Canary Wharf alone will eventually have obtained £500 million from public funds.

In launching 'Action for Cities' the government assembled an organization of major construction and property development companies which it named 'British Urban Development'. Each member of the group, which included McAlpine, Laing, Wimpey, Tarmac, Taylor Woodrow and Trafalgar House, was asked to subscribe £5 million in share capital to create a fund which would pump-prime some large inner-city development schemes. The path would be smoothed by the relaxation of planning controls and the enforced sale of council-owned land. A close working relationship between the state and the big corporations is a feature of twentieth-century monopoly capitalism.

Monopoly is one of the paradoxes of the capitalist system. Theoretically, the system receives its stimulus from free competition, which is said to increase efficiency and keep costs down. In practice, competition results in the more successful companies increasing production at the expense of the

# capital accumulation

**Marx's General Formula** for Capital

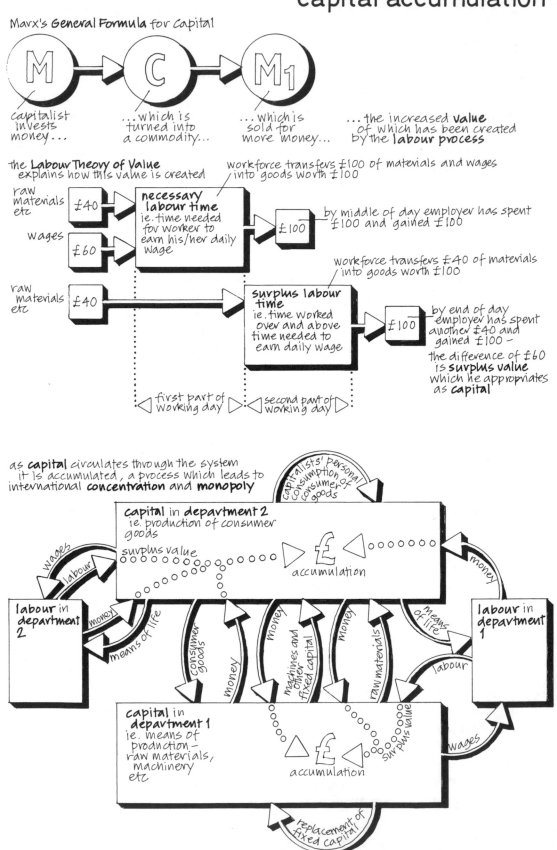

M — capitalist invests money...

C — ...which is turned into a commodity...

M₁ — ...which is sold for more money...

...the increased **value** of which has been created by the **labour process**

the **Labour Theory of Value** explains how this value is created

workforce transfers £100 of materials and wages into goods worth £100

raw materials etc — £40

wages — £60

**necessary labour time** ie. time needed for worker to earn his/her daily wage

£100 — by middle of day employer has spent £100 and gained £100

workforce transfers £40 of materials into goods worth £100

raw materials etc — £40

**surplus labour time** ie. time worked over and above time needed to earn daily wage

£100 — by end of day employer has spent another £40 and gained £100 — the difference of £60 is **surplus value** which he appropriates as **capital**

◁ first part of ▷ working day

◁ second part of ▷ working day

as **capital** circulates through the system it is accumulated, a process which leads to international **concentration** and **monopoly**

capitalists' personal consumption of consumer goods

**capital** in **department 2** ie. production of consumer goods

surplus value

£ accumulation

wages

labour

money

money

**labour** in **department 2**

means of life

consumer goods

money

machines and other fixed capital

money

raw materials

means of life

labour

**labour** in **department 1**

**capital** in **department 1** ie. means of production — raw materials, machinery etc

£ accumulation

surplus value

wages

replacement of fixed capital

less successful; the former take controlling interests in the latter, or buy them up, or force them out of business, so that there emerge fewer and larger firms controlling an ever-increasing proportion of the total production. The process of accumulation results both in concentration – the tendency of firms to grow in size – and in centralization – the tendency of firms to reduce in number – thus concentrating capital into fewer hands.

If competition is supposed to lead to lower prices, then monopoly means the opposite: that prices can be fixed, so that it is not necessary to strive for efficiency or to increase productivity to maximize profit. This does not necessarily mean that pressure is taken off wage levels, however; it is still important to extract the greatest amount of surplus-value from the workforce and to keep the quality of the product as low as possible. In 1982 it was possible to say that the high level of corporatism in the British building industry had both positive and negative aspects: 'on the one hand offering the prospect of a sustained programme of house production, but on the other hand taking the real risk that the finished products (such as the British industrialized high-rise housing of the 1960s) take anti-social and minimal forms associated with building for profit.'[14]

Now, with the 'sustained programme of house production' a thing of the past, we are left simply with the low standards 'associated with building for profit', applied this time to a series of questionable commercial developments which the state, through such things as 'Action for Cities', is trying to persuade us to accept.

The economist J. K. Galbraith noted[15] that the large corporation seeks to control the price of all goods, both inputs and outputs. To this end it substitutes long-term planning for the uncertainties of the open market. Fulfilment of its long-term targets depends on the performance of the corporation's 'technostructure', its managers and researchers. Their priorities and outlook become those of the corporation itself, and ultimately of society in general, which cannot be allowed to choose to buy the products of its own will but must be conditioned through advertising and other means to believe it needs them.

In the interests of the system as a whole, the state will lend its support to monopoly capital. One role it can play is to secure the acquiescence – or at least neutralize the dissent – of the mass of the people through, as we have seen, legislation, persuasion and the discriminatory allocation of resources. Another is to respect the international nature of capital. Monopoly does not necessarily lead to greater productivity but often to the deliberate limitation of productivity in order to maintain high prices. In this case, surplus capital is not reinvested in the normal way, but takes on a 'missionary role', being exported to other industries, to other sectors of the economy – or to other countries hitherto free from monopoly conditions.

The British Conservative government of the eighties had a close relationship with the multinational corporations. Only five months after it took office in May 1979, exchange controls were abandoned; between 1979 and 1983 £50 billion flowed out of the country as British companies invested overseas.[16] At the same time foreign multinationals were encouraged into Britain. A government handbook produced in 1983[17] pointed to low wages and to reduced trade-union rights as an incentive to foreign companies to locate here. In 1985 the British subsidiaries of foreign multinationals employed nearly 14 per cent of Britain's industrial workforce. At the same time overseas banks and financial institutions were steadily expanding in the City of London.

The 'petrodollar' phenomenon was typical of the movement of capital about the world. Heavy consumption of the world's primary energy sources, mainly by the USA and Japan, generated immense wealth in the OPEC countries, particularly in Saudi Arabia, responsible for a quarter of the world's oil exports. Some 40 per cent of Saudi Arabia's output went to the USA and Japan, the rest to Europe. The income from this was too large to be consumed locally by a tiny ruling class and a small indigenous population; much of it was exported to the west where it helped to shore up dilapidated First World economies. From here it was re-exported, often in the form of bilateral aid, to poverty-stricken Third World countries, which incurred mounting debts to the First World banks and governments.

Minster Court, Broadwalk House and all the other new buildings of the City of London, with their polished granite and travertine, and the tinted glass of their sub-tropical 'atria', are good examples of the international movement of capital. Many major schemes are directly financed from overseas. The original proposals for Canary Wharf were by a consortium which included Credit Suisse/First Boston. After that the initiative passed to the Canadian company Olympia and York, known as the world's largest commercial landlord, one quarter of whose holdings were in New York City. Olympia and York themselves, and the Chicago architects Skidmore, Owings and Merrill have offices in the development. The proposals for Paternoster Square promoted by the Prince of Wales are to be financed jointly by the British Greycoat PLC, by the American Park Tower Group and by the Mitsubishi Estate Company of Japan. Park Tower own office buildings in New York, Washington and London, while Mitsubishi own the Rockefeller Group and have projects in Florida, California, Portland and Los Angeles, as well as in London.

Foreign construction firms are increasingly involved with commercial development in Britain, and the eighties saw a number of Japanese construction sites in the City. Architectural experts were imported too, often for their experience in new methods of construction and contract management. American architects and contractors as a whole have more experience than the British in steel-frame construction, which is quick to erect and, in the competitive arena of commercial building, is becoming more popular, following recent relaxations of the Building Regulations. 'Fast-track' management too is becoming more common; here, the site-work is begun before the design is complete, and components are not stored on site but incorporated into the building as soon as they are delivered. The technique saves time, space and money – all at a premium on a city-centre development site – but requires sophisticated management. American architects are successful here, and Skidmore, Owings and Merrill have handled most of the Broadgate development.

The reverse process, the export of British capital abroad, shows similar links: with the USA, Japan, Canada, and the European Community. Of the £11.6 billion invested overseas in 1986 by all British companies, both industrial and financial, some £6.8 billion went to the USA. About £1 billion, by contrast, went to all developing countries, and most of this was to the newly industrializing, and therefore more lucrative, places like Brazil, Argentina, Nigeria, Hong Kong and Singapore. High-quality architecture has always been an exportable product, and contemporary British architects have won a number of well-known commissions abroad: the Pompidou Centre in Paris, for example, on which Richard Rogers collaborated; Norman Foster's Hong Kong and Shanghai National Bank in Hong Kong; and James Stirling's Staatsgalerie in Stuttgart. Less recognized by the public are the major commercial architects whose long-standing links with the Foreign Office and Commonwealth governments have, over the years, obtained them a large volume of work in African and Asian countries. And extraordinary circumstances occasionally bring to light the involvement of British firms in still less publicized commissions; Saddam Hussein's palaces, bomb shelters and Arch of Triumph in Baghdad being recent examples.

During the sixties, architects were deeply involved in the inner city and with the solution of housing problems because their social role, in those days of economic growth, coincided with their commercial one. Since then, commerce has led them elsewhere and, though some architects are as involved with social issues as they ever were, the profession as a whole has understandably drifted towards the most financially rewarding areas of work: from the inner city to the city centres, from the stagnating economies of the world's developed north to the oil-rich states of the Middle East or southeast Asia, or to the rapidly growing monopoly-capitalist outposts implanted in the Third World. Capitalism ensures that of architecture's two manifestations as a commodity – use-value and exchange-value – the latter will predominate.

# importing capital

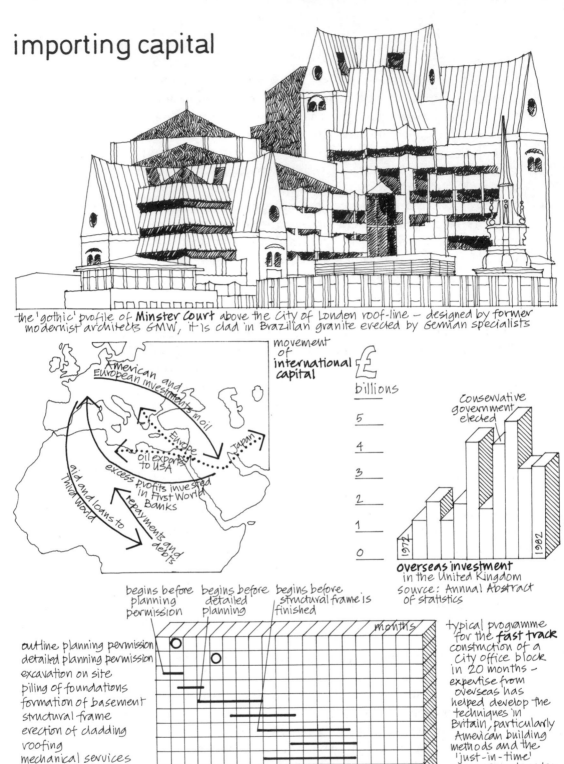

the 'gothic' profile of **Minster Court** above the City of London roof-line – designed by former modernist architects GMW, it is clad in Brazilian granite erected by German specialists

movement
of
**international** £
**capital**

billions

Conservative
government
elected

5
4
3
2
1
0

1972          1982

**overseas investment**
in the United Kingdom
source: Annual Abstract
of statistics

American and
European investments roll

Europe
oil exports
to USA

Japan?

excess profits invested
in First World
Banks

aid and loans to
Third World

repayments and
debts

begins before
planning
permission

begins before
detailed
planning

begins before
structural frame is
finished

months

outline planning permission
detailed planning permission
excavation on site
piling of foundations
formation of basement
structural frame
erection of cladding
roofing
mechanical services
electrical services
installation of lifts
internal wall panels
first tenant moves in
practical completion
developer fits out interior

typical programme
for the **fast track**
construction of a
City office block
in 20 months –
expertise from
overseas has
helped develop the
techniques in
Britain, particularly
American building
methods and the
'just-in-time'
management system
of the Japanese
car industry

can begin on
lower levels
before roof
is on

interior not
designed by
architect of
the building

can move in while
work still going
on on the
upper floors

contractor leaves site,
except for purposes
of making-good
any defects

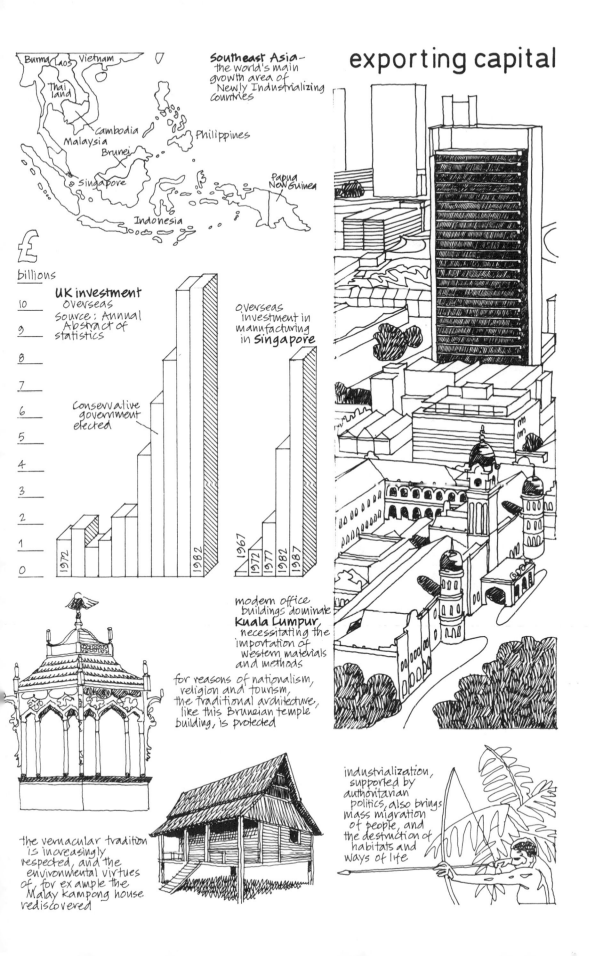

# exporting capital

Burma  Laos  Vietnam
Thailand
Cambodia
Malaysia
Brunei
Singapore
Philippines
Papua New Guinea
Indonesia

**Southeast Asia—** the world's main growth area of Newly Industrializing Countries

£ billions

**UK investment** overseas
Source: Annual Abstract of statistics

10
9
8
7
6
5
4
3
2
1
0

Conservative government elected

1972          1982

overseas investment in manufacturing in **Singapore**

1967  1972  1977  1982  1987

modern office buildings dominate **Kuala Lumpur**, necessitating the importation of western materials and methods

for reasons of nationalism, religion and tourism, the traditional architecture, like this Bruneian temple building, is protected

the vernacular tradition is increasingly respected, and the environmental virtues of, for example the Malay kampong house rediscovered

industrialization, supported by authoritarian politics, also brings mass migration of people, and the destruction of habitats and ways of life

# 6 The Fountainhead Syndrome – architectural attitudes

A successful building project depends, needless to say, on the creativity and co-operation of all those involved. Yet distrust between, for example, architect and contractor is almost a commonplace. It is not surprising. The alienated system within which they all work separates the architectural schools from the profession, the profession from the building industry and, within the industry, the employer from the employed. The lack of contact and understanding between students and educators, professionals, contractors and labourers, to say nothing of the wider gulf between all of these and the public who use their buildings, is one reason our environment displays the problems it does.

In 1974 Malcolm MacEwen wrote a short book which remains one of the most perceptive analyses of the problem of modern architecture and of the role of the architect in society.[1] Essentially it is about alienation. The problems addressed included the profession's lack of concern with the energy crisis of the seventies, its identification with 'the property racketeer and the bureaucracy' rather than with the wider community, its inability to make the best use of the skills and enthusiasm of its members, and the inappropriateness of its own institutions. Despite the positive and practical nature of the book's recommendations, the criticism it levelled at the profession in general and the RIBA in particular remain apposite.

If anything, the profession has become more commercialized and less concerned with wider social and economic issues than before. Under a succession of presidents with flourishing commercial practices, the RIBA has lifted the restrictions on advertising and company directorships which had belonged to its gentler, more 'professional' days, and has attacked the planning system as a restriction on architectural enterprise. Its activities and publications reflect a weakening of its role as learned society and an emphasis on being a commercial pressure group. In 1985 it co-operated with the government in an attempt to close down three schools of architecture in order to limit entry into the profession at a time of recession. For Louis Hellman the RIBA has become the 'Royal Institute of Businessman Architects'.

The American sociologist Herbert Gans, reviewing the role of architects in general in the seventies and eighties,[2] writes of their continued lack of concern for users of buildings, of their predilection for aesthetics rather than practicalities, and that 'professional imperialism has perhaps been greater, or at least more visible, in architecture than in other professions, partly because some architects felt that their role was to express the contemporary culture or the philosophy of society through their buildings. This is what Gans, after the well-known Ayn Rand novel, calls the 'Fountainhead' syndrome.

But not only does the architect express society; society also makes the architect. Society creates the architectural profession in its own image and thus gets an architecture which reflects its social priorities. A class society creates an architecture of inequality.

This is also true of architectural education. Architectural schools have always been social mirrors – the Beaux Arts of bourgeois Paris, the VKhUTEMAS of revolutionary Moscow, the Bauhaus of the Weimar Republic – and British schools since World War II have reflected the progress of contemporary capitalism.

In 1957 the critic John Smith visited all seventy-four of the schools then offering some kind of architectural training in the United Kingdom, and reported on an anarchic situation.[3] He found a wide variety of courses, with varying standards and philosophies, few of which appeared to be facing up to the needs of an expanding modern economy and its social implications. He concluded that architectural education was 'a disgrace', and proposed a radical re-organization of the system, capable of providing a supply of 'highly skilled and talented architects, to serve the urgent needs of the country'. The same year, there was an Oxford conference on architectural education, which proved to be a turning point. Under the guidance of Leslie Martin and Llewellyn Davies a new system was set up and criteria for higher standards laid down. The aim was to produce the technical and managerial skills which the country as a whole was considered to need. In principle, that system remains today. A group of thirty-six schools, in polytechnics and universities 'recognized' by the RIBA, offer high-quality degree and diploma courses. The schools' right to grant exemption from the RIBA's own examinations carries with it the duty to respect the RIBA's curriculum, so all offer a broadly comparable training.

It can be seen that the debates within such a system will always be defined by the academic institutions on the one hand and the professional body on the other, each with its own set of priorities. And since the priorities of learning institutions, in parallel with those of the profession, have increasingly been affected by market forces, the schools' agenda have become less socially responsible than originally anticipated in 1957. In the sixties and early seventies some radical architectural groups – like the Architects' Revolutionary Council and the New Architecture Movement – briefly flourished and it was at least possible for the schools to be active agents of social progress. It was a time when, both in Britain and the USA, 'the traditional goals and structures of the professions came under strong criticism from students and young practitioners ... they defined improvement as drastic if not revolutionary change ... and they rejected the traditional professional alliance with the elite.'[4]

If this was true of the schools then, it is not now. The need to concentrate on income-generation, to compete with each other for full-fee-paying students, has affected the ethos of all higher education establishments. The general drift of politics to the right, and the fear of unemployment, have tempered student radicalism, never widespread among architects anyway. The architectural schools have become more marginal.

There are, of course, honourable exceptions to this generalization, which almost all schools could claim. Here and there, imaginative projects seek to unite theory and practice. The Polytechnic of North London, for example, acted as host to the trade-union sponsored Centre for Alternative Industrial and Technological Systems, and still runs the respected access course Women into Architecture. Oxford Polytechnic has a strong research tradition and has done valuable work, for example, into alternative funding methods for public sector development and into the reasons for building failures. The Martin Centre at Cambridge is still one of the country's most important places of research into energy conservation. Masters courses are offered to help strengthen teaching at Diploma level, at York and London Universities, at Oxford Polytechnic, at the Polytechnic of East London and other places. At Liverpool University the remodelling of the old architecture building to provide high-tech studio space was carried out by an outside consultant in close association with staff and the students themselves.

But increasingly there is a general tendency to concentrate on imaginative 'design', on paper architecture, on the architecture-into-art that looks good in advertising brochures and at the end-of-year show, but which has little relationship with the process of building, still less with the satisfaction of society's urgent material needs.

The Architectural Association is perhaps the clearest example of these market forces at work in architectural education. Following a financial crisis in 1971 when a merger with Imperial College of Science and Technology was proposed, the AA successfully kept its independence. Under the inspired leadership of the late Alvin Boyarsky, it worked hard at its perceived role as the major intellectual force in British architecture. Its jealously-guarded independence from the public sector gave it a freedom and an air of creativity which its precarious financial position made all the more febrile.

Like all private-sector institutions the school is available only to those who can afford high fees, mostly relatively wealthy, middle-class males. As in all such regimes, a wide choice is offered. The AA system is based on a rich menu of activity from which students may choose almost at will. A good example of this is the 'unit' system, in which students opt to be taught design by the particular group of tutors whose philosophy appeals to them – and in which the tutors themselves choose the students they wish to teach. The tutors themselves are often poorly paid, and their continued employment dependent on 'results'.

This microcosm of the open market is said to create both variety and excellence but paradoxically, as in the macrocosmic market, both variety and excellence are often illusory, due to the dictates of marketability. In the marketing of aesthetic quality, other aspects of architecture can all too easily be lost sight of: technical rigour, critical method, managerial competence, social and political awareness. The fact that all this may be on offer somewhere or other at the AA, often from brilliant exponents, does not mean that it is either valued by the school or assimilated by the students.

The AA's main product is not so much building, or even architecture, as 'design'. As Alvin Boyarsky said, 'We fight the battles with the drawings on the walls', drawings which have a commercial currency in exhibitions, galleries and magazine pages. It is here more than on the building site that the historicism of Dalibor Vesely, the Constructivism of Bernard Tschumi, the modernism of Elia Zenghelis or Rem Koolhaas, and the Suprematism of Zaha Hadid have had their greatest validity.

> Despite the quality and prestige of its other ventures and of its graduates, teachers and their output, the AA accords pride of place to, and sees its major justification in, the student projects it produces. Here is where the stimulus of lecture and discussion, and the findings of private and communal research have their final flowering.[5]

The AA and other similar schools are often criticized from within the profession and the industry. They are accused of being unrealistic, of a dilettante approach which has little in common with the practical, competitive 'real world' of commissions and building contracts. This is true in one sense; architectural education can justifiably be criticized as an imperfect preparation for practice, and particularly for giving the young architect an inadequate understanding of the building industry, separated from the profession by barriers of education and class.

On a different level though, one might question how real the 'real world' actually is, or indeed how real anything is under capitalism, the system in which real relationships between people are turned daily into unreal ones, defined by money and objects. On this level, even the eminently practical world of the building industry is no more nor less real than the schools are, no more nor less alienated, exploiting and objectifying as it does the potential creativity of all those involved in it.

The building industry is obviously important in the economy, but in some ways it is very untypical of British industry as a whole. Compared, say, with the motor or electronics industries, it is highly labour intensive, with a low level of mechanization. Because its products are very site-specific, each one different from the rest, it does not lend itself easily to Fordist or Taylorist production techniques. By comparison with such high-tech industries it is perceptibly inefficient and its products unsatisfactory.

The building industry is frequently criticized, often in contrast to those of Scandinavian countries, with their much higher levels of mechanization, as technically backward. Its fragmented organization, low productivity and lack of long-term investment might lead one to the conclusion that its problems are internal, and that what it requires is some sort of radical reorganization. In fact the overhaul and even nationalization of the industry have occasionally been discussed.

However, this would be to disregard the role of capital at both national and international levels, which exert external pressures on the industry far more significant than its own internal problems. The main features of twentieth-century capitalism – monopolistic accumulation, repeated crises, and worsening inflation – all have their effects. So do the monetary policies through which the government tries to control the instability.

Accumulation, the main activity of modern capitalism, leads to market domination in the British building industry by a few very large firms, often multinational in scope. The monopolistic conditions they create allow the perpetuation of inefficiencies in the industry, and make for a volatile programme of investment, as resources are switched from one area to another in search of profit. The industry becomes polarized between a few very large firms and a large number of very small ones, with little organizational continuity in the shape of medium-sized firms between them.

Crisis conditions increase this polarity; medium-sized firms tend to lose out to the multinationals who move down market in search of work. Crises discourage long-term investment even more, and encourage the movement of capital out of the country or out of the industry altogether. The British establishment's long-standing interests in land provide an alternative to construction; the biggest companies will speculate in land and property when building contracts are scarce.

The development process is a key factor in government policy on inflation; it is seen as a regulator through which economic activity can, in the short term, be controlled. Monetarist policies like interest-rate rises will have a more immediate and more drastic effect on the building industry than on any other sector, to the great detriment of those – such as the badly housed – who need the products of the industry, and of the large number of building workers who lose their jobs as a result.

The aggressive market system within which the industry operates makes things difficult for the workforce. Periodic unemployment is only one of the problems faced by building workers. Pay is low and conditions of employment are poor; sick pay, for example, is very limited and there is no pension scheme. Working conditions are also poor; the industry has a bad health and safety record, and building work falls into the most dangerous class of employment for which insurance is normally available.

One reason for all this is the low level of unionization. It is sometimes said that the fragmentary nature of the building process itself makes union organization difficult, though union membership in the Swedish industry, for example, is 90 per cent, three times the British rate at the best of times. Sweden also has much better industrial relations, a reflection perhaps of the real reason for the British predicament, the exploitative attitude of the employer. It is common for building employers to victimize union organizers, and the fluid nature of the work makes it comparatively easy to strike them off the payroll. The employment of 'labour-only' sub-contractors or 'lump' labour – well paid but in other respects heavily exploited – in preference to unionized labour, has been another common tactic. And the Conservative government's reform of council direct-labour organizations, which has forced them to compete against private contractors with less compunction about their workforces' pay and conditions, has all but abolished the one section of the industry offering reasonable working conditions and non-discriminatory employment policies.

The industry is covered by four main unions. The smallest, the Furniture, Timber and Allied Trades Union, is the last survivor of the craft unions which dominated trade unionism in the nineteenth century, and were responsible for many of the early struggles for recognition and rights. Building-craft unions have declined as a result of the new techniques of the twentieth century, and the need to organize on a large scale. Most unionized building workers are now in sections of the two general unions, the Transport and General Workers' and the General and Municipal Workers', or the large building-industry union, the Union of Construction Allied Trades and Technicians. A merger between the T&GWU and UCATT has been discussed.

As general unemployment has increased and the building workforce has declined, union membership has suffered and union organization has become more difficult. So far, the big unions and the TUC have proved unequal to the task of protecting pay and conditions. While essential in one respect – that of matching the strength of the multinational employers – large-scale union organization also poses a problem. The

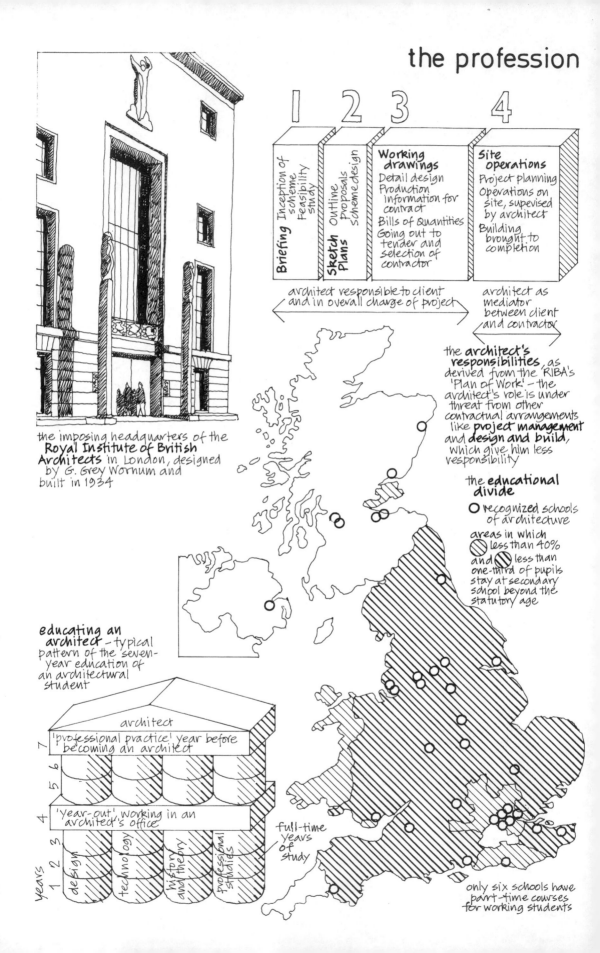

# the profession

**1**

**Briefing** Inception of scheme Feasibility study

**2**

**Sketch Plans** Outline proposals scheme design

**3**

**Working drawings**
Detail design
Production information for contract
Bills of Quantities
Going out to tender and selection of contractor

**4**

**Site operations**
Project planning
Operations on site, supervised by architect
Building brought to completion

← architect responsible to client and in overall charge of project →

architect as mediator between client and contractor

the **architect's responsibilities**, as derived from the 'RIBA's 'Plan of Work' – the architect's role is under threat from other contractual arrangements like **project management** and **design and build**, which give him less responsibility

the **educational divide**

○ recognized schools of architecture

◑ areas in which less than 40% and ◐ less than one-third of pupils stay at secondary school beyond the statutory age

the imposing headquarters of the **Royal Institute of British Architects** in London, designed by G. Grey Wornum and built in 1934

**educating an architect** – typical pattern of the 'seven-year education of an architectural student

architect

7 'professional practice' year before becoming an architect

6
5

4 'year-out' working in an architect's office

full-time years of study

3
2
1

years

design   technology   history and theory   professional studies

only six schools have part-time courses for working students

# the industry

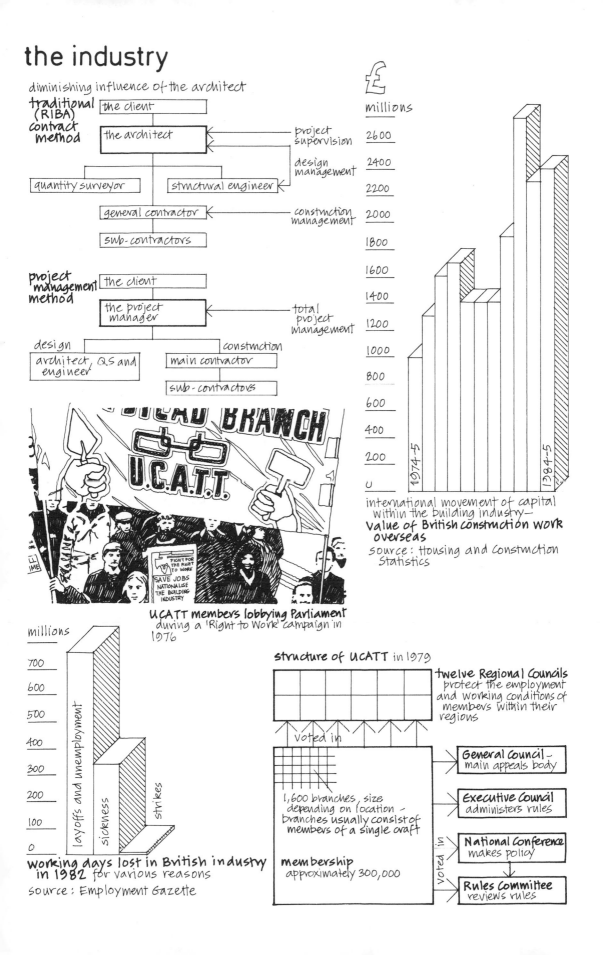

diminishing influence of the architect

**traditional (RIBA) contract method**

- the client
- the architect — project supervision
  - design management
- quantity surveyor
- structural engineer — design management
- general contractor — construction management
- sub-contractors

**project management method**

- the client
- the project manager — total project management
- design
  - architect, QS and engineer
- construction
  - main contractor
  - sub-contractors

£ millions

2600
2400
2200
2000
1800
1600
1400
1200
1000
800
600
400
200
0

1974-5 ... 1984-5

international movement of capital within the building industry—
**Value of British construction work overseas**

source: Housing and Construction Statistics

UCATT members lobbying Parliament during a 'Right to Work' campaign in 1976

millions

700
600
500
400
300
200
100
0

layoffs and unemployment
sickness
strikes

**working days lost in British industry in 1982** for various reasons

source: Employment Gazette

**structure of UCATT** in 1979

**twelve Regional Councils**
protect the employment and working conditions of members within their regions

voted in

1,600 branches, size depending on location - branches usually consist of members of a single craft

**membership**
approximately 300,000

**General Council** - main appeals body

**Executive Council** administers rules

**National Conference** makes policy

voted in

**Rules Committee** reviews rules

British trade-union system has become part of the establishment and, unwilling to disturb the corporate balance of power too much, acts as a brake on the militancy of the workforce. At the best of times, shop stewards, working at local level, often feel isolated from decision making at union headquarters.

The government's anti-union legislation between 1980 and 1984 increased problems for local organizers. Workers' freedom of action was curtailed by their loss of union immunities, by a narrowed definition of what constitutes a legal strike, by the outlawing of secondary picketing, and by the obligation to hold strike ballots. As a result genuine grievances may in future have to be pursued outside the law. Despite or because of all this, some successful actions have been fought, notably the building workers' strike in Docklands in 1989.

The capitalist system is expressly divisive of the building industry. It is in the interests of profit that the relationships between students, architects, contractors and workers should be marked by exploitation, confrontation and mutual ignorance. Under the circumstances, close links between theory and practice, and between designers and constructors, are difficult to achieve; sensitive, co-operatively designed and constructed buildings are rare. It is not surprising, under the circumstances, that our environment should be so deficient.

# 7 Theories and History – linking theory and practice

The preceding chapters have described British architecture today as the product of a monopoly capitalist system in crisis and of a conservative ideology. They have created a picture of an alienated profession, its theory concentrating on stylistic controversy, its practice on short-term expediency. Both theory and practice seem unconcerned with society's most urgent needs, particularly those of the exploited poor, a situation which the theorists, the educators, the profession and the industry seem, on the whole, to accept.

The following chapters offer a more hopeful view. They will look at attempts being made to criticize not only the environment but also capitalist society itself, to construct alternative theories and to engage in alternative practice. Here and there, theorists and practitioners are trying to discover new roles for themselves, to make better use of techniques and resources, to create the strategies necessary to match the scale of today's problems, to involve the community itself in the creation of its own environment.

Bourgeois theory confuses our view of society; a critical theory could help to clarify it. And if theory and practice could be more closely linked, the critical theorist could have an important influence on the direction taken by the practitioner.

First and foremost, such a theory would be concerned with people and their needs; it is these and not architectural dogma that should provide the criteria against which to judge the success of the built environment.

Architecture is unique among the arts in its potential for satisfying human physical needs. This is often lost sight of by self-interested designers and technologists, for whom architecture is merely a means of practising an arcane craft, or ignored by those for whom building is merely a matter of profit. It needs to be rediscovered as a basic principle of architecture, so that the gap between human physical needs and the ability of the building process to satisfy them may begin to narrow rather than continue to widen.

This is not to say that building should only satisfy physical need. Like all the other arts it should meet a spiritual need as well. Up to a point, the architects I have discussed so far have tried to address this question. The whole post-modern experiment, for example, or the revival of classicism, might generously be described as attempts to discover some of the poetry seen to be missing from modern architecture.

Up to a point, that is, because architecture could be much more than the system allows it to be. Capitalist divisions of labour have alienated ordinary people from large areas of everyday life, including the production of buildings, which they experience principally as commodities. People do not develop their inherent potential by acquiring commodities, however well designed, however 'poetic'. They do this only by being fully involved in the production of their own lives – which includes being in control of the production of their own environment.

> Everlastingly chained to a single little fragment of the Whole, man himself develops into nothing but a fragment; everlastingly in his ear the monotonous sound of the wheel that he turns, he never develops the harmony of his being, and instead of putting the stamp of humanity upon his own nature, he becomes nothing more than the imprint of his occupation or his specialized knowledge.[1]

Such alienation is accepted, even promoted, by bourgeois theorists, but a critical theory of architecture would challenge this, confronting the practitioner with alternative views of the nature of building.

Secondly, architecture would be seen not as an isolated, finite discipline, but as a part of the overall economic system. Bourgeois architectural analysis emerges from narrow aesthetic, academic or commercial considerations; behind it, certain political agenda often lie concealed. Architecture, it is said, is individual not social, depending more on personal inspiration than collective effort. Thus, architectural history, to adapt Carlyle, is the biographies of great architects. This kind of theory stresses elitism as a moving historical force, and helps perpetuate such a view of society, all the more persuasive for being apparently non-political.

To make the economic structure of society the starting point is to make such subtle forms of concealment more difficult; real reasons can be discovered, rather than the mystifying ones offered by bourgeois history. As Engels has said,

> the production of the means to support human life and, next to production, the exchange of things produced, is the basis of all social structure ... the final causes of all social changes and political revolutions are to be sought, not in men's brains, but in changes in the modes of production and exchange. They are to be sought, not in the philosophy, but in the economics of each particular epoch.[2]

The work of a group of socialist theorists at University College, London, stresses the relationship between architecture and the mode of production. Since 1979 the Bartlett International Summer School has been organized from there, and its published proceedings represent the largest body of current research into capital accumulation in the building industry, the role of the state and of private property, and the organization of building labour. The school draws together the experience of architects, economists and activists from a range of backgrounds – eastern and western Europe and developing countries – and emphasizes architecture as a function of a rapidly developing economic system.

Thirdly, then, a critical theory of architecture could offer a view of society that is dynamic and dialectical, in which tensions occur between the changing economic system and the inability of the existing social fabric to accommodate these changes.

Bourgeois theory will tend to conceal even the possibility of social change. It will deny the existence of class conflict by representing a community of interest among all classes. The work of Mark Girouard on the Victorian country house has already been mentioned. David Watkin[3] points approvingly to the increased popularity of television dramas about life above and below stairs. Such works create the impression of being popularly democratic because they deal with servants as well as masters; they seem to be social history because of their use of the class terminology which the subject demands.

But there is a clear difference between class terminology and class analysis. The latter rejects the idea of community of interest between rulers and ruled; it investigates the class struggle as a reality. Like William Morris, it takes the view that 'individuals of good will, belonging to all classes' are not able to accomplish positive changes in society. Instead, 'the antagonism of classes, which the system has bred, is the natural and necessary instrument of its destruction ... Here are two great classes, face to face with each other ... No man can exist in society and be neutral ... you must either be a reactionary ... or you must join in the march of progress.'[4]

When Morris said that 'no man' could be neutral, he might also have said 'no woman'. Some feminist architectural writing has shown considerable class awareness. Although feminist theory in general depends on gender-based rather than class-based politics, one of the best-known architectural analyses from a woman's point of view,[5] by the architectural co-operative Matrix, not only criticizes the sexist basis of our male-dominated city design, but also makes it clear that working-class women suffer most. To Matrix, it is the capitalist mode of production which has determined the relative social roles of men and women, has created an elitist architectural profession dominated by white, middle-class men, and has ensured 'the invisibility of women's lives to the professionals who plan buildings and cities'. Matrix looks towards the creation of a more equal society, in which 'the activities of bringing up children and running the home become socialized', and social attitudes towards children, and between families, become 'radically changed'. Only this way 'the fundamental problems of loneliness and alienation, which often accompany responsibility for young children, will be overcome'.

The ideas of Matrix, perhaps because they are practitioners first and theorists second, are expressed clearly and concisely. The same cannot be said of most architectural theory. Among the more difficult texts are those of Manfredo Tafuri, whose department at Venice University has made an important investigation into the relationship between architecture and ideology. Tafuri and his colleagues have produced a penetrating analysis of the culture of the capitalist city,[6] while Tafuri's own *chef d'œuvre*[7] is perhaps the most respected of all socialist analyses of architectural theory – though it does not yield its message easily. Tafuri identifies an important role for the architectural critic, one of class awareness, in which he or she confronts the architectural practitioner with the implications of helping to create a ruling-class ideology. He says 'that to find out what architecture is ... is the only purpose with any historical sense.'

And what is architecture? In our society, according to Tafuri, it is 'a discipline historically conditioned and institutionally functional to, first, the 'progress' of the pre-capitalist bourgeoisie and, later, to the new perspectives of capitalist "Zivilisation".'[8]

Tafuri gives the word 'progress' a certain irony. Bourgeois critics will often imply a synonymity between the creation of wealth on the one hand and social progress on the other. This was never true, and the eighties, in which the gap between rich and poor increased, made it even less tenable. Nevertheless, the bourgeois view is that the continued health of capitalism is good for society as a whole. Architectural critics who offer formulae, whether 'traditional values' or 'technical progress', as a means of improving society are practising a deception. There is nothing inevitable about history, no scenario which says that economic growth, merely by continuing, will improve the quality of life for the mass of the people.

A fourth feature of our critical theory, then, is one which Marx makes clear:

> History does nothing. It possesses no immense wealth, it wages no battles.
> It is man, real living man, that does all that, that possesses and fights;
> history is not a person apart, using man as a means for its own particular
> aims; history is nothing but the activity of man pursuing his aims.[9]

If the aim is to create a fairer society, then this cannot be left to chance; it must be worked for and, if necessary, fought for. History is a highly contingent process. A critical theory can help us understand not only the problems, but also the opportunities for social change, which the system creates. It is concerned with alternative ways forward.

In the British periodical *A3 Times*, one of the very few radical architectural magazines, there is a certain amount of sharp criticism of the architect's current role under capitalism, but the main concern is to defend the social and political idealism of the early Modern Movement, and to promote the parallels – few as they are – which exist today. Whether it is campaigning on behalf of the much-criticized avant-garde 9H Gallery in London, for example, or discovering the work of young architects for whom modern design and social progress go together, or debating the decline and possible regeneration of the contemporary city, *A3 Times* is positive and propagandist in its search for an alternative future.

One Bartlett paper should be mentioned in this context, written for the Summer School of 1989 in Paris. In 'Ideology, Production and Architecture', Jonathan Charley suggested

> that some ideas as produced and represented in buildings are ideological in that they mask contradictions. These ideas may help to reproduce the interests of the ruling class, though sometimes ideas may be represented in buildings that whilst serving the interests of the ruling class do not mask contradictions. This also raises the question of the possibility of the production of design ideas that do neither.

The paper continued by referring to

> those kinds of social production, be it of paper images or buildings, where the process of their production involves practices that either openly confront the ideas of the ruling class ... or, by carving little niches in the fabric of society, challenge the social order in offering an alternative vision and way to practice.

Charley cites examples as diverse as the building workers' strike in Docklands, the co-operative movement, the Soviet avant-garde in art and design, the Civil Rights movement in the USA, the Lucas Aerospace shop stewards' combine, and Acid House music.

If we believe with Morris that individuals do not accomplish changes in society, then the task of creating the future must be socialized. All these isolated movements, essential in themselves, must also be part of a more general, popular movement. Architectural theory must discover how to be relevant to a wider audience.

Morris scorned the view that architecture can be defined in terms of great buildings and of the superficialities of style. This remains a common failing among critics, which even Pevsner has helped to perpetuate. 'A bicycle shed is a building. Lincoln Cathedral is a piece of architecture. Nearly everything that encloses space on a scale sufficient for a human being to move in, is a building; the term architecture applies only to buildings designed with a view to aesthetic appeal.'[10]

In our society, 'aesthetic appeal' is, by definition, for those with a privileged education. Fifthly, then, a critical architectural theory would be pluralist rather than elitist. Instead of offering narrow definitions of

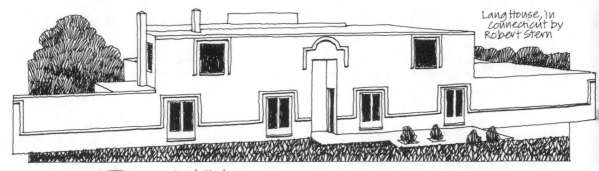

Lang House, in Connecticut by Robert Stern

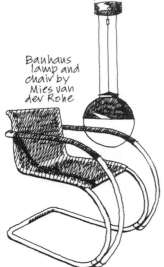

Bauhaus lamp and chair by Mies van der Rohe

post-Modern design may be an attempt to bring 'stylistic multivalence' to architecture — but architectural theory should be about much more than design — architecture is about **people and their needs**

the Bauhaus designers attempted a marriage between design and industrial production — but commodity production is an alienating process and an imperfect way of meeting human need

Frank Lloyd Wright

failure to recognize the **economic system** as the basis of society distorts history — architectural history ends up by being no more than a succession of monographs on 'great architects'

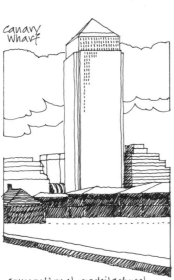

Canary Wharf

conventional environmental theory does not address the needs of women and children

conventional architectural history and theory is concerned essentially with aesthetic debate — the social and economic effects of architecture go largely unremarked

theory should take a **dialectical** view of society, identifying it as unequal and exploitative

modern buildings like Broadwalk House may be innovative technically and in terms of organization — but technical progress may not indicate social progress

# critical theory 1

history has no scenario—instead it is highly **contingent**, offering opportunities for social change which have to be worked for, and grasped when they occur

the architects of the early Modern Movement worked for social change

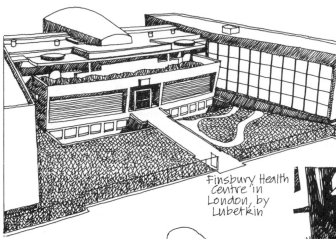

Finsbury Health Centre in London, by Lubetkin

theory should be **pluralist** not elitist—there are too many examples of 'professional' design which ignore ordinary people

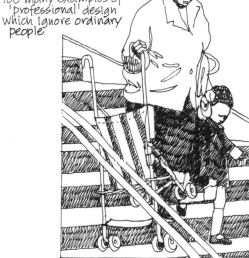

Malevich (centre) with Ermolaeva and Lissitzky and the UNOVIS group at Vitebsk in 1920—architects saw themselves at the centre of the class-struggle—

today's architects need to rediscover a community of interest with building workers

Bertolt Brecht

history and theory should not be about the past—Brecht's 'Worker who reads' asks pertinent questions about the past so that it can illuminate the **present** and help create the **future**

critical theory 2

architecture, of who may create it and who comment on it, its scope would be much wider. It would deal with humble buildings as well as great ones, take account of economic, political and social evidence as well as stylistic, and involve people at large as well as the academic and the professional. Many conventionally-held views about architecture would be challenged, most particularly the 'professionalism' which makes it remote, middle-class, white and male-dominated, and which helps to create the alienated design described by Matrix: 'It may be that the nuclear family is the most "economical" way for capitalist society to reproduce itself. And in a privatised society the suburban semi is probably the most "efficient" solution for housing the nuclear family ... But ... it does not fulfil the needs of the woman.'[11]

Architectural theory should contribute to an architectural practice in which the needs of underprivileged and minority groups in western society, and of the needy in poorer societies, are given their full value.

Lastly, and above all, a critical theory would be concerned about the future. Too often, architectural history and theory deal only with the past. And too often they are carefully selective, concerning themselves only with matters which pose no challenge to the way our society is run. As a result, they may well seem irrelevant to, and disconnected from, the real problems of today. But our knowledge of today's problems can be used as an entry into the past and can help us decide which of the many strands of history are relevant to us, as distinct from the ones which bourgeois history offers us. If the past somehow seems disconnected from the issues of today – and architectural history as taught in our schools is often particularly so – this is because we are extracting from it only the irrelevancies.

Separation of past and present can be a political act. For the formulators of the government's National Curriculum for schools, history stops at 1969, and its use as a means of criticizing present society is thereby limited. A number of rightist American commentators, taking heart from the demise of Stalinism, have declared history to be at an end; this way capitalism can be represented as the final fulfilment of human development.

Even some former progressives seem to have taken this view. The British Communist Party renames itself 'Democratic Left' and declares that we live in 'New Times'. The whole project of post-modernism, in literary theory, architecture and art, seeks to persuade us that our modernist past, with its strong social commitment, is dead. When Daniel Bell speaks of the post-industrial society, and André Gorz of the end of the working class, they are expressing the frustration of a generation of intellectuals who have forgotten even the illusory hopes of 1968, and have no other means of explaining or confronting the present.

Yet history is full of relevant material. The history of class struggles, for example, though half hidden, or concealed from us by bourgeois historical methods, can be rediscovered and used to help create the future. As the French Marxist historian Jean Chesneaux says, the past is a 'reference point' that makes it possible for us to carry out 'a radical critique of the present' and allows us to make steps towards 'the definition of a qualitatively different future'.[12]

The main characteristic of the materialist conception of history described in this chapter and attempted in this book is that it recognizes the capitalist mode of production as the main factor on which the social structure and its supporting theories depend. But matters do not end there; the mode of production also creates the conditions for the political changes that are needed to make social progress. Thus we devise a social theory not merely to describe and criticize the present system, but also as a necessary prelude to critical practice. The next three chapters look at some current attempts to turn theory into practice.

# 8 The New Spirit – architecture and technology

For Richard Rogers, Norman Foster, Nicholas Grimshaw and others, modernism is alive and well. The work of Rogers in particular, such as the Beaubourg Centre which he designed in conjunction with Renzo Piano, or his building for Lloyd's of London, has attracted the attention of a wide public. Foster's Hong Kong and Shanghai National Bank, or his terminal at Stansted Airport, and Grimshaw's Sainsbury superstore in London have become almost as well known. With their structural inventiveness, their unconventional, mechanistic forms and their spatial dynamism, they seem to represent what modern architecture is all about. The very epithet 'high-tech', which has been applied to them, connotes the last word in popular modernity.

This representative role is one which today's high-tech architecture shares with that of the Soviet Constructivists of the twenties. In both cases, the visual power of modern technology is, or was, being used to make a statement, both futuristic and utopian, about society. Constructivism was probably the strongest visual expression of modernity this century, and today's high-tech architects seem to see themselves as its inheritors. Rogers, for example, wrote in an architectural manifesto, in 1969: 'Technology offers the possibility of a society without want, where for the first time, work and learning need only be done for pleasure, and the age-old capitalist morality of earning one's keep, the backbone of the existing power structure, would be eliminated.'[1]

The utopianism of this is reminiscent of the Constructivists, and visually at least, the architecture which accompanies it is the equivalent of the Constructivists' 'destruction of the traditional'. But there the resemblance ends; the economic, social and political circumstances of the October Revolution were so different from today's experience that no further parallels can be drawn.

The Constructivists were participating in an actual revolution. Their designs celebrated technology not for its own sake but for the sake of the new social order it represented. The new architectural forms devised by Lissitzky, Ginsburg and the Vesnins were attempts to give the social and economic revolution greater immediacy.

This was, and still is, untrue of modernism in the west, despite its utopian claims. Modern technology and social progress were very much associated in theory, but the realities dictated otherwise. By the time the political problems of the thirties had been resolved through World War II, any synonymity between technical and social progress had been lost. The main purpose of the Keynesian economic system, with its insistence on a strong public sector, was not altruistic; the underlying purpose was to ensure the future of capitalism. Technology was used to increase output, not primarily to build a better world. However, the vast surplus-value created could be ploughed back into capital investment – which included a big building programme. And the rapidly developing technology could of course spin off into the building process itself.

The prefabrication of buildings, presaged by the theoreticians of the twenties and thirties, now became a reality. Heavyweight precast concrete panel construction came into common use for high flats, and lightweight steel frames with clip-on claddings for low-rise buildings such as schools. The terminology of factory production – output targets, quality control, economies of scale – was much in evidence. For school building, many local authorities were able to pool their resources and to strike a happy balance between efficiency and quality. In the case of council flat-building, competition between scores of private-sector manufacturers contributed to a high output, but achieved neither economies of scale nor quality of product.

The opportunity was taken to transfer technology from other fields into the building industry. Materials developed for the war effort made their appearance, including plastics, synthetic sealants and lightweight metals. The high strength-to-weight ratios demanded by the aircraft industry stimulated new forms of construction too, such as stressed-skin construction and geodesics.

This last area is particularly associated with Richard Buckminster Fuller, for many years the architectural world's most famous technical innovator and its greatest prophet of the benign use of technology. Fuller began his research in the twenties, inventing both the Wichita House and the Dymaxion Car, in which he sought the maximum performance from a minimum of fuel and materials. He came into prominence after World War II with his space frames and geodesic domes. He designed his own geodesic house and sang 'Roam Home to a Dome' to the tune of 'Home on the Range'. He designed an aluminium dome 44 metres in diameter for Honolulu, and one of 114 metres, made from folded sheet-steel hexagons, for Baton Rouge, Louisiana. He even devised a project for a transparent dome three kilometres wide to cover, and control the climate of, New York City. Many of his domes were of cheap materials like plywood or paperboard and were mass-produced in quantity for the US government, which found them easily transportable and capable of being lifted intact by helicopter.

# industry and technology

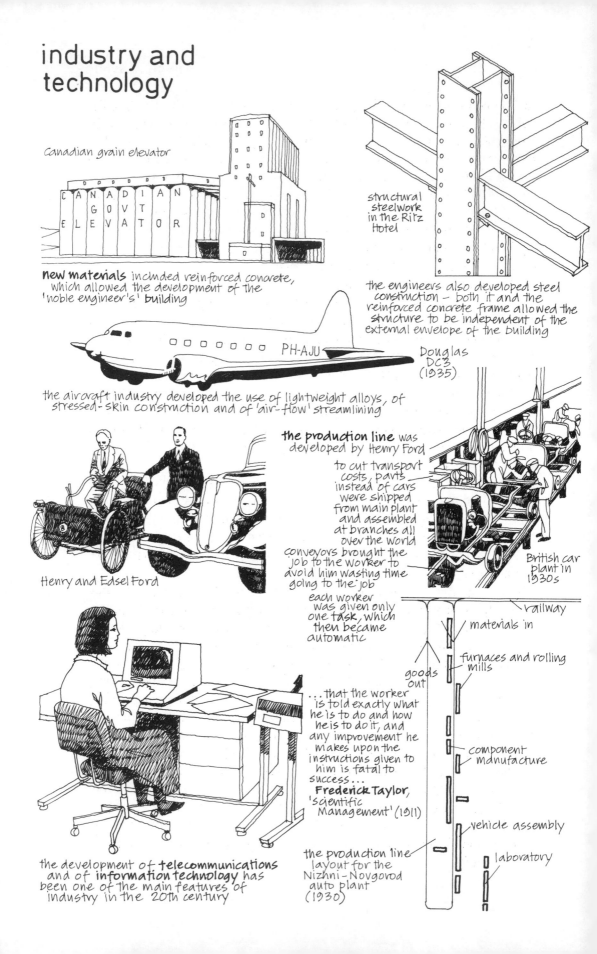

Canadian grain elevator

CANADIAN GOVT ELEVATOR

**new materials** included reinforced concrete, which allowed the development of the 'noble engineer's' **building**

structural steelwork in the Ritz Hotel

the engineers also developed steel construction – both it and the reinforced concrete frame allowed the structure to be independent of the external envelope of the building

PH-AJU

Douglas DC3 (1935)

the aircraft industry developed the use of lightweight alloys, of stressed-skin construction and of 'air-flow' streamlining

**the production line** was developed by Henry Ford

to cut transport costs, parts instead of cars were shipped from main plant and assembled at branches all over the world

conveyors brought the job to the worker to avoid him wasting time going to the job

Henry and Edsel Ford

British car plant in 1930s

each worker was given only one **task**, which then became automatic

...that the worker is told exactly what he is to do and how he is to do it, and any improvement he makes upon the instructions given to him is fatal to success...
**Frederick Taylor**, 'Scientific Management' (1911)

railway
materials in
furnaces and rolling mills
goods out
component manufacture
vehicle assembly
laboratory

the production line layout for the Nizhni-Novgorod auto plant (1930)

the development of **telecommunications** and of **information technology** has been one of the main features of industry in the 20th century

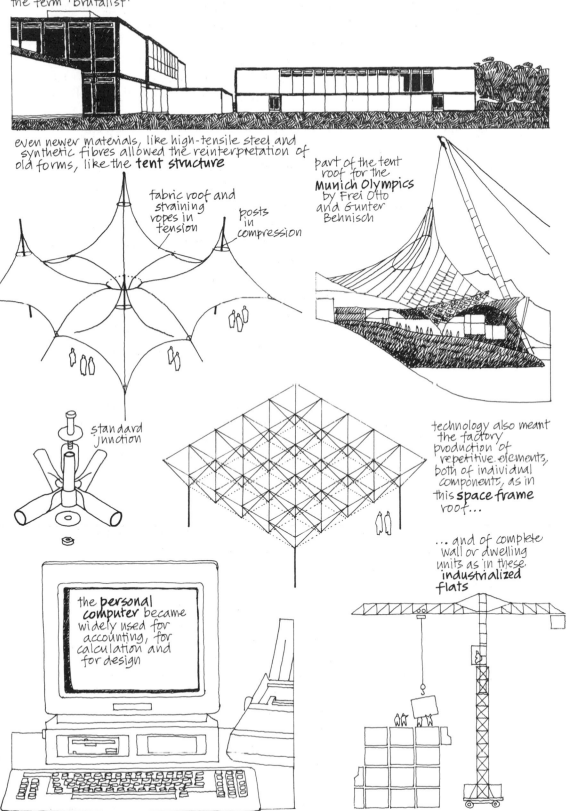

in the fifties, the Smithsons' **Hunstanton School** in Norfolk was an architectural demonstration of the materials of modern technology – its exposed steel frame and internal brickwork earned it the term 'brutalist'

even newer materials, like high-tensile steel and synthetic fibres allowed the reinterpretation of old forms, like the **tent structure**

fabric roof and straining ropes in tension

posts in compression

part of the tent roof for the **Munich Olympics** by Frei Otto and Gunter Behnisch

standard junction

technology also meant the factory production of repetitive elements, both of individual components, as in this **space frame** roof...

the **personal computer** became widely used for accounting, for calculation and for design

... and of complete wall or dwelling units as in these **industrialized flats**

Fuller combined an intuitive technical brilliance with a utopianism both sincere and naive. Deeply concerned about the future of the environment, he put his faith in the enterprise and creativity of the young, and in the positive use of technology. Yet at the same time he put his skills at the disposal of the multinational corporations and the Pentagon. To him, 'The invention and systems-design revolution must come before political adjustments. Revolution by design and invention is the only revolution tolerable to all men, all societies, and all political systems everywhere.'[2]

Technologists very easily learn to suspend political disbelief for the opportunity to develop their craft. One great contemporary of Fuller, however, was much less equivocal. Paul Goodman, perhaps the most acute environmental critic of the sixties, had a much clearer perception of what the problems were and of where the future lay. At a symposium organized in 1967 by the National Security Industrial Association, an organization founded to enhance communications between the USA's armaments industry and the government, he ungratefully said to his hosts, 'you are the military-industrial of the United States, the most dangerous body of men at present in the world'. He saw that because most of the world's scientific effort had been taken over by the military state, it was impossible to put any faith for the future in the social use of technology:

> it is your companies who have oversold the planes, and the cars, polluted the air and water, and baulked at even the most trivial remedies, so that I do not see how you can be morally trusted with the job ... Your thinking is never to simplify and retrench, but always to devise new equipment to alleviate the mess that you have helped to make with your previous equipment.[3]

Like Fuller, Goodman also thought the future lay with the young, but only if they had the wit to challenge the existing power structures. 'If the young continue to be in conflict, to try out innovations, and to study professionally what ought to be done with our technology and ecology, mores, and authority structure, and the fact of one world, they will gradually shape for themselves a good inheritance to come into.'[4]

In the sixties there were many attempts by the young to challenge existing power structures, from Prague to Paris, from Kent State to Grosvenor Square; the struggles of Ho Chi Minh or of Che Guevara were common ideological currency. But it was still very difficult for those engaged in architecture not to be seduced by technology and therefore by the power structure which lay behind it. It was much easier to hold the view, like Fuller, that technical progress would itself open doors to a utopian future than, like Goodman, to make the political connections and to see that the most important question about technology was who controlled it, and for what purpose.

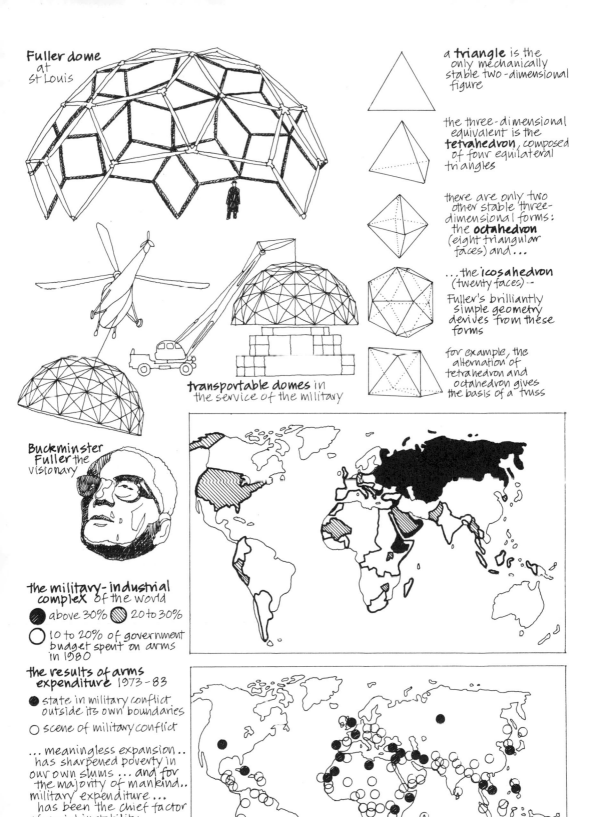

**Fuller dome** at St Louis

a **triangle** is the only mechanically stable two-dimensional figure

the three-dimensional equivalent is the **tetrahedron**, composed of four equilateral triangles

there are only two other stable three-dimensional forms: the **octahedron** (eight triangular faces) and...

...the **icosahedron** (twenty faces) --

Fuller's brilliantly simple geometry derives from these forms

for example, the alternation of tetrahedron and octahedron gives the basis of a truss

**transportable domes** in the service of the military

**Buckminster Fuller** the visionary

**the military-industrial complex** of the world

● above 30%   ▨ 20 to 30%

○ 10 to 20% of government budget spent on arms in 1980

**the results of arms expenditure** 1973-83

● state in military conflict outside its own boundaries

○ scene of military conflict

... meaningless expansion.. has sharpened poverty in our own slums ... and for the majority of mankind.. military expenditure ... has been the chief factor of social instability
Paul Goodman 1967

# Fuller and Goodman

Take *Architectural Design.* In some ways the most progressive architectural magazine there has been in postwar Britain, AD tried in the sixties to deal seriously with issues of housing, community action, the inner city, democracy and social change. But the magazine also had an uncritical enthusiasm for technical imagery, celebrating technology for its own sake and seldom seeming to question its military-industrial provenance. The issue of June 1968 is one example of many. With the Paris events in full swing, AD published an article by Utopie, a group of young French radicals, which attempted to define a new socially critical role for architects. But the main part of the issue was devoted to the high-tech excitements of pneumatic structures, in a series of seductive images from a variety of sources, including not only Utopie themselves but also multinational companies, the aerospace and defence industries, the fashion scene and the neocolonial world of Walt Disney.

Most young architects were no doubt aware of the difficult social tasks of the day. Maybe because of the difficulties, it was easier to concern oneself with more esoteric pursuits. It is safer to work in isolation or in small groups on designs or ideas that purport to change society than to involve onself in the actual social struggle. In the sixties it was an exciting diversion from the real world to concern oneself with the imagery of flight, space travel, undersea exploration, motorcar production, science fiction, cybernetics and computers.

'Archigram' emerged, as a magazine and an architectural group, in 1961. The group included designers like Peter Cook, Ron Herron, Warren Chalk and Cedric Price, and was given support by the writings of, among others, Reyner Banham. In some respects, it was the architectural equivalent of the Pop Art movement, with its interest in the technology of the acquisitive society, and its general desire to rethink the image of architecture – though there was little enough of Richard Hamilton's caustic social comment in Archigram's enthusiastic celebrations of consumerism.

Archigram was a loose grouping, bound together by the predilection of its members for lively visual images, though certain so-called 'preoccupations' recurred in its work. One of these was its fascination with a high-energy urban society, consumptive and wasteful. Another, related to this, was its view of cities as dynamic enterprises, reflections of the rapid changes and the physical movement which went on in them, and of buildings themselves as energetic mechanisms. From this grew the concept of non-architecture – of architecture as an amalgam of the functions and services that go on in it – in which the traditional concept of a building was destroyed.

To these should be added the tendency to treat the whole process of design as an abstract exercise, so that the drawn project rather than the

# Archigram

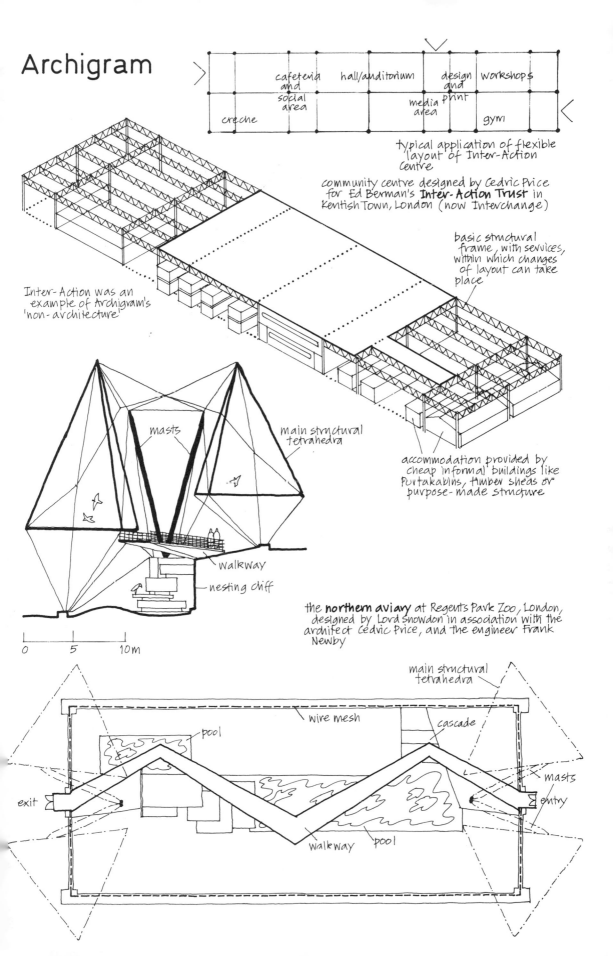

cafeteria and social area | hall/auditorium | design and print | workshops

creche | media area | gym

typical application of flexible layout of Inter-Action Centre

community centre designed by Cedric Price for Ed Berman's **Inter-Action Trust** in Kentish Town, London (now Interchange)

basic structural frame, with services, within which changes of layout can take place

Inter-Action was an example of Archigram's 'non-architecture'

accommodation provided by cheap 'informal' buildings like Portakabins, timber sheds or purpose-made structure

masts

main structural tetrahedra

walkway

nesting cliff

0  5  10m

the **northern aviary** at Regents Park Zoo, London, designed by Lord Snowdon in association with the architect Cedric Price, and the engineer Frank Newby

main structural tetrahedra

wire mesh

pool

cascade

exit

masts

entry

walkway  pool

built object became the preferred currency. Archigram designers did produce some buildings, notably the Snowdon Aviary in Regents Park Zoo and the building for the Inter-Action arts trust in Kentish Town in London, both by Cedric Price. But they became better known for their enticing paper images, which long influenced students and practitioners alike: the Sin Centre in Leicester Square, the Plug-in City, the Walking City, the Potteries Thinkbelt.

Archigram belonged essentially to a world apart, one of unreal architecture, of unbuilt schemes published in the glossy magazines, of competition entries and of ideas which went the rounds of the architectural schools. Such is the power of the media, even in architecture, that one could make a reputation without ever facing the realities of the building site or coping with users' needs. Influential magazines and fashionable schools of architecture have always tended to encourage such self-referential aesthetic creativity and to discourage, for example, critical awareness of the role of architects and architecture in a consumer society.

In August 1986 the *Architectural Review* detected that a 'New Spirit' had come into architecture, supplanting the post-modernism which had itself claimed to have ousted modern architecture. 'Post-Modernism is dead', claimed the leading article, having become 'no more than the pretty plaything of rampant capitalism'. Architecture was looking forward again, it seemed, becoming 'vigorous, exploratory and, although it takes no heed of fashion, very much an architecture of now'.[5]

This new architecture, it was said, had diverse roots. It owed much to the 'heroic' modernism itself, especially to Constructivism, but also to the more anti-heroic movements like Dada, Surrealism, Pop, Punk and New Wave. The biggest claim was that it avoided the 'reductivist morality' of modernism by being somehow more 'real', in that it embraced 'the grimy, godforsaken realities of contemporary urban existence' and celebrated 'the power of the "found" environment'.

The work which illustrated this argument included a small number of built projects and a greater number of conceptual images, unconventional, often dynamic, crude or elegant by turns, making use of harsh modern materials, often in very poetic ways. They ranged from experimental fantasies, with descriptions like post-Constructivist or neo-Suprematist, to the built forms of high-tech modernism. The main theoretical link between them all was the concept of 'deconstruction'.

This term, applied to architecture, brings an instant reaction, for what is architecture if not construction? Like structuralism, of which deconstruction is a development, the term is of course primarily literary, and does not translate smoothly into architectural terms – though this has not stopped theorists from trying.

I commented above on the adoption of structuralism by architectural critics and how its concern for language and signs helped create an interest in the idea of 'meaning' and 'metaphor' in architecture. Structuralism, in which signs were said to consist of the two closely related components of 'signifier' and 'signified', very soon developed into post-structuralism, in which this close relationship was broken down.

Many signifiers, like the French word *mouton*, which is sometimes chosen as an example, have more than one signified – in this case 'sheep' and 'meat'. For post-structuralists, it became clear that signifier and signified were separate, and related to each other in more complex and elliptical ways than the early structuralists had allowed. Nevertheless, both structuralists and post-structuralists took it as axiomatic that language does have a structure.

However, the French critic Jacques Derrida[6] developed a branch of post-structuralism in which even this was questioned. Western philosophy, from Plato to post-structuralism, said Derrida, presupposed certain fixed 'centres of meaning' around which all else revolved: absolute concepts like 'goodness', 'consciousness' or 'truth'. To him these presented a philosophic paradox; each concept had an opposite, like good had evil, the latter challenging the absoluteness of the former. He developed the idea of 'deconstruction', moving into a world of relativity in which a proposition 'transgresses the laws it appears to set up for itself'. This implied a critical gap between a text and its meaning; it was in the nature both of writing and of language as a whole that they were not to be confined to specific centres of meaning. The text has its own life, and 'reads' the reader as much as the reader reads it.

The whole structuralist project was critical and radical. It set itself up in opposition to mainstream criticism for which 'the text' was autonomous, sacrosanct and value-free. The relativities and uncertainties promoted by the structuralists were attempts to widen this view, and in effect were a criticism – if a mild one – of the bourgeois system.

This approach struck a chord with many architectural theorists of the seventies and eighties: European progressives disillusioned by the death of the hopes of 1968; modernists uneasy about the rigid, prescriptive way in which modernism had been applied; intellectuals seeking a theory which would adequately express the baffling complexities of a 'new age'; fashionable critics looking for something impressive and new.

> The magnitude of the events dealt a devastating blow to our collective unconscious; our species was faced with having to make new associations with rules of instability and perplexing abstraction ... For now, an architecture of no fixed theory or doctrine, with a visual vocabulary of instability – an architecture that cannot be codified and turned into a style – can escape consumption and retain historical relevance.[7]

'The New Spirit' took a more public form as projects began to be built.

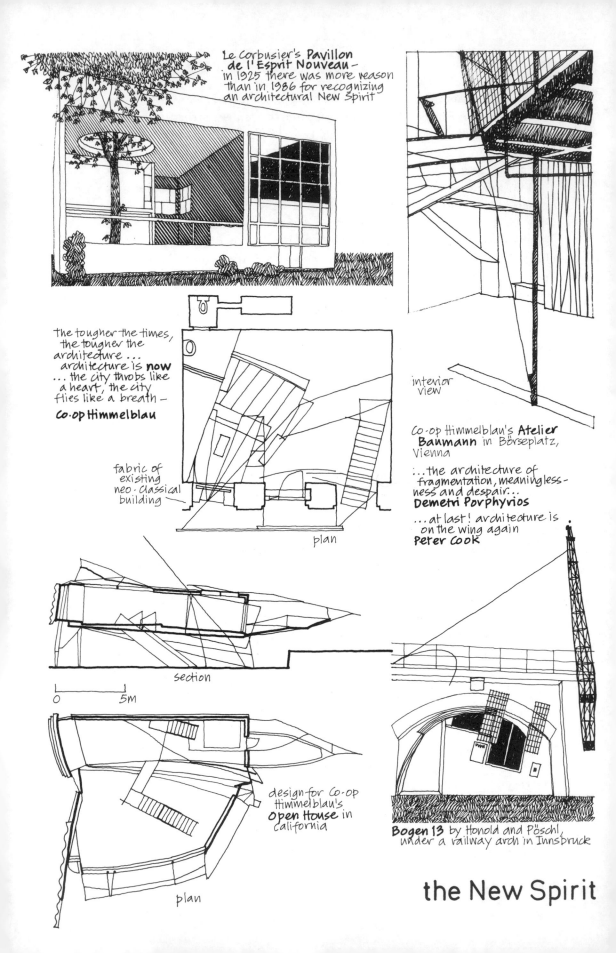

Le Corbusier's **Pavillon de l'Esprit Nouveau** – in 1925 there was more reason than in 1986 for recognizing an architectural New Spirit

the tougher the times, the tougher the architecture ... architecture is **now** ... the city throbs like a heart, the city flies like a breath –
**Co·op Himmelblau**

fabric of existing neo·classical building

plan

interior view

Co·op Himmelblau's **Atelier Baumann** in Börseplatz, Vienna

... the architecture of fragmentation, meaningless-ness and despair ... **Demetri Porphyrios**

... at last! architecture is on the wing again **Peter Cook**

section

0    5m

design for Co·op Himmelblau's **Open House** in california

plan

**Bogen 13** by Honold and Pöschl, under a railway arch in Innsbruck

# the New Spirit

Most of them were modest in scale though often spectacular in effect. Among the most interesting designers, and best known among aficionados, was a two-man team of Viennese architects, Wolfgang Prix and Helmut Swiczinsky, known as Co-op Himmelblau, who began their joint career in the early seventies by setting fire to a specially-built tower in a Viennese courtyard, in protest at architectural convention. They became known internationally through a lecture-presentation *Architektur ist Jetzt* (Architecture is now), held in Frankfurt and London in 1984. Through their complex, informal geometry, rich use of homely materials and intricate spatial arrangements, Himmelblau tried to create 'open architecture', which they saw as an expression of today's complex, uncertain society. This approach was taken in the design of a cocktail bar, *Der Rote Engel*, and in the Atelier Baumann, a studio for a graphic artist, both in Vienna.

Less complex but even more extreme geometrically was another bar, *Bogen Dreizehn*, designed by Reinhardt Honold and Wolfgang Pöschl as a violent collision of metal sheets and I-section beams under a railway arch in Innsbruck. Projects like this were in some respects the architectural equivalent of Punk Rock or New Wave: rather aggressive, embracing the 'reality' of a difficult and dangerous urban society, while at the same time being a protest against it. Himmelblau's *Architektur ist Jetzt* manifesto criticized not only the closed mentality of public-sector functionaries and myopic preservationists, but also the real-estate speculators and their architects, while Honold and Pöschl saw their railway-arch project as something 'hard' in what they called 'a town of commercialised lies and exploitative, soft-sell tourism'.[8] The 'deconstruction' here was almost literal, of buildings whose elements were visually disengaged, blown apart, floating at uncommon angles and levels: the architecture of a decadent civilization cracking up. Critical acclaim and commercial success, however, subsequently reduced Himmelblau's appetite for caustic social comment. Their later project for a private house in California, the 'Open House' at Malibu, was a soft-sell speculation for the luxury market.

These were all small projects, the comments of a few individuals who saw themselves, however misleadingly, as critics of society. There were also much larger ones, sponsored by the state itself, in the form of grand architectural competitions – events in which central and local governments in Germany, Catalonia and France were particularly active. The former pursued for some years a project called 'Living in the Inner City', notably by setting up an International Building Exhibition (IBA) in Berlin, with built contributions from a number of internationally known architects. One of the grandest proposals to emerge from this project was the development of the declining industrial area of Moabit, on the banks of the Spree, with a new 'metropolitan resort'. A competition-winning

# Berlin

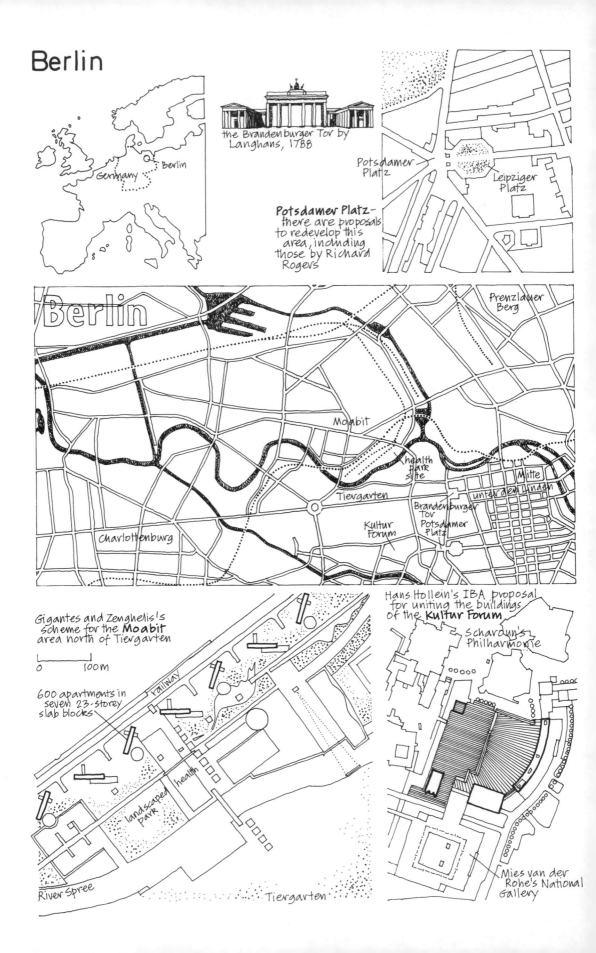

the Brandenburger Tor by Langhans, 1788

**Potsdamer Platz** —
there are proposals to redevelop this area, including those by Richard Rogers

Potsdamer Platz

Leipziger Platz

Prenzlauer Berg

Moabit

health park site

Tiergarten

Mitte

unter den Linden

Brandenburger Tor
Potsdamer Platz

Kultur Forum

Charlottenburg

Gigantes and Zenghelis's scheme for the **Moabit** area north of Tiergarten

0      100m

600 apartments in seven 23-storey slab blocks

railway

health

landscaped park

River Spree

Tiergarten

Hans Hollein's IBA proposal for uniting the buildings of the **Kultur Forum**

Scharoun's Philharmonie

Mies van der Rohe's National Gallery

entry by Eleni Gigantes and Elia Zenghelis proposed seven 23-storey slab blocks containing 600 apartments, set in a landscaped 'health park' of hydrotherapy pools, saunas and aerobics centres. The slab blocks would float insubstantially on pilotis, while a museum, designed in the form of a gigantic cantilever beam, would jut out over the nearby railway track, defying both gravity and the traditional form of the city: deconstruction on a grand scale.

Further south, in Baden-Württemburg and Bavaria, the work of the successful firm Behnisch and Partners displays similar characteristics. Behnisch came into prominence with his competition-winning design for the 1972 Munich Olympics. His 'roof over the landscape', a gigantic tensile structure, for which the engineer Frei Otto was technical consultant, linked all the Olympic stadia into a continuous whole. In his work, most of it for the public sector and much of it gained through winning competitions, Behnisch has always seen structure and environmental control as integral to design. In many of his later buildings, like his library for the Catholic University of Eichstätt, or his Hysolar Institute at the University of Stuttgart, he has created dramatic, mechanistic forms very expressive of technical and functional complexity.

Barcelona, having rediscovered its pre-Franco role as the centre of Catalan culture, emerged during the eighties as an important sponsor of modern design. The Catalan magazine *Quaderns* became an important focus of progressive debate on architecture and urbanism. Then, following the appointment of Oriol Bohigas as city planner, over 100 separate civic design schemes were set in motion in Barcelona, while preparations for the 1992 Olympics changed the city still further. Typical of the improvements were the new squares and parks, ranging from the cool palm-lined avenues of the Parc Joan Miró to the mechanistic fantasy of the Plaça dels Països Catalans at Sants railway station, from the transformed seafront promenade of Moll de la Fusta to the suburban park of Plaça de la Palmera. The Olympic works included not only new stadia, by Isozaki, Bofill and others, but also a complete reconstruction of the Poble Nou industrial suburb to the east of the city centre, to provide an Olympic village in the short term and subsequently a complete residential quarter. The refurbishment or transformation of the classic buildings of Catalan *Modernisme* included metallic sculpture on the roof of the Tàpies Museum and modern extensions to the Palau de la Música Catalana.

Of all European cities, however, Paris saw the most dramatic changes – and ones in which the architectural avant-garde played the biggest part. The grand-manner planning of Paris has always reflected the desires of successive heads of state to make it an expression of *La Gloire*. Major projects were begun under De Gaulle, Pompidou and Giscard d'Estaing, including the establishment of a business complex at La Défense with its

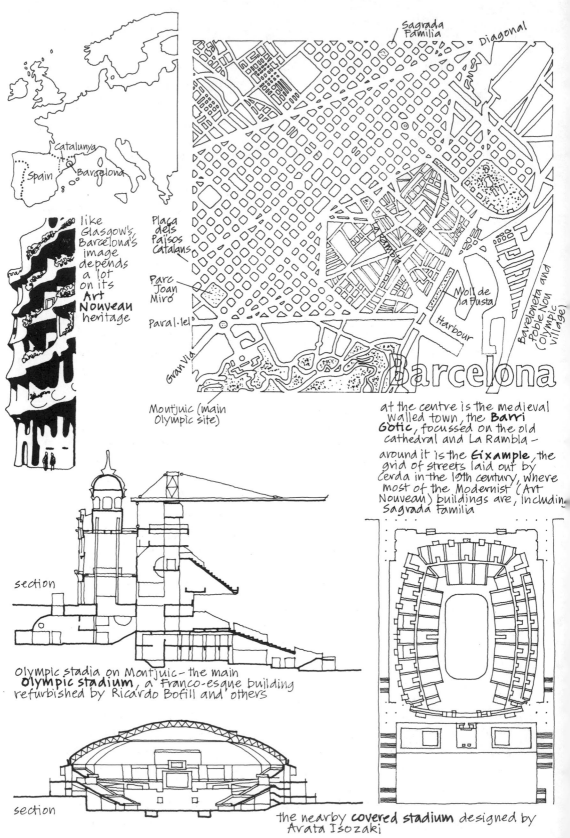

Sagrada Familia

Diagonal

like Glasgow's, Barcelona's image depends a lot on its **Art Nouveau** heritage

Plaça dels Països Catalans

Parc Joan Miró

Paral·lel

Gran Via

Montjuïc (main Olympic site)

Nyoll de la Busta

Harbour

Barceloneta (Poble Nou and Olympic village)

Barcelona

at the centre is the medieval walled town, the **Barri Gòtic**, focussed on the old cathedral and La Rambla –

around it is the **Eixample**, the grid of streets laid out by Cerda in the 19th century, where most of the Modernist (Art Nouveau) buildings are, including Sagrada Familia

section

Olympic stadia on Montjuïc – the main **Olympic stadium**, a Franco-esque building refurbished by Ricardo Bofill and others

section

the nearby **covered stadium** designed by Arata Isozaki

# Barcelona 1

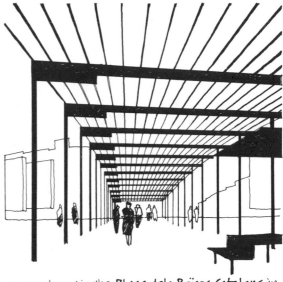

covered way in the **Plaça dels Països Catalans** in front of the Barcelona Sants railway station

newly laid-out quay-side promenade of **Moll de la Fusta**

spectacular wire sculpture on the roof of Domenech's 1881 publishing house for Montaner y Simon, now the **Tapies museum**

Calatrava's **Bac de Roda - Felip II** bridge over the railway to the north of the city centre

# Barcelona 2

remarkable CNIT building, and the redevelopment of Les Halles, of which the Beaubourg centre became such a popular focus. Paradoxically, however, the main Gaullist contribution to planning in Paris has probably been the development of an integrated subsidized public-transport system, worthy almost of Moscow, while it has been the role of the socialist Mitterrand to pursue the grand architectural projects which have begun to invest the townscape with a new kind of glory.

Recently Les Halles has been further developed and La Défense has grown into a giant office city with the CNIT building now dwarfed by J. O. von Spreckelsen's Grande Arche, a 35-storey, 110-metre hollow cube of offices sitting astride the triumphal way from the Champs Elysées. A new 'people's' opera house has been built at the Bastille, cradle of the Revolution. A major refurbishment of the Louvre includes I. M. Pei's extraordinary glass pyramid. In all these projects no compromise has been made with architectural tradition, often controversially, with *L'Architecture d'Aujourd'hui* calling the Grand Arche 'the disfigurement of the very horizon where for the patriotic soul the bloody sun of Austerlitz still sets'. Paris has become the envy of modernists in Britain, where large-scale public support for modern architecture is a thing of the past.

Intellectually and socially, the most impressive scheme of all is that for a gigantic 55-hectare park at the old slaughterhouse area of La Villette, which like most of the projects was the subject of a competition. A distinguished proposal was put forward by the OMA team of Rem Koolhaas and Elia Zenghelis, but the winner was an inspired and complex solution by Bernard Tschumi, an epic of deconstruction which he developed with none less than Jacques Derrida.

This solution is less a park than an enormous building, one of the biggest ever built. The list of activities is too large to describe, but it includes cinema, restaurants, computer gallery, libraries, exhibition halls, swimming pool, ice-rink, play-spaces and athletics areas. The entire project consists of three overlaid systems: of 'lines', in which roads, paths and linear buildings reflect the routes through the site; of 'surfaces', which are large, geometric spaces to accommodate outdoor activities; and of 'points', a multiplicity of basically cubic buildings at the intersections of a 120-metre grid. These buildings are based on a ten-metre cubic frame and have extensions and accretions to house the various activities – shops, crèches, bars – which go on in them. Each of the three overlaid systems has its own logic, so that the contacts between them are intentionally accidental, giving an impression of the multifarious complex and contingent relationships of modern life. 'Layering' is an architectural concept developed out of structuralist theory to express ambiguity, contradiction and complexity. At La Villette it is used to considerable effect, reflecting the alienation of modern society.

The entire deconstructionist project, like its social background, is full of contradiction. Its architecture is 'modern', but in a rather superficial sense. It appears to use all the techniques of modernism – exposed frameworks, industrial materials, buildings which float, cantilever or span unsupported across space – and achieves great spatial expressiveness. At the same time, its origins in the schools, magazines and international competitions – where poetic, visual values seem to count above others – tend to make it peculiarly unconvincing technically. To conceive building primarily as form, and only to solve the technical problems afterwards, if at all, does not achieve – as modernism originally set out to do – a close conceptual relationship between aesthetics and technology. The forms may be modern but the thinking is post-modern.

Nor, to the modernists, was this to be the only role for technology. The productionist theories of the twenties sought, through the factory process, to match the scale of society's needs; designers like Fuller had made genuine attempts to follow this path. Technology was as much the repetitiveness of mass-construction as it was the spectacular solution of a one-off problem. Here again, the deconstructionist agenda fell short. The preciousness of each project, and the lack of concern for solutions to wider problems, ensured this. Visual images which challenge the aesthetic assumptions of bourgeois society are all very well, as are public monuments sponsored by social-democratic governments. Many of them, like La Villette, for example, or many of the urban spaces in Barcelona, may be very successful locally, and of real benefit to a deprived local population. But they still remain peripheral to the real problems of the capitalist city: homelessness, industrial decline, congestion, pollution and the squandering of finite resources. If built, the projects ran the risk of becoming – to turn the *Architectural Review*'s comment round on itself – the playthings of capitalism; if unbuilt, they remained simply the currency of an arid aesthetic debate.

This last point could never be made, of course, about the works of the 'high-tech' designers. These above all were successful, realizable schemes. Richard Rogers's early success with the Beaubourg Centre and with the Inmos factory near Newport was surpassed by the brilliance of his well-known office block for Lloyd's, which led to an international portfolio of commissions. Norman Foster's early offices for Willis, Faber and Dumas in Ipswich and his arts centre for the Sainsbury family at the University of East Anglia led to schemes for the redevelopment of the centre of Nîmes and of the Langham Hotel in central London, while his *chefs-d'œuvre* became the spectacular Hong Kong and Shanghai National Bank in Hong Kong and the elegant Stansted airport terminal. Nicholas Grimshaw, designer of the Brentford Homebase store and the Oxford ice rink, produced his best work in the Sainsbury superstore in Camden

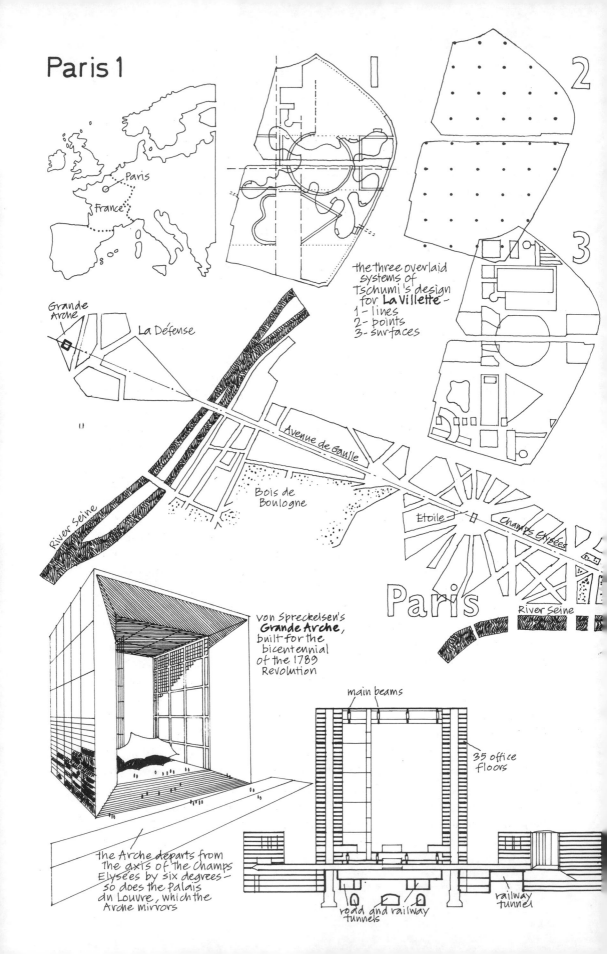

# Paris 1

Paris
France

La Défense

Grande Arche

La Défense

Avenue de Gaulle

Bois de Boulogne

River Seine

Etoile

Champs Elysées

Paris

River Seine

the three overlaid systems of Tschumi's design for **La Villette** –
1 – lines
2 – points
3 – surfaces

von Spreckelsen's **Grande Arche**, built for the bicentennial of the 1789 Revolution

main beams

35 office floors

the Arche departs from the axis of the Champs Elysées by six degrees – so does the Palais du Louvre, which the Arche mirrors

road and railway tunnels

railway tunnel

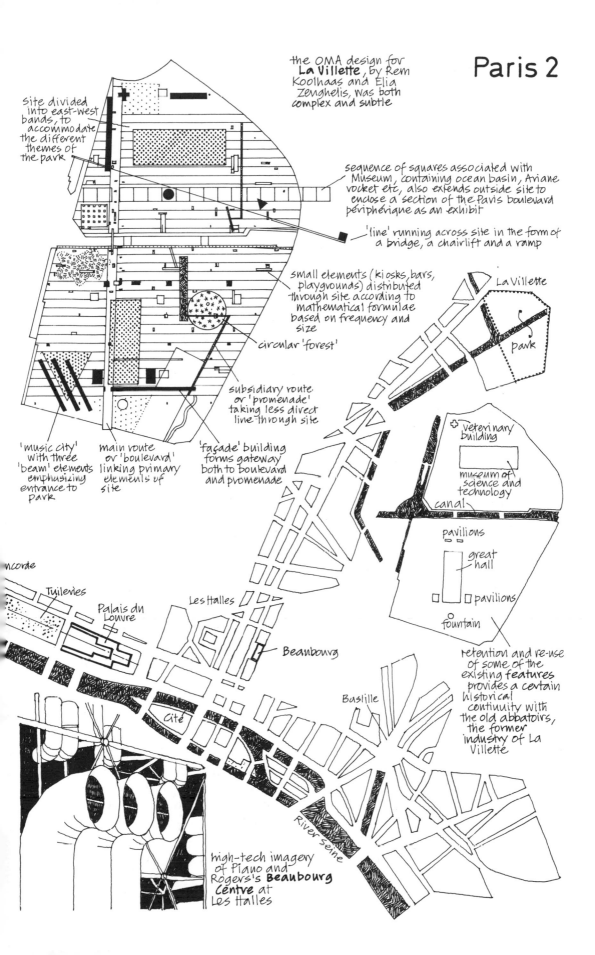

the OMA design for **La Villette**, by Rem Koolhaas and Elia Zenghelis, was both complex and subtle

Site divided into east-west bands, to accommodate the different themes of the park

sequence of squares associated with Museum, containing ocean basin, Ariane rocket etc, also extends outside site to enclose a section of the Paris boulevard périphérique as an exhibit

'line' running across site in the form of a bridge, a chairlift and a ramp

small elements (kiosks, bars, playgrounds) distributed through site according to mathematical formulae based on frequency and size

circular 'forest'

subsidiary route or 'promenade' taking less direct line through site

'music city' with three 'beam' elements emphasizing entrance to park

main route or 'boulevard' linking primary elements of site

'façade' building forms gateway both to boulevard and promenade

La Villette

Park

veterinary building

museum of science and technology

canal

pavilions

great hall

pavilions

fountain

retention and re-use of some of the existing features provides a certain historical continuity with the old abbatoirs, the former industry of La Villette

ncorde

Tuileries

Palais du Louvre

Les Halles

Beaubourg

Cité

Bastille

River Seine

high-tech imagery of Piano and Rogers's **Beaubourg Centre** at Les Halles

Town. Michael Hopkins's remarkable tensile structures included the Schlumberger research centre in Cambridge, and the west stand at Lord's cricket ground.

To some extent, all these buildings have been conceived in a way which closely integrates design and technology, with the technical component forming the very basis of the building's expressiveness. At East Anglia the design is based on the logic of climatic control, at Lloyd's on the complex services, at Camden Town on the highly-stressed clear-span roof structure. In most of them the technical element is creative and experimental, pushed very close to the edge of what is practically possible, and carrying the threat of failure.

Conceptually, many of the buildings are not unprecedented. High-tech architecture is international, and the work of Jean Nouvel in France, such as his clinic in Bezons, his hotel in Bordeaux and his Institut du Monde Arabe in Paris, explores many similar themes. It is a feature of the international trade in architectural ideas that they quickly cross national boundaries, or that the unbuilt schemes of one generation reappear as the realized projects of the next. Lloyd's, for example, though obviously a building of the eighties, with its disturbing *Bladerunner* aesthetic, owes much to the 'Bowellist' fantasies of the early Archigram designers. Nevertheless, it forms part of the most spectacular group of British buildings today. Some high-tech buildings are controversial, but they have attracted wide public interest, in Britain and overseas, and also the approval of the mainstream of the profession, glad at last to know that the buildings they like are also striking a chord among non-architects.

With critical acclaim has come commercial success; corporate clients everywhere have commissioned high-tech buildings to advertise their progressiveness in the international marketplace, such as Michael Manser's Sterling hotel at Heathrow Airport. Existing sixties office blocks are being extensively refurbished, not only to contain the hardware that electronic trading demands but also, like the former Rank Xerox building in London's Euston Road, to present new high-tech façades to the public. And on every ring-road, factories and warehouses are being tricked out in networks of exposed pylons, lattice beams and cross-braces to resemble Inmos or Homebase.

High-tech architecture presents some major problems. The first is the uneasy relationship between the social aspirations of the architects and their commercial success. The quotation from Richard Rogers at the beginning of this chapter suggests a utopian, even revolutionary agenda: an end to want, and the elimination of capitalist morality, 'backbone of the existing power structure'. 'The New Spirit', apparently, represents 'the determined rejection of the conformist ideals the establishment would have us adopt, and the refusal to be manipulated by the huge anonymous forces of authority.'[9] These are idealistic views but how do they work in practice? Are not all these corporate clients – banks, insurance brokers, national and international companies – part of the establishment, the forces of authority, the existing power structure? And what kind of challenge is one mounting on them if one's living depends on providing them with buildings which both facilitate and celebrate their hold on society?

We are back to the ever present dilemma of the architect under capitalism: how to practise his or her craft and still express political dissent. Buildings cost money and the architect is by definition in the hands of the ruling class. This problem intensified under the Thatcher and Major governments; only the private sector could now build in any quantity and, within it, only the very wealthiest clients could afford the expensive product offered by the experimental architect. It is no accident that the best built examples of high-tech architecture were sponsored by this minority, however much the architects themselves might wish it were otherwise. The occasional high-tech foray into low-cost social architecture, such as Foster's housing in Milton Keynes, where the roofs leaked and had to be rebuilt, is less successful.

The dominance of the marketplace leads liberal-minded architects into impossible situations, as when Rogers, for example, is obliged to take up a position of opposition to the local community, over the development of the 'Kite' area of Cambridge, or Coin Street in London. This is anything but the elimination of 'the age-old capitalist morality'.

Another question remains: how responsive high-tech buildings are to society's ecological needs. Buildings with large areas of glass, high heat losses or high solar-heat gain, expensive electronic climate controls, scarce and sophisticated materials and high maintenance costs, may raise more problems than they solve, wasteful in themselves and inappropriate as prototypes for the future.

These two issues – social responsibility and appropriate technology – clearly belong together. From time to time they coincide to produce architecture sophisticated yet humane, inventive yet informal – in a word, appropriate. Examples were seen in the work of the French engineer, Jean Prouvé, in the thirties. His People's Palace, designed for the socialist municipality of the Clichy district of Paris in 1939, was an adaptable building to be used both as a commercial market and as a hall for local entertainments and political meetings. Simply framed in steel, with movable floors, sliding partitions and a retractable glass roof, it subordinated all architectural histrionics to the nobler purpose of meeting the needs of its users. After World War II, Prouvé helped produce prefabricated emergency housing, of which a good example still remains at Meudon, near Paris. With their lightweight steel framing, and metal

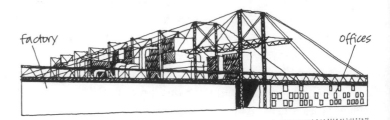

Richard Rogers Partnership's factory for **Inmos** at Newport in Gwent - the central spine provides not only the structure for the suspended roof but also the services to ventilate the factory in which the microchips are put together

Structural mast on the building for **Renault UK**, Swindon, by Foster Associates

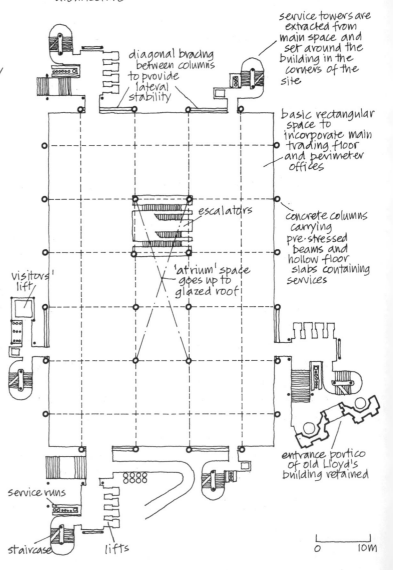

the office block for the insurance brokers **Lloyd's** in Leadenhall Street, London, by Richard Rogers Partnership - it has become Britain's main exemplar of high-tech architecture

service towers are extracted from main space and set around the building in the corners of the site

diagonal bracing between columns to provide lateral stability

basic rectangular space to incorporate main trading floor and perimeter offices

escalators

concrete columns carrying pre-stressed beams and hollow floor slabs containing services

'atrium' space goes up to glazed roof

visitors' lift

entrance portico of old Lloyd's building retained

service runs

staircase      lifts

0          10m

Foster Associates' high-tech shed for the **Sainsbury** arts centre at the University of East Anglia - the interior is environmentally controlled - the high-performance cladding of glass and sandwich panels can easily be removed and changed

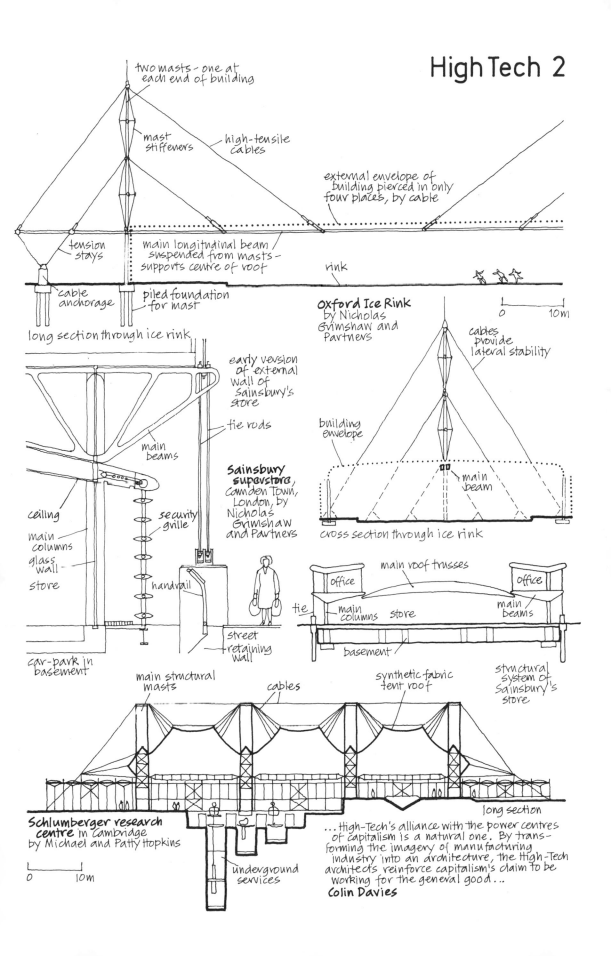

two masts - one at each end of building

mast stiffeners

high-tensile cables

external envelope of building pierced in only four places, by cable

tension stays

main longitudinal beam suspended from masts - supports centre of roof

rink

cable anchorage

piled foundation for mast

**Oxford Ice Rink** by Nicholas Grimshaw and Partners

0   10m

cables provide lateral stability

long section through ice rink

early version of external wall of Sainsbury's store

tie rods

main beams

building envelope

main beam

ceiling

security grille

main columns

glass wall

store

handrail

**Sainsbury superstore,** Camden Town, London, by Nicholas Grimshaw and Partners

cross section through ice rink

car-park in basement

street retaining wall

main roof trusses

office

tie

main columns

store

main beams

office

basement

structural system of Sainsbury's store

main structural masts

cables

synthetic fabric tent roof

long section

**Schlumberger research centre** in Cambridge by Michael and Patty Hopkins

0   10m

underground services

... High-Tech's alliance with the power centres of capitalism is a natural one. By transforming the imagery of manufacturing industry into an architecture, the High-Tech architects reinforce capitalism's claim to be working for the general good...
**Colin Davies**

floors, roof and cladding panels, these little buildings were designed to achieve economy and adaptability and at the same time to provide decent living spaces.

In Holland too there is a long tradition of humane architecture, which the designs and writings of Aldo van Eyck have done much to maintain. His interest in child development has led him to design a large number of play areas, while his well-known Mothers' House in Amsterdam, a refuge for single parents and their children, displays all the humanity of which modern architecture is capable, with its free forms, its warm colours and textures, and its respect for the street scene. Similarly humane is Hermann Hertzberger's Centraal Beheer office building in Appeldoorn, where the open planning of the work-spaces, over which the workers themselves have design control, are a direct response to the concept of industrial democracy.

The earlier work of Behnisch and Partners in south Germany, especially their smaller projects, often displays a sense of restraint and appropriateness missing from their later, larger buildings. This includes their secondary school on the 'Schafersfeld' at Lorch, school extensions at Alfdorf, in Welzheimer Wald and at Marbach am Neckar, an old-people's home at Reutlingen, and a kindergarten at Stuttgart-Neugereut.

Sometimes considered a direct inheritor of the Prouvé tradition is the Catalan engineer Santiago Calatrava Valls, who works mainly in Switzerland. Like Prouvé's and those of Behnisch, his projects and commissions have often been municipal ones, and also like Prouvé, he has often done collaborative rather than individual work. A concert hall in Bährenmatte Suhr, in Switzerland, bus shelters in St Gallen and railway stations for Zurich and Lucerne show the range of his skill. He has designed a number of elegant bridges, ranging from an enormous project for an east London river crossing to the small Bac de Roda-Felip II bridge and even a traffic-sign gantry in Barcelona. At its best, his work is unspectacular but poetic, in the sense that the beauty of poetry derives from its economy and appropriateness. Poetry, as Keats said, 'should be great and unobtrusive, a thing which enters into one's soul, and does not startle it or amaze it with itself, but with its subject.'

Equally poetic is the work of the Italian architect Renzo Piano. He came into prominence as the partner of Richard Rogers when they won the competition for the Beaubourg centre – of which Jean Prouvé, incidentally, was one of the judges. It was an impressive start but his work has since become much more understated and thoughtful. Concerned with social issues, with appropriate technology and with the historic context of his buildings, Piano has diverged from his former partner. He combines a sculptor's sensibility for materials with a rigorous approach to scientific research. His work includes a cheap and elegant extension to a factory in

# Jean Prouvé

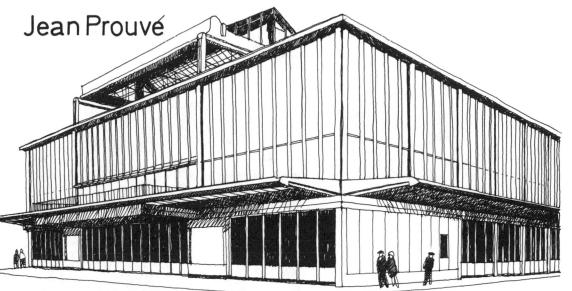

Prouvé's **Maison du Peuple** at Clichy in Paris, designed in association with Eugène Beaudouin (architect), Marcel Lods (engineer) and Vladimir Bodiansky (aero engineer) in 1939

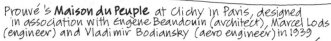

concierge · to offices above

market

ground floor plan

0   10M

sliding roof designed by Bodiansky, to open the hall to the sky on hot days

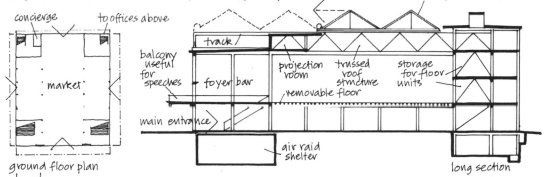

track

balcony useful for speeches · foyer bar · projection room · trussed roof structure · storage for floor units

main entrance → · removable floor

air raid shelter

long section

@ **a**

void

market balconies

canopy · balcony outside

© **b**

screen

700 seat cinema or meeting room

foyer + bar

upper floor plans showing arrangement as
**a** market hall and
**b** Maison du Peuple

...Long before 'Beaubourg' the Maison du Peuple sought to provide an everyday cultural and communication venue for local people, a free forum for our epoch. No doubt the design was ahead of its time and, to begin with, the administration of such a versatile building was a difficult matter. As it reaches the prime of life, techniques (particularly audio-visual ones), demand, management techniques and users have matured to the point that this building could now hope to meet its calling as a People's Palace...
**Jean Prouvé** in 1981

**emergency housing** at Meudon, 1950 - size 12m X 8m

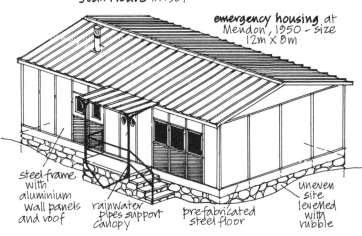

steel frame with aluminium wall panels and roof · rainwater pipes support canopy · prefabricated steel floor · uneven site levelled with rubble

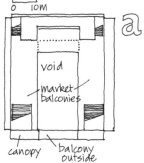

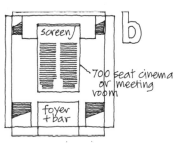

# Van Eyck and Hertzberger

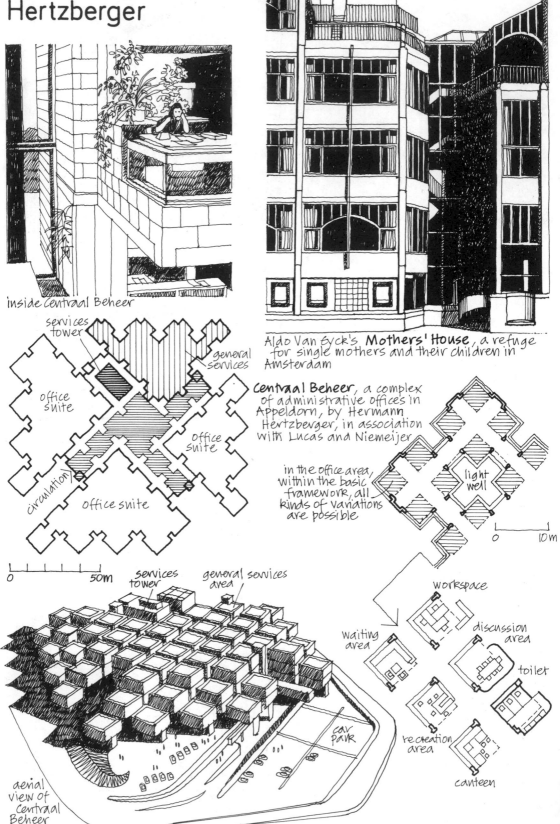

inside Centraal Beheer

Aldo Van Eyck's **Mothers' House**, a refuge for single mothers and their children in Amsterdam

**Centraal Beheer**, a complex of administrative offices in Appeldorn, by Hermann Hertzberger, in association with Lucas and Niemeijer

services tower

general services

office suite

office suite

circulation

office suite

in the office area, within the basic framework, all kinds of variations are possible

light well

0          10m

0                    50m

services tower

general services area

car park

aerial view of Centraal Beheer

workspace

waiting area

discussion area

toilet

recreation area

canteen

# Calatrava

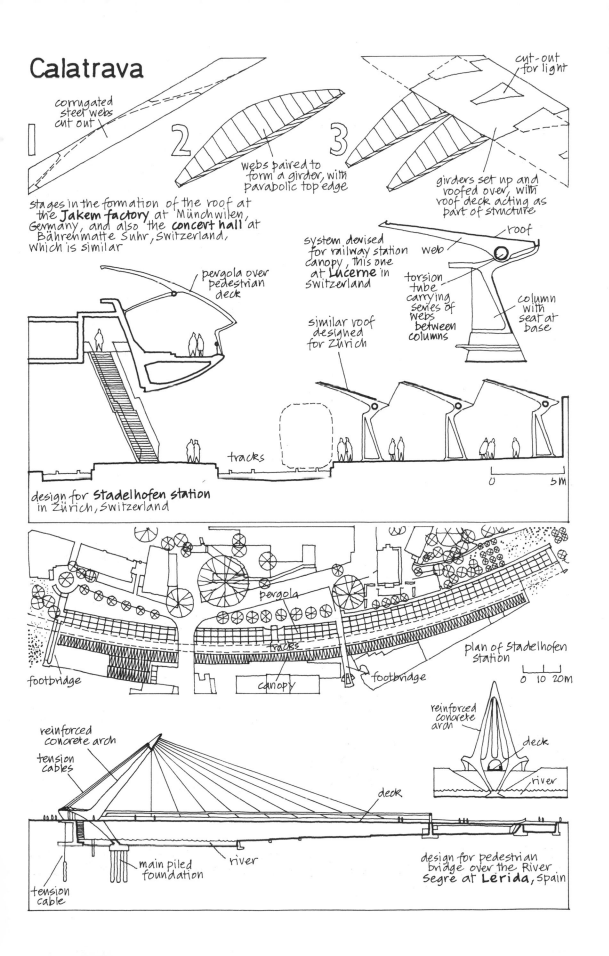

corrugated steel webs cut out

1

2 webs paired to form a girder, with parabolic top edge

3

cut-out for light

girders set up and roofed over, with roof deck acting as part of structure

stages in the formation of the roof at the **Jakem factory** at Münchwilen, Germany, and also the **concert hall** at Bährenmatte Suhr, Switzerland, which is similar

pergola over pedestrian deck

system devised for railway station canopy, this one at **Lucerne** in Switzerland

roof

web

torsion tube carrying series of webs between columns

column with seat at base

similar roof designed for Zürich

tracks

0    5M

design for **Stadelhofen station** in Zürich, Switzerland

pergola

tracks

canopy

footbridge

footbridge

plan of Stadelhofen station

0 10 20M

reinforced concrete arch

tension cables

reinforced concrete arch

deck

river

deck

river

main piled foundation

tension cable

design for pedestrian bridge over the River Segre at **Lérida**, Spain

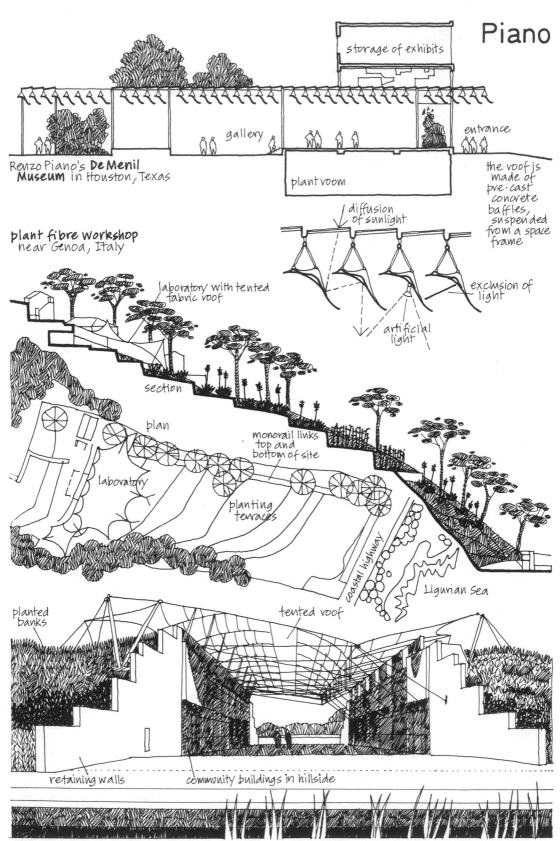

# Piano

storage of exhibits

gallery

entrance

**Renzo Piano's De Menil Museum** in Houston, Texas

plant room

the roof is made of pre-cast concrete baffles, suspended from a space frame

diffusion of sunlight

exclusion of light

artificial light

**plant fibre workshop** near Genoa, Italy

laboratory with tented fabric roof

section

plan

laboratory

monorail links top and bottom of site

planting terraces

coastal highway

Ligurian Sea

planted banks

tented roof

retaining walls

community buildings in hillside

**Forum**, consisting of covered space and community buildings designed for the Schlumberger Corporation, to act as a focus to the Montrouge industrial park, near Paris

Vicenza, a sports hall in Ravenna and a workshop for the study of plant-fibres – a subject of personal interest – in Genoa. His works of urban rehabilitation include a scheme for improving the ancient city walls of Rhodes, and his well-known revitalization of Palladio's basilica in Vicenza for use as a public hall.

In Britain there are a small number of architects who work in the same careful way, placing more stress than usual on the users' needs and on meeting them as simply and directly as possible. I have already mentioned Ralph Erskine's Byker Wall as an example of collaboration between architect and users. In London's East End, Florian Beigel designed the bold little Half Moon Theatre, and Matrix the Jagonari Centre, a refuge for Bengali women. The Half Moon, only partly built, was a radical design, not only in terms of its experimental approach to theatrical technique, but also in its very advanced technology. Both it and the Jagonari Centre, purposely a much more traditionalist design, were developed in close co-operation with the users. This approach is unusual in working-class areas like Byker or the East End, where as a rule the bourgeois system offers architecture both crude and exploitative.

The London Borough of Camden is well known for its grand-manner housing schemes of the late sixties and early seventies, such as Alexandra Road and Maiden Lane. The uncompromising and spectacular nature of these buildings contrasts with the small-scale sensitivity of, for example, Colquhoun and Miller's Caversham Road housing and the council's own Bartholomew Road health centre, designed by Peter Watson. This informal, pragmatic approach is also seen in the early work of Edward Cullinan, in his own house in Camden Mews, his house for a musician in Bartholomew Villas, and his council flats in Leighton Crescent, Kentish Town.

Cullinan has become well known as a 'community architect'. The term may be difficult to define, but it is clear that both his methods and his buildings have a democratic emphasis. His office is run as a co-operative and his commissions have often been public-sector ones, for which he has developed a modernist yet informal and accessible style, making use of a variety of simple materials in an imaginative way and deriving his aesthetic from a builderly concern about the way buildings are put together. His early Minster Lovell conference centre in Oxfordshire used traditional Cotswold materials. Many of his buildings are imaginative re-workings of traditional forms, such as his extension to St Mary's church, Barnes, and his residential buildings for the MacIntyre charity at Westoning in Bedfordshire. One of his best-known recent buildings is the elegant and humane Community Care Centre, one of a number of health buildings designed for Lambeth Council. In his hands, modernism is not a matter of style, but of the honest use of simple materials.

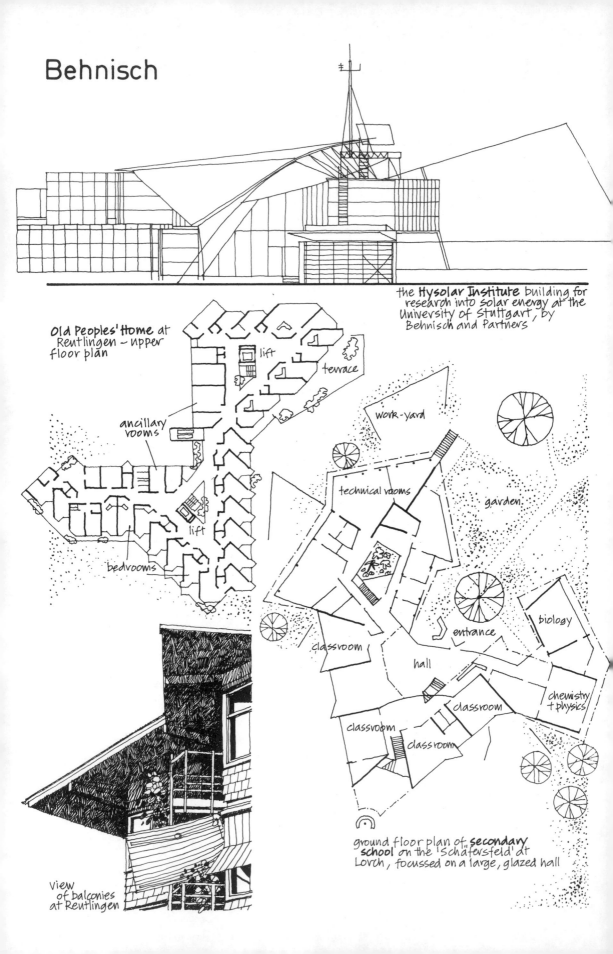

# Behnisch

the **Hysolar Institute** building for research into solar energy at the University of Stuttgart, by Behnisch and Partners

**Old Peoples' Home** at Reutlingen – upper floor plan

lift

terrace

ancillary rooms

lift

bedrooms

work-yard

technical rooms

garden

classroom

entrance

biology

hall

chemistry + physics

classroom

classroom

classroom

view of balconies at Reutlingen

ground floor plan of **secondary school** on the 'Schäfersfeld' at Lorch, focussed on a large, glazed hall

# social architecture

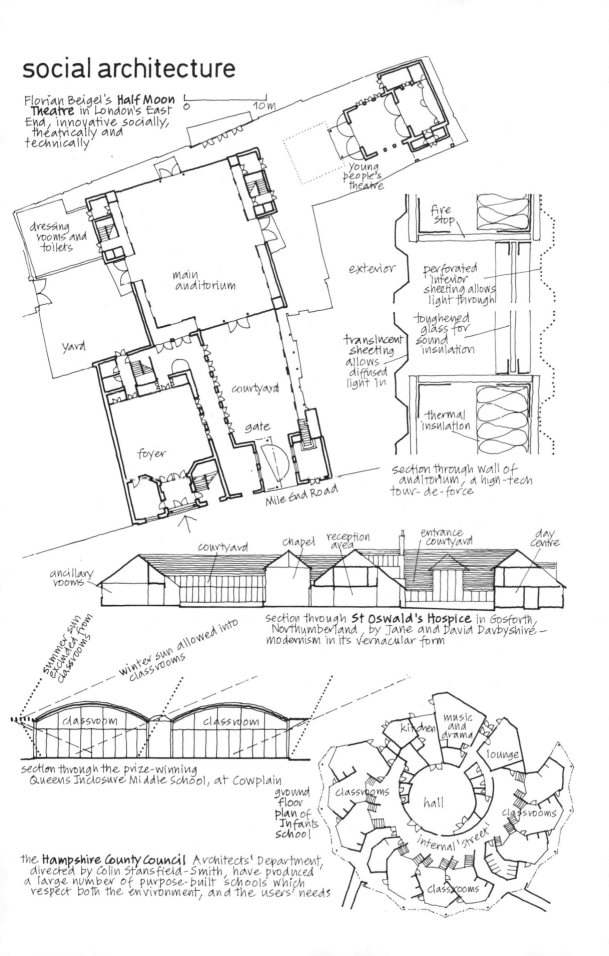

Florian Beigel's **Half Moon Theatre** in London's East End, innovative socially, theatrically and technically

young people's theatre

0    10 m

dressing rooms and toilets

main auditorium

yard

courtyard

foyer

gate

Mile End Road

exterior

fire stop

perforated interior sheeting allows light through

toughened glass for sound insulation

translucent sheeting allows diffused light in

thermal insulation

section through wall of auditorium, a high-tech tour-de-force

ancillary rooms

courtyard

chapel

reception area

entrance courtyard

day centre

section through **St Oswald's Hospice** in Gosforth, Northumberland, by Jane and David Davbyshire – modernism in its vernacular form

summer sun excluded from classrooms

winter sun allowed into classrooms

classroom    classroom

section through the prize-winning Queens Inclosure Middle School, at Cowplain

ground floor plan of Infants school

kitchen

music and drama

lounge

classrooms

hall

classrooms

'internal street'

classrooms

the **Hampshire County Council** Architects' Department, directed by Colin Stansfield-Smith, have produced a large number of purpose-built schools which respect both the environment, and the users' needs

Cullinan is part of a humane tradition in British architecture, in which modernism is combined with local pragmatism. It is often found in small-scale public or voluntary-aided sector buildings, and can be seen all over the country from Gosforth to Gwent: from Jane and David Darbyshire's St Oswald's hospice to the Abertillery comprehensive school. Its best-known manifestation is the programme of school-building in Hampshire, co-ordinated by the County Architect Colin Stansfield-Smith, in which well-researched design and the appropriate use of technology combine to produce an architecture both elegant and humane.

Another well-known experiment in architectural democracy has been the redevelopment of various derelict sites in the Vauxhall area of Liverpool. In the face of bureaucratic delay and political difficulties a group of local residents calling themselves the Eldonians arranged finance, assembled the land, appointed architects and embarked on an ambitious development, to meet some of the area's housing needs. The results may not be great architecture but have been more democratically arrived at, and reflect local needs better, than most corporation schemes.

Co-operative schemes can strike a blow at the alienation of the municipal housing system. An extra dimension is added when the occupiers are involved not only in the planning and design but also in the construction. Self-build projects, though not appropriate to all – or even most – circumstances, have attracted considerable interest in recent years, both for the freedom and for the self-fulfilment they offer. I have already mentioned Lucien Kroll's experiments at Louvain, and he has done a similar collaborative project at the technical college in Belfort. Peter Sulzer has organized the design and construction of a hall and social centre in Landau for and by the local Protestant Youth Choir, and with Peter Hübner has organized self-build housing for students of Stuttgart University.

But perhaps the most interesting contribution in this field has come from the late Walter Segal. His early houses in Highgate in north London were honest and pragmatic explorations of modernism. In 1963 he constructed a temporary house for himself in simple timber framing and uncut standard sheet materials. Its speed of construction – two weeks – and its cheapness – £800 – led him to experiment further with self-build methods. This led him through a number of self-build projects culminating in a housing scheme in Lewisham in south London, co-designed with Jon Broome and completed in 1986, shortly after Segal's death.

The clients were families from Lewisham's housing waiting list. Attending classes in the use of tools and materials, the tenants constructed the houses themselves, using Segal's system and expertise, and layouts agreed between them and the architects. Wet construction, such as concreting and plasterwork, was kept to a minimum and even

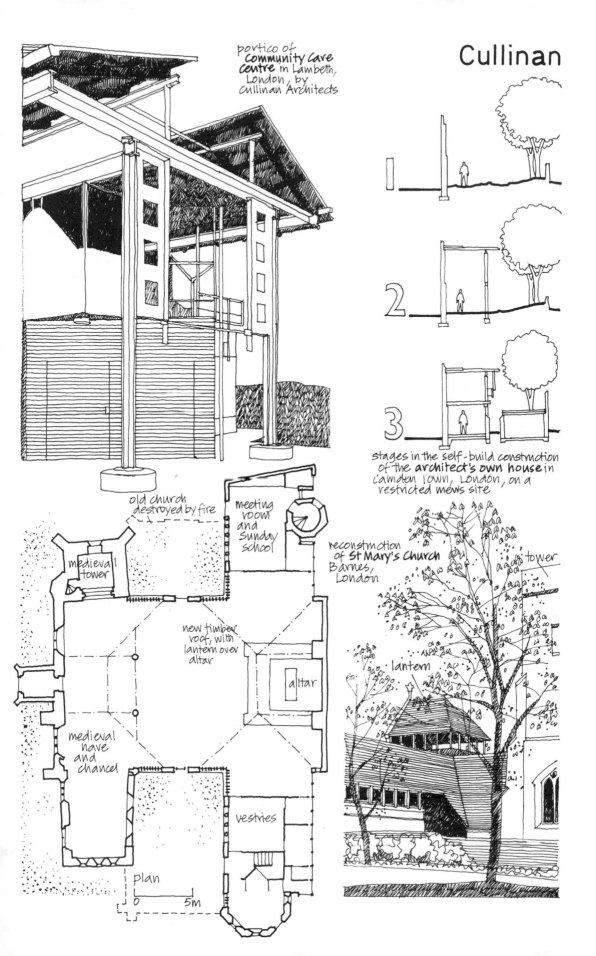

# Cullinan

portico of **Community Care Centre** in Lambeth, London, by Cullinan Architects

2

3

stages in the self-build construction of the **architect's own house** in Camden Town, London, on a restricted mews site

old church destroyed by fire

meeting room and Sunday school

medieval tower

reconstruction of **St Mary's Church** Barnes, London

tower

new timber roof, with lantern over altar

altar

lantern

medieval nave and chancel

vestries

plan

0          5m

# Segal

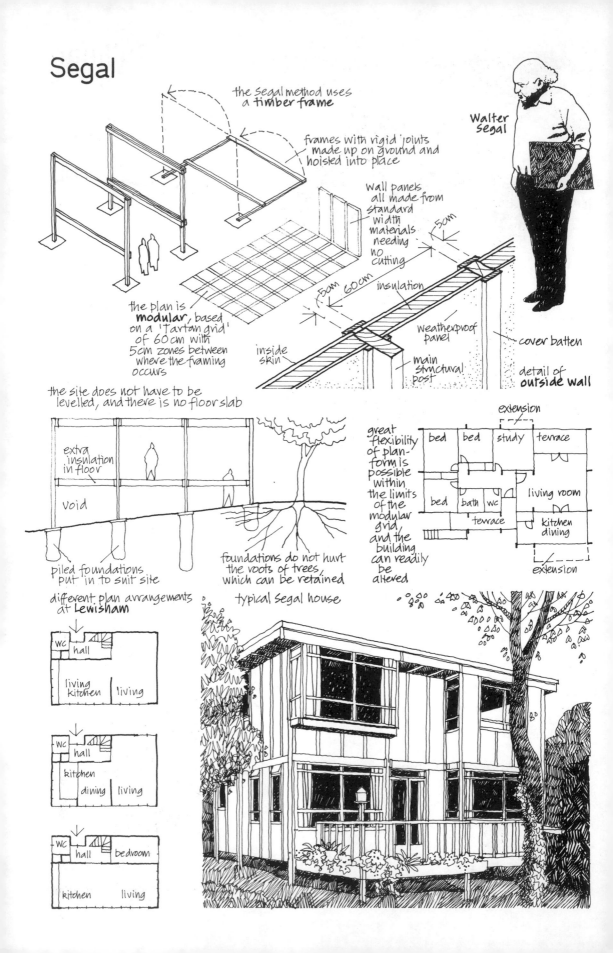

the Segal method uses a **timber frame**

frames with rigid 'joints' made up on ground and hoisted into place

Wall panels all made from standard width materials needing no cutting

Walter Segal

the plan is **modular**, based on a 'Tartan grid' of 60cm with 5cm zones between where the framing occurs

5cm

60cm

5cm

insulation

inside skin

weatherproof panel

main structural post

cover batten

detail of **outside wall**

the site does not have to be levelled, and there is no floor slab

extra insulation in floor

Void

piled foundations put in to suit site

foundations do not hurt the roots of trees, which can be retained

great flexibility of plan-form is possible within the limits of the modular grid, and the building can readily be altered

extension

| bed | bed | study | terrace |
| bed | bath | wc | living room |
| | terrace | | kitchen dining |

extension

different plan arrangements at **Lewisham**

| wc | hall | |
| living kitchen | living | |

| wc | hall | |
| kitchen | dining | living |

| wc | hall | bedroom |
| kitchen | living | |

typical Segal house

# self-build

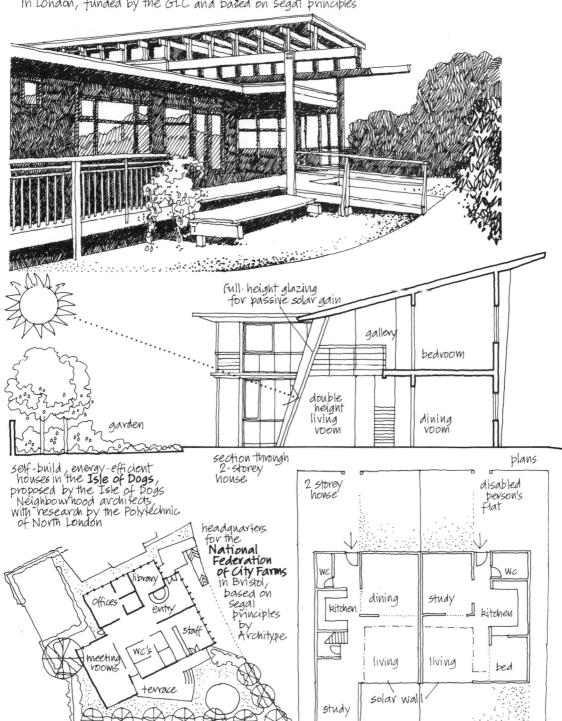

the work of many self-build co-operatives mimics the products of the commercial house-building sector, like these houses by the **Eldonians** in Liverpool

the community centre of the **Calthorpe Project** at Kings Cross in London, funded by the GLC and based on Segal principles

full-height glazing for passive solar gain

gallery

bedroom

double height living room

dining room

garden

section through 2-storey house

plans

self-build, energy-efficient houses in the **Isle of Dogs**, proposed by the Isle of Dogs Neighbourhood architects with research by the Polytechnic of North London

headquarters for the **National Federation of City Farms** in Bristol, based on Segal principles by Architype

library

offices

entry

staff

meeting rooms

WC's

terrace

2 storey house

disabled person's flat

wc

dining

study

wc

kitchen

kitchen

living

living

bed

study

solar wall

excavation was largely avoided by suspension of the ground floors above the earth. Within the limits of the two-storey, timber-framed, modular construction, with standard junction details, a considerable variety was achieved; the houses clearly belong to the same architectural family but are also as individual as their client-builders. Their intricacy, warmth and humanity are a strong contrast to the alienated environments of the more normal municipal housing. A Walter Segal Trust now exists to promote his ideas.

Here and there, his principles are taken seriously. A tiny project in London's Isle of Dogs contrasts poignantly with the overwhelming display of commercialism all around. A pair of council houses designed by Nasser Golzari and his colleagues at Tower Hamlets derive structurally from the principles of Prouvé, use a Segal-type timber-frame and panel construction, and are intended to be highly energy-efficient. The ground floor accommodation is designed around the needs of the physically disabled. It takes some integrity to pursue appropriate design given the great economic and professional pressures which push architecture in the other direction.

The local authority system has produced one winner however. This is the CLASP system of school building, which began with the prefabricated school buildings designed in Hertfordshire, under the County Architect, C. H. Aslin, in the late forties. A few years later, led by the Nottinghamshire County Architect, Donald Gibson, a number of Midland local authorities set up the Consortium of Local Authorities Special Programme to build standard school buildings for themselves. Rigorous technical research – for example into the problems of building in areas of mining subsidence – and careful user consultation resulted in a building system of great quality. The buildings are prefabricated, framed in steel, with standard joints and facing panels. Great flexibility is obtained, and there is high acoustic and thermal performance. A CLASP school building won the *Gran Premio* at the Milan Triennale of 1960. Since then, some 3,000 buildings have been built in Britain, Europe, South America and North Africa, including schools, universities, community buildings and offices, and the system has had an influence on the development of the successful Hampshire schools building programme. Of the hundreds of building systems available in Britain during the sixties, CLASP is – deservedly – one of the very few survivors.

Piano's success brought him wealthy corporate clients; in his more expensive and spectacular buildings his social values have become rather more obscure: his laboratories in Grenoble for 'marketing' X-rays; his luxurious Menil museum in Houston, Texas; his 'ladybird' demountable pavilions for the IBM Corporation; his scheme to improve the image of the Schlumberger Corporation in Montrouge. Multinational corporations

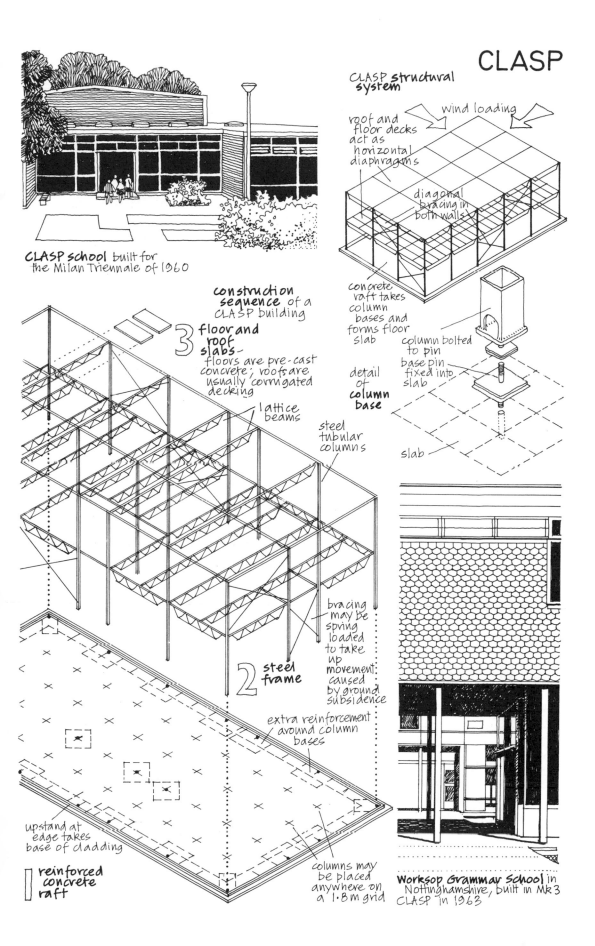

# CLASP

**CLASP school** built for the Milan Triennale of 1960

**CLASP structural system**

wind loading

roof and floor decks act as horizontal diaphragms

diagonal bracing in both walls

concrete raft takes column bases and forms floor slab

**detail of column base**

column bolted to pin

base pin fixed into slab

slab

**construction sequence** of a CLASP building

**3 floor and roof slabs** - floors are pre-cast concrete; roofs are usually corrugated decking

lattice beams

steel tubular columns

**2 steel frame**

bracing may be spring loaded to take up movement caused by ground subsidence

extra reinforcement around column bases

upstand at edge takes base of cladding

☐ **reinforced concrete raft**

columns may be placed anywhere on a 1.8m grid

**Worksop Grammar School** in Nottinghamshire, built in Mk3 CLASP in 1963

tend to demand the hard-headed exploitation of technology rather than its appropriate use; there can often be conflicts between an aspiring designer's best intentions and his client's ambitions. Mike Cooley describes 'the manner in which scientists and technologists are used as mere messenger boys of the multinational corporations whose sole concern is the maximisation of profits.'[10]

To the aspiring appropriate technologist, these conflicts are never far from the surface. The best-intentioned experiments – the Lucas Aerospace shop stewards' corporate plan, the Centre for Intermediate Technology at Machynlleth, the Martin Centre at Cambridge – are continually faced with the need to compromise. Short of funds, they may be pushed into alliances with the commercial sector; lacking the support of the establishment, they work under continued threat of closure. The experimental administration of the small town of Davis in the USA, whose local democracy, conservation and self-sufficiency have made it justly famous, contrasts ironically with that of its immediate surroundings in the state of California, the world's most conspicuously consumptive community.

Meanwhile the technological establishment has interested itself in the green movement, either to present a caring face to the public, or to adapt alternative technology to its own purposes. Privatization has made it all the more necessary to sell, rather than save, energy. At Burry Port in South Wales there is an experimental wind generating station set up by the electricity industry, an organization well known for its commitment to nuclear power. The gas industry, concerned at its own association in the public mind with the problem of greenhouse gases, sponsors well-publicized research into global warming. And at Sellafield, British Nuclear Fuels present an exhibition favourably comparing nuclear power with alternative sources.

At the same time, preventable environmental catastrophes continue to underline the irresponsible way technology is used. In 1984 3,000 people were killed and 200,000 injured by the release of dioxin gas from the Union Carbide plant at Bhopal in India. In 1986 the nuclear explosion at Chernobyl in the Ukraine caused deaths in the locality and a cloud of fallout from Finland to Italy. In 1988, most of Bangladesh was covered by catastrophic flooding. In 1991 the Gulf War brought massive environmental damage. Every year there is famine in Africa, acid rain in northern Europe, the loss of rain-forest, oil pollution, food poisoning, polluted drinking water and the ever-present threat of chemical, biological or nuclear war.

It is often difficult to uncover the truth behind such catastrophes. The problem is that information, like many other things in our society, is a commodity, to be withheld or distorted when it offers advantage, or to be sold when it makes money. The state uses information to achieve military or political supremacy, and monopoly capital uses it in the accumulation process. The development of information technology, one of the main features of postwar capitalism, has been motivated essentially by politics and profit. The manufacturers of silicon chips – Texas Instruments, Fairchilds, Intel and a few others – together with the manufacturers of the machinery in which the chips are used, now play a crucial part in the capitalist economy. It has been necessary to capture huge markets in order to recoup the enormous development costs, and to form close links with major clients, such as the American aerospace and defence industries. The international financial sector too, depends on up-to-date information. Two of the 24 transponders of the Westar satellite launched in 1982 were bought outright by the world's biggest bank, Citicorp, for its own exclusive use. Information technology now dominates world markets, and IBM has become the fifth largest company in the USA and the most profitable; in 1985 its sales were over $50 billion and it made a clear profit of $6 billion.

Yet at the same time, information technology has enormous social potential. It can help release people from the drudgery of repetitive tasks; the workplace could be greatly improved by its considerable use. It offers data bases, modelling systems and other techniques to improve the speed and quality of decision-making; the physical environment is only one of many aspects of life which could benefit from hard information being collected, understood and used by the community.

At present, this rarely happens. Most ordinary people's experience of information technology is through the entertainment and leisure industries, in which information is for the most part soft, and often exploitative. In the workplace, the new technology has been introduced primarily to cut costs, by cutting the workforce, rather than to improve the quality of decisions. Here it has created unemployment, and compromised health and safety standards, especially for the poorly-paid women workers who are its main users.

Information technology is a relative newcomer to architecture, but computers are now in common use. As in the larger world outside, market forces predominate. The most common application, in both schools and architectural practices, is in CAD, or Computer Aided Design. The schools use it as an extension of their essentially aesthetic predilections, while the profession uses it as a drafting tool, to cut down the number of staff and increase profitability. The idea of using computers to improve the information base, to strengthen scientific methods of analysis, and to improve the quality of decision-making, is relatively uncommon. Yet all this is urgently needed, not only for architecture, but also for environmental practice on a larger scale.

The point about twentieth-century technology is not how brilliant it is – though it clearly is – but for whose benefit it is used. Technology in the hands of the bourgeois state or the corporate machine can never be more than exploitative, whether it deals with information, or the built environment, or the environment as a whole. What it offers is soft information and a hard environment. Only if society progresses beyond this current system can it develop a socially responsible technology – one which offers the hard information and the soft environment that is necessary to its survival.

# 9 According to Plan – strategies for the future

In 1990, the capitalist press celebrated the end of the planned economy and the spread of the 'free market' into eastern Europe. The terms for German unification were dictated by the Christian Democrats in West Germany, while the break-up of the Soviet Union in 1991 was presided over by the USA and its NATO allies. Even long-standing communists, such as Eric Hobsbawm in Britain, found themselves admitting that world Communism had been a 'detour' and that the Russian Revolution had been one of a number of 'freak results' of a cataclysmic period of world unrest.[1]

Yet at the same time, the US Census Bureau and other government organizations were reporting that the gap between rich and poor in the USA was continuing to widen. The incomes of the top 1 per cent had risen by 75 per cent over ten years; the top 2.5 million families were now, on average, twenty times as wealthy as the poorest 50 million. In Germany 'the march of the mighty Mark', as Günter Grass called the political takeover, offered only 'coarse exploitation'.[2]

The contradictions were clear; western capitalism seemed to be winning the economic struggle, but could offer neither stability nor social justice. Even so, very few voices were being raised against market forces and in defence of the planned economy. Was planning a thing of the past, appropriate only to historic circumstances which had now been swept – and bourgeois commentators relished re-using Lenin's phrase – into 'the dustbin of History'? Who now wanted a return to New Deal USA, or to Britain's postwar Keynesianism, still less to the bureaucracy and stagnation of the Stalinist system? In the minds of most commentators, economic planning, the public sector and socialism were closely linked, and there was widespread agreement that all three were undesirable.

This begged three major questions, however. Firstly, economic planning is not predominantly socialist. Central planning had characterized Hitler's Germany and Mussolini's Italy during peacetime, and most western capitalist countries during both World Wars. And central planning in the postwar world, though associated by its critics with socialism, was not primarily socialist in intent. The New Deal had been the USA's response to the Wall Street crash and the Depression; a federally-run public sector would, it was hoped, stimulate productivity and employment. In postwar Britain, a strong public sector was intended to create a demand for goods and services and revitalize the declining traditional industries.

Secondly, economic planning continues to flourish in the capitalist system, though not primarily in the public sector. I have already mentioned Galbraith's analysis of the 'new industrial state' and how the long-term aims of the multinationals are imposed upon society as a whole. The fact that the annual turnover of each of the four largest European companies, for example, is higher than the yearly budget expenditure of Spain, emphasizes the economic power of the multi-nationals. The scale and efficiency of central planning within the biggest multinationals are probably superior to any government planning in the world.

Thirdly, and most importantly, what died in eastern Europe was not in any real sense socialist. Socialism must be a complete system; it cannot coexist with capitalism in the same economy, where inevitably the competitive market distorts it. And what is true within an individual economy is also true between the economies of a world system. Stalin had destroyed Bolshevism, and created a new ruling class to control the workers. He had undermined the international socialist revolution, replacing it with the illusory 'socialism in one country'. The Soviet Union, forced into the international marketplace, had a planned economy right enough, but one subordinated to the needs of competition and capital accumulation. International pressure to spend, for example, on arms rather than on housing, welfare and the domestic economy, created instability and misery, which had to be kept in check by the state apparatus. The two fundamental Marxist-Leninist principles of the 'withering away' of the state and of giving 'to each according to need', were never remotely approached by Stalinism. Successive attempts by most Soviet leaders since 1945 to move ever nearer to western-style capitalism culminated in Gorbachev's policy of *perestroika*, the market-led restructuring needed to shore up an ailing state-capitalist economy.

In Britain, like many other western economies, economic planning had been a crucial feature of the World War II war effort. From 1945, a big public sector was maintained, and many forms of government control were still thought necessary – though comprehensive economic planning by the state was only half-hearted. Public-sector economics and a planned economy imply – though they do not necessitate – a welfare state. The wartime economy had had both the former but not the latter. Nevertheless, the welfare state was politically appropriate in a postwar, Depression-weary world. Public-sector economics provided the mechanism for it while it in turn became a popular ideological justification for them. In Britain, the task of welfare was to extend some of the benefits of national prosperity to all sections of society. Capitalism would solve the problem of production and a powerful welfare state would distribute the products more fairly. Individuals, groups and entire regions would benefit, through subsidies, policies and proposals which directed resources to areas of need.

In the capitalist system, welfare has often been used as a social and economic mechanism, but welfare capitalism is to some extent a contradiction in terms. The logic of capital accumulation, involving as it does the maximization of surplus-value, is basically inimical to welfare. The priority is to preserve the health of capitalism; a welfare programme is appropriate only if it assists this aim.

The British land-use planning system is a good illustration of the interlinked contradictions of economic planning, of the public-sector economy and of the welfare state. Its development over more than a century into what is vauntingly described – usually by planners – as the best planning system in the world, has reflected the priorities of capitalism itself. During the nineteenth century, the first public-health legislation was introduced; whatever its motivation, its actual effect was to aid production and consumption, by protecting the working population from some of the worst environmental aspects of industrialism.

Planning legislation enacted between 1909 and 1932 was intended to improve housing and the environment through a certain amount of public sector intervention. The Town and Country Planning Act of 1932 gave powers to local authorities to prepare development plans, and required landowners to obtain permission for developments which deviated from the plan, with the aim of creating a more productive and orderly environment. This was not altruism; one of the state's main motives was to stifle the working-class unrest created by World War I and the October Revolution. 'If you do not give the people Social Reform,' Quintin Hogg told Parliament in 1918, 'they are going to give you Social Revolution.'

The planning system reached maturity with the postwar welfare state legislation, which included both the New Towns Act of 1946 and the Town and Country Planning Act of 1947, the former presaging an enormous programme of new-town planning and construction, the latter providing a legislative framework for new and old towns alike and for the mining, industry, forestry and agriculture which supported them. The Barlow report of 1940 had argued for the efficient location of productive industry as a precondition to economic recovery, and of course full employment was fundamental to the Keynesian economists' rescue plan for Capital.

It was also fundamental to welfare. The Beveridge report of 1942, on which the welfare state was largely based, had identified five great evils. As well as 'Want, Disease, Ignorance and Squalor', there was 'Idleness'.

Social harmony, in a capitalist system, depended on people having the opportunity to work hard and provide for themselves.

One of the main tasks of the planning system therefore, like the welfare state as a whole, was to cope with the long-term decline of Britain's traditional industries by providing a good framework for new growth. Thus, a lasting link was established between economic planning for the needs of Capital, and the land-use planning system.

Considerable powers were given to the new planning authorities. The 1947 Act turned the 1932 Act around. Instead of development plans being optional, all authorities were now obliged to prepare them. Instead of a landowner having a right to develop provided he infringed no plan, now any kind of development needed planning permission, which need not necessarily be given. The new act was supported by a large and growing body of legislation, including the General Development Orders, which defined what was or was not 'development', and the Use Classes Orders, which indicated when and when not a 'change of use' was involved.

To work this vast machine, a large planning bureaucracy was set up which attracted many of the ablest minds of the day, including many zealous young architects. Large amounts of public money were directed into regional industrial development, housing and public building programmes, road-building and the New Towns. On the face of it, this was a powerful and well-resourced system, capable of achieving great social changes.

However, the contradictions remained. First, the planning system was uncontentious as long as it coincided with the interests of Capital, but was subject to reconsideration at times of crisis or change. Second, as an important part of the public sector, the planning system was subject to government control; again, this might be uncontentious at times of consensus, but was also a potential source of conflict if local needs and the government's political priorities lay in different directions. And thirdly, the planning system, like the welfare state as a whole, was based, ideologically at least, on the concept of social justice. If this were ever to be achieved, it would entail the radical redistribution of resources within society and the creation of a new economic environment. Its powers, however, controlled only the physical environment – land-use, the size and shape of buildings, the layout of towns.

With the overall aims so ill-defined, and in any case subject to rapid political reappraisal almost at will, and with the powers of the planning system so ill-suited to its social task, there can be little wonder at its inadequacies. Despite all the debate during World War II about nationalizing the land, or clawing back development value in the public interest, postwar property relations remained intact and there was no challenge to the pre-eminence of the process of capital accumulation. Even the mildly

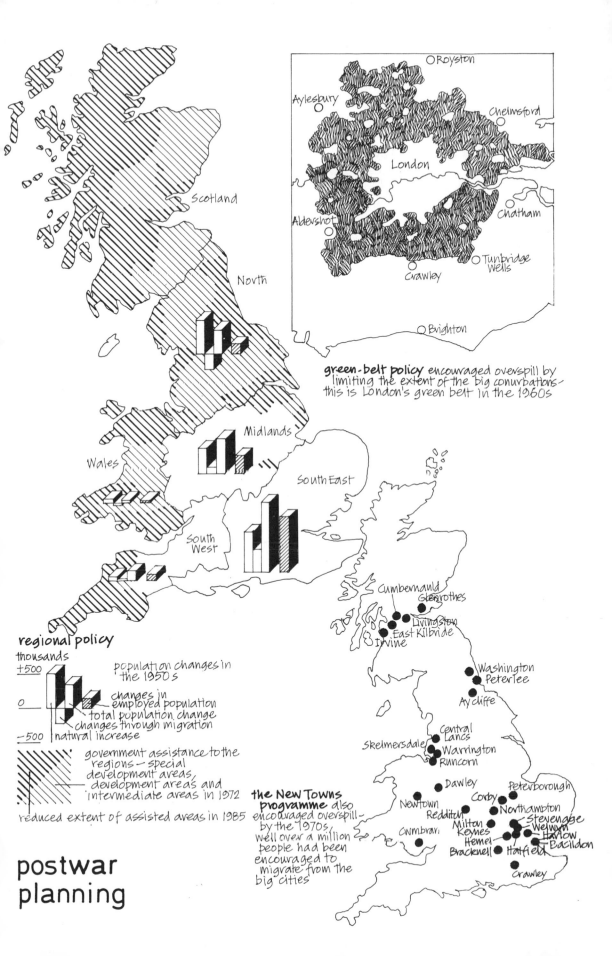

O Royston

Aylesbury

Chelmsford

London

Aldershot

Chatham

Crawley

Tunbridge Wells

Brighton

**green-belt policy** encouraged overspill by limiting the extent of the big conurbations - this is London's green belt in the 1960s

Scotland

North

Wales

Midlands

South East

South West

**regional policy**

thousands

+500

0

-500

population changes in the 1950s

changes in employed population

total population change

changes through migration

natural increase

government assistance to the regions - special development areas, development areas and intermediate areas in 1972

reduced extent of assisted areas in 1985

Cumbernauld
Glenrothes
Livingston
East Kilbride
Irvine

Washington
Peterlee
Aycliffe

Central Lancs
Skelmersdale
Warrington
Runcorn

Dawley
Peterborough
Corby
Newtown
Northampton
Redditch
Milton Keynes
Stevenage
Cwmbran
Hemel
Welwyn
Harlow
Bracknell
Hatfield
Basildon
Crawley

**the New Towns programme** also encouraged overspill - by the 1970s, well over a million people had been encouraged to migrate from the big cities

# postwar planning

egalitarian provisions which did find their way into the 1947 Act, such as the development tax, were quickly repealed when the Conservatives came back to power in the fifties.

As a result, postwar planning was shaped in the image of capitalism. The conventional wisdom was that major programmes of profitable urban renewal were needed: slum-clearance, city-centre redevelopments, major urban motorways. Profit dictated the form taken by the vast postwar housing programme, greatly to the detriment of the social needs. Profit also dictated the office-led property boom of the sixties, and the subsequent one during the eighties, which the planning system proved powerless to control.

I have already mentioned the misgivings which affected architects during the late sixties, when the effectiveness of postwar reconstruction began to be questioned. In the wider field of planning, a similar reassessment took place. Ordinary people's demands for involvement in the planning process led to the Skeffington report and to the authorities' reluctant acceptance of 'public consultation'. The work of sociologists – of Rex and Moore in Birmingham, of Willmott and Young in Bethnal Green, of Townsend and Abel-Smith on poverty – had its influence and, as in architecture, 'social' planning became respectable. The more progressive British planners, following an American lead, took up 'advocacy planning', in which they took up the cause of deprived minorities in inner-city areas.

But as with architecture, the reluctance of professionals and politicians to surrender any real power negated any moves towards local democracy by this means. Behind advocacy planning there often lay the assumption that the experts knew best. And within planning as a whole, the creation of development opportunities for the private sector still remained a priority. The way forward for the country was said to lie through the 'white-heat of technology'. The government's South-East Study, published in 1964, was based essentially on commercial growth. The official Planning Advisory Group's report, 'The Future of Development Plans', published in 1965 and enacted in effect in 1968, suggested that a new form of 'structure plan' would be quicker and easier to implement, and less of a restriction on economic expansion. Planners attempted to improve their own efficiency by developing a technocratic 'systems' approach to decision-making.

The profession continued to insist that its work was apolitical, uncommitted, value-free, that the planner's job was to mediate in a disinterested way between society's conflicting demands for land and property. But in practice, the system as a whole worked against the interests of the less privileged. An 'apolitical' planning system, intentionally or not, supported the establishment.

This is well illustrated by the office-development process in London. Offices are a major feature of modern cities. Rapid growth of the commercial sector, especially in an administrative centre like London, together with increasing space standards, have created a legitimate need for more office floorspace. However, office buildings, as well as being use-values, are particularly important as exchange-values. The profits are very high and the conflict often fierce, not only among developers, but also between developers, the planners and the local community. The latter suffers from the construction process, from the traffic congestion and visual ugliness which offices bring and, most importantly, from the economic impact they have on the locality, as they bid up the value of land and price out other, more useful, local activities.

The planning system should be able to resolve this conflict. Indeed, from time to time, local planners and, less frequently, government planners have attempted to strike a balance between competing uses by controlling office developments, either refusing them planning permission or encouraging their relocation out of the city entirely.

Success has been very limited. Relocation policies have been advisory rather than compulsory, and in practice have been more successful with government departments, which have no choice but to go if required, than with private developers. Local authorities' powers to refuse office applications are limited by the appeal process, whereby a sympathetic government may end up granting permission to a development previously opposed by hostile local planners. It takes an extremely committed kind of planner or planning authority to do more than simply accept the inevitability of office development.

Local people are at a particular disadvantage. The complicated nature of the planning legislation has created a system through which developers and their architects have learned to move with ease but which is ill-suited to the needs of lay-people. By institutionalizing dissent, by placing time-limits on public consultation and by prescribing the methods by which objections may be made, the planning process places obstacles in their path. Further, its emphasis on purely physical questions often directs the debate into side-issues; when the main question is whether or not a development should take place, it is a diversion if the discussion is about the number of storeys or the colour of the cladding.

If the planning system, despite its originators' best intentions, has ended up by favouring the developer and hampering the local communities, this has not, however, prevented it from being a means of trying to achieve some kind of equity and order in our decaying capitalist society. It is, with all its deficiencies, the only framework we have for environmental debate. In the last few years, progressive planning authorities seeking to do their duty by the most deprived members of their community, and progressive theoreticians seeking to build on the lessons of the urban struggles of 1968, have at times pushed the planning agenda beyond the limits of the legislation.

I have already mentioned the formidable body of social theory developed over the last twenty years or so by the French school of urban sociologists and their British counterparts. Manuel Castells has called for a move away from the 'street-fighting' image of social struggle, and for an effort to 'integrate all the means available for exercising pressure, including the management of sectors or levels of the state'. He identifies the working class as the group which is best organized and most politically conscious, but considers that they cannot, on their own 'pose a socialist alternative in western Europe'. 'This can be possible only by the organisation of popular classes objectively interested in going beyond capitalism and subjectively conscious of this necessity and possibility.'

For Castells, the way forward involves an alliance both of the working class and the salaried classes, and 'it is in urban protest that they most easily discover a similarity of interests ... and a common opposition to the logic of the system.'[3]

This approach formed a theoretical base for much of the experimental local planning work of the eighties. A dissenting approach to planning practice has always been easier outside the framework of government, and the independent Town and Country Planning Association has long been known for its opposition to the spread of nuclear power, its development of planning aid for local communities, and its support for projects like the tenants' campaign in Belfast to get the Divis Flats demolished. During the eighties however, some local authorities, impatient with the government's negative attitude to local planning, and spurred on by demands from an increasingly deprived local community, themselves promoted radical local schemes, often in the face of government opposition.

Practical examples of progressive local planning could already be seen and visited, for instance, in Italy, in cities controlled by local PCI (*Partito Communista Italiano*) administrations. The city of Bologna had become justly famous in the late seventies for its social policies, incorporating employment, housing and health provision, accessible education and free public transport. The integrated public transport system of Paris, pedestrian schemes and cycle routes in Dutch cities and experiments in decentralized democracy in northern Spain also provided examples.

In Britain, the theories of protest found acceptance among left Labour authorities anxious to hold the line against impending government cuts and among planning authorities trying to respond to increasing local demands for more control of the environment. Walsall and a number of other local authorities decentralized council services to local offices, to make them more accessible. Manchester Council developed imaginative public consultation techniques which were followed elsewhere. Camden, in north London, set up a number of local people's area committees, with budgets and devolved, decision-making powers. And the Greater London Council became well known for its experiments in popular planning, its industrial training schemes and employment enterprise, its night-time lorry bans, bus-only lanes and subsidized bus and Underground fares.

Much of this work lay outside the statutory duties imposed on planning authorities simply to prepare development plans and to control development in the context of these plans. But at least the planning system provided a framework for such things to happen. The egalitarian aims of the original welfare state could be addressed more effectively by authorities which thus stepped outside their strict statutory roles.

The planning system also provides our only framework, imperfect though it may be, for confronting strategic planning issues, some of which are large and complex, and deserve full debate. Major public debates were held over the Roskill Commission's inquiry into the site for London's third airport, the inquiry into the Windscale plant, and the Greater London Development Plan. There are justifiable misgivings about the subsequent political decisions on all of these issues, but at least debates took place. People's growing concerns about employment, public transport, pollution and greenhouse gases make it increasingly necessary for future decisions on transport or power generation to be taken after full, effective debate.

The fact is, however, that for the last ten years or more, government policy has been to dismantle the planning framework and to shift the balance of power to the developer and the commercial sector. As a result, using the planning system to achieve either social equity or the proper husbandry of national resources has become progressively more difficult. The Conservatives have abolished many socially-directed environmental projects, have changed the planning legislation in many ways to make control more difficult and development easier, have reduced planning authorities' resources through rate- and charge-capping, surcharge and privatization, and have abolished the GLC and the Metropolitan Counties, the last remaining agents of strategic public-sector planning. London became the only major world city without a unified local administration.

Loss of all these functions has generally been to the disadvantage of ordinary people – whose position has been further worsened by measures like the 'poll tax' – while the stifling of strategic debate has allowed the country's long-term environmental and energy problems to remain unaddressed. The government's philosophy speaks of freedom but at all levels freedoms have been removed. Public sector environmental planning has largely been subordinated to the long-term planning of the

# popular planning 1

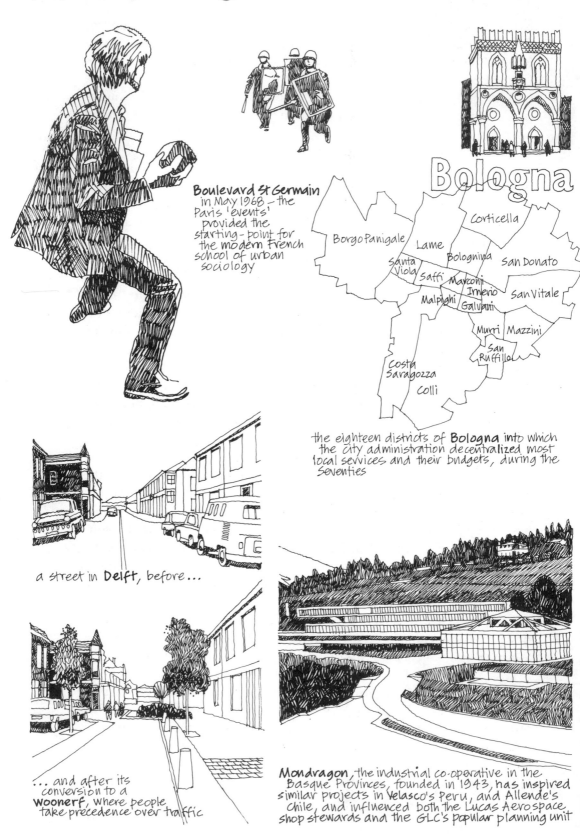

**Boulevard St Germain** in May 1968 — the Paris 'events' provided the starting-point for the modern French school of urban sociology

Bologna

Borgo Panigale · Lame · Corticella · Bolognina · San Donato · Santa Viola · Saffi · Marconi · Imerio · San Vitale · Malpighi · Galvani · Murri · Mazzini · San Ruffillo · Costa Saragozza · Colli

the eighteen districts of **Bologna** into which the city administration decentralized most local services and their budgets, during the seventies

a street in **Delft**, before...

... and after its conversion to a **woonerf**, where people take precedence over traffic

**Mondragon**, the industrial co-operative in the Basque Provinces, founded in 1943, has inspired similar projects in Velasco's Peru, and Allende's Chile, and influenced both the Lucas Aerospace shop stewards and the GLC's popular planning unit

the **Crowndale Centre**, Camden Town, London, a former postal sorting office converted by Ko€k Townsend for community use

為根德委
分區委
公開會

十一月二十日 星
在 Church Hall, F€
於 Lady Margare

publicity for a public meeting in **Kentish Town**, London, reflecting the area's ethnic mix

some important **transport initiatives** during the seventies and early eighties

**Tyne and Wear** Metro

**Middlesbrough** cycleways

**South Yorkshire** Subsidized bus fares

**Runcorn** new housing in a pedestrian environment

**Nottingham** free bus experiment

**Norwich** city centre pedestrian scheme

**Oxford** major traffic management

**Windsor** heavy lorry ban

**London** Subsidized bus and tube fares cycle routes night-time lorry ban Opposition to nuclear transport

GLC WORKING FOR LONDON JOBS FOR A CHANGE

**DEVELOPMENT** OF **30 INDUSTRIAL UNITS**

ENQUIRIES TO 01-000 0000

COMPLETION 0000000 0000

through the **Greater London Enterprise Board** and the **London Industrial Strategy** the GLC tried to promote local industrial jobs for local people, by building factories, financing enterprise and sponsoring training schemes

multinational corporations, the finance companies, the big building contractors and the newly-privatized utilities.

In its different way, the welfare state of the Soviet Union has experienced the same problems. The housing and land-use planning systems, though fundamental to Soviet ideology, were allowed to exist only so far as the economy could support them. There were many problems. The housing was of low quality, the jobs often stultifying and the public transport overcrowded, but the successes too were undeniable. The housing output was prodigious, and rents were pegged at 4 per cent of a family's income. Unemployment was low. Public transport was efficient and extraordinarily cheap.

In theory the planned economy of the Soviet Union was intended to avoid one of the main problems of capitalism: the fact that profit is not only its motivating force but is also crisis-ridden. The control of consumer demand would, it was hoped, avoid this. In practice, the planned economy was volatile, with resources being switched at will from one sector to the other. Competition within the world capitalist system forced the hands of the economic planners, so that industrial output, or the arms trade, or the space race, always had priority over welfare and the environment. The priorities of the multinational corporations indirectly affected decisions in the Kremlin as well as in the White House. *Glasnost* and *perestroika* were responses to the world economic crisis, a final attempt to hold the Soviet system together. With the switch to a market economy, welfare could not continue. Unemployment went up; so did prices, fares and rents, crime, vandalism and disease.

No one need lament the collapse of a repressive bureaucratic system. In Britain the current crisis of the local state is not wholly unwelcome; the local-government system was long due for an overhaul. The GLC was probably not the best strategic planning authority for London, which needs to be planned on a regional scale, over an area much wider than the conurbation. And the present form of the borough councils makes them less responsive than they should be to local needs and conditions. However, there is no democratic gain if the inefficiencies and excesses of local government are replaced by similar ones at national level. Closing legitimate channels of local democratic expression, however imperfect, merely directs the pressures elsewhere.

Likewise, there can be no justification for the repression of the old Stalinist regimes, but the people of the Soviet Union and eastern Europe have not overthrown Stalinism, at appalling cost, merely to replace one form of exploitation with another. It is ironic that eastern Europe is turning from state capitalism to market capitalism at a time when, throughout the world, the effects of the latter have never been more open to question.

# strategic planning

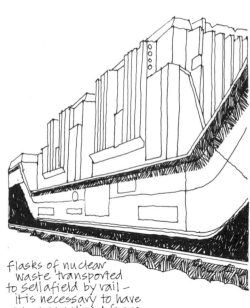

flasks of nuclear
waste transported
to Sellafield by rail –
it is necessary to have
a proper national forum
to debate issues like
nuclear power

nuclear power
stations

route of nuclear
waste to Sellafield

Windscale (Sellafield)
nuclear reprocessing
plant

Stansted

Heathrow
Gatwick

Channel
Tunnel and
rail link – the
decision to
choose this
route was not
the subject of
a public
inquiry

the impact of
air travel on
the living
environment

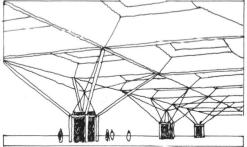

Stansted airport building, by Foster
Associates – the Roskill commission's
preferred location of Cublington for
London's third airport was rejected by
the government after little national
debate

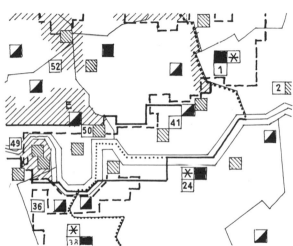

the East End of London, shown in an
extract from the 'key diagram' of the
revised Greater London Development Plan –
the Plan was the subject of a two-year
inquiry process – with the abolition of
the GLC, the Plan was set aside by the
government – there is now no public
forum for debating the future of London

the symbol on the Isle of Dogs indicates an
area of office 'restraint'

The European Community, which some former Soviet states have expressed interest in joining, is a case in point. At first sight, the Treaty of Rome appears to offer many benefits to the people of its signatory states. Britain's EEC membership since 1973 has stimulated a great number of initiatives, many of them environmental and social. Britain's slow postwar progress in research and development in the building industry, for example, was given impetus by metrication, by the dimensional co-ordination of building components, and by the need for 'quality assurance'. EC directives on the environment, which require environmental assessments of large projects to be made, have been used to challenge British government schemes. Debate in Britain at the time of the 1991 Maastricht summit centred on the 'Social Charter', and seemed to define a choice between a progressive, socially responsible, 'united Europe' and a conservative 'little-England'.

But it is still a capitalist Europe. It is not only in Britain that the working class and the underprivileged minorities are bearing the brunt of the recession. Some 20 million Europeans are out of work. In many countries, immigration laws are being strengthened – as in the case of the British Asylum Bill – while government policies of discrimination – as in Germany – are giving encouragement to neo-Nazism. The 'unity' that today's Europe fosters is little more than the unity of its own capitalists to enable them to compete with the USA and Japan.

It is important to guard against the illusory belief that, in either east or west, people are achieving freedom. The state continues to survive in eastern Europe; one ruling class has been replaced by another. And in most of western Europe, especially Britain, the state has become stronger than at any time since 1945. In Britain, major problems now exist at both local and national levels: local democracy has been eroded, and the growing state power is being used for narrow political ends. Both local and strategic planning have suffered, and with them, the interests of ordinary people.

The problem before us is how to create a system which combines democracy at local level with large-scale planning at national level and beyond. There is an undeniable need for greater local autonomy in planning. There is a need for a strong welfare programme to provide the measure of social justice which the market cannot and will not offer. And there is also a need for a democratic system of large-scale economic and social planning, to create the coherent strategy for the future which the state has failed to provide. None of these is possible in an economy dominated by the needs of international Capital. Planning for the people's future should be entrusted not to the state, and still less to the multinational corporations, but to the people themselves.

# 10 Beyond Perestroika – the dialectics of change

In the three previous chapters I looked at ways in which theorists and practitioners were attempting to go beyond bourgeois society. I identified attempts to construct a more progressive and critical environmental theory, on which action could be based. I looked at the problems of developing an environmentally responsive technology, both for buildings themselves and for the decision-making which leads to them. And I emphasized the need to recapture the ability to think strategically, devoting energy and resources sufficient to match the enormous scale of the tasks.

As to the tasks themselves, one need not look far. Most people, other than right-wing leader writers and their public, would identify issues like homelessness, the decay of the urban environment and the global energy crisis. They might point to the declining quality of people's living conditions, especially in the cities, with their pollution, congested transport systems and rotten housing. They might point to the profligate – and uneven – use of the world's resources, whereby the USA, per person, consumes about three hundred times as much of the world's primary resources as does Bangladesh.[1]

To all of these tasks the architect, educated at considerable social cost, to a high professional standard, might reasonably be expected to make a contribution. Were it not, that is, for the process of capital accumulation. As I have tried to show, the capitalist mode of production, with its competition, accumulation and concentration, is the cause, not the solution, of the environmental crisis; the owners of the means of production – and all those who serve them, including architects – respond to the crisis only by turning it to further profit, creating worse problems as they do so.

Our education and culture, which architects themselves help to foster, makes it difficult for them to see what is going on, and what to do about it. The architects of the early Modern Movement were erroneously certain they had the answers to many of society's problems. Architects today may be less prone to that particular mistake, but meanwhile, architectural theory and practice have become so narrow that they are of little relevance to the major tasks in hand. Here and there, as we have seen, individual architects or groups of architects are trying to offer alternatives, but are too often overwhelmed by the mass of commercialism.

As a result, many ordinary people now realize that the environment cannot be entrusted to business interests, to the bureaucracy, to the white, male-dominated professions and all the other agents of the state, and have begun seriously to question the way environmental decisions are made. This questioning process can take three main forms: rejecting today's society in favour of alternative ways of life; attempting to work within the system to ameliorate it; attempting its subversion or overthrow. The state in its turn will react in different ways, according to the seriousness of the challenge, but its main aim, one way or another, will be to neutralize dissent.

Some people have despaired of achieving a sane environment through conventional means and have reacted by dropping out. By trying to set up tipi communities or organic farms in remote valleys in Wales or Scotland, they hope to escape, or to educate society into different ways. One problem with all such hopes, as Robert Owen found in the nineteenth century, is that although society might grudgingly admire the sentiments, it finds it easy enough to ignore the message. Another is that such communities are never as independent as they might wish. To a large extent they depend on capitalist society to provide the social and material context in which their protest can take place. Ultimately, they depend on society for its tolerance.

Potentially more challenging than simply dropping out are the numerous attempts, some of them noted in previous chapters, to reform and humanize the system from within. This kind of activity has an undoubted value, but raises one major problem. As long as the system remains intact, it is all too easy for protest to be neutralized; the state will seek to contain it, and the commercial sector to turn it to profit. Since the days of Titus Salt and W. H. Lever, capitalists have known the value of populist gestures. So today, multinationals will sponsor community enterprise awards, or major property developers get involved in community schemes.

The so-called 'community architecture' movement is a case in point. I have already mentioned some of the spontaneous community action which took place in the sixties and early seventies: the concept of architecture by and for the community dates from that time. Over the last few years however, 'community architecture' has gradually become dominated by business interests, the architectural establishment and HRH The Prince of Wales. Thus, a movement which at first sight seems to challenge the establishment contributes in the end to class hegemony.

Brought up in an elitist tradition, the Prince of Wales is an unlikely people's champion. Yet that is how he seems to see himself, and how many people see him. He attracted some public approval with his speech at Hampton Court in 1984 (see p. 2), but he drew further attention with his intervention in the competition for Paternoster Square, his criticism of the design of Canary Wharf, his television appearances, his book,[2] his proposals for the development of his own Duchy of Cornwall estates and, above all perhaps, his promotion of 'community architecture'. With such advocates as the Prince of Wales and his expert advisers, who include the populist RIBA ex-President Rod Hackney, community issues might seem to be in safe hands.

Yet 'the community' can be a specious idea. Politicians talk of 'the international community' when they refer to the interests of western capitalism, and of 'returning health-care to the community' when they mean reducing public-sector health provision. Likewise, 'community architecture' – local people banding together to improve their housing through their own efforts – sounds admirable, but needs examination. The movement is said by Charles Knevitt and Nick Wates to have emerged 'from a growing realisation that mismanagement of the built environment is a major contributor to the nation's social and economic ills, and that there are better ways of going about planning and design.'[3]

At Hampton Court, Prince Charles was specific about what community architecture offered. 'Apart from anything else,' he said, 'there is an assumption [by community architects] that if people have played a part in creating something, they might conceivably treat it as their own possession and look after it, thus making an attempt at reducing the problem of vandalism.'

Knevitt and Wates see the Prince's speech, with its explicit linking of 'social unrest' with 'the degree of control people have over their environment', as a breakthrough for community architecture. The royal endorsement 'gave the community architecture movement the respectability and credibility it so badly needed'. One aspect of this respectability is said to be that 'while community architecture demands a radical change in the relationships between those involved in development, it transcends traditional Left/Right politics. It is not rigidly pro nor anti public or private ownership of land, public or private development agencies, high or low rise building.'[4]

Community architecture is said to give people what they want, and

> has shown ordinary people that their views are worth having ... that they need not be made to feel guilty or ignorant if their natural preference is for the more 'traditional' designs – for a small garden, for courtyards, arches and porches – and that there is a growing number of architects prepared to listen and offer imaginative ideas.[5]

There is a lot of practical good in community architecture, but its apologists often hold naive views. One of these is their concern for the social health of 'the nation'. A class society is not one nation but two, as even Disraeli recognized, and its environment is the direct result of the one imposing its priorities on the other. This is not 'mismanagement' but deliberate intention. It is indeed true that if ordinary people exert control over their own environment they will improve their circumstances, but in this society it will be necessary to exert control over a lot more besides. It is a nonsense that ordinary people should rely on the establishment – the royal family, the professions, or anyone else with a vested interest in the status quo – to change anything significant. Architecture does not transcend politics.

The capitalist system having failed to provide an adequate environment for the working class, the more energetic of them are encouraged, rather than fight against it, to associate themselves more fully with it, by becoming bourgeois property owners. In the name of choice, they are offered not choice of political future but choice of architectural style. There is a genuine community architecture, but it must lie higher up the scale of awareness.

The problem of achieving significant change while leaving the system intact is an insuperable one. In 1985 the Church of England published a report[6] on inner-city problems. Its title 'Faith in the City' has at least two connotations: how the Christian can discover his or her faith while living in the difficult environment of the city; how the church can help society rebuild its own faith in the idea of the city. The report gave an unequivocal picture of urban deprivation. Though it was mainly an exhortation to Anglican parishioners to get more involved, to carry out 'social audits', and to contribute to a Church Urban Fund, the report was also an implicit criticism of government policy.

Its appearance therefore attracted defensive fire from government ministers and Conservative backbenchers. The Archbishop of Canterbury, Robert Runcie, had already become a target in 1982 when he had preached reconciliation at the otherwise triumphalist Falklands victory celebrations. The Bishop of Durham, David Jenkins, was also under attack, both for his progressive theological views and for his championship of social justice. There was much comment about the desirability of the church staying out of politics.

This is ironic, since the procedures of the Anglian church and its key appointments are either controlled or influenced by the government. The church is expected to show its 'apolitical' nature by tacitly supporting the state. But so obvious had the social divisions now become that the church's duty to the poor had begun to override its loyalty to the state. It no longer seemed to be 'the Conservative Party at prayer'.

How far this was or was not true, how far the church really is able to break away from its bourgeois associations, is a matter of debate. Apart from the obvious question, that is, the church's close legal relationship with the state, a matter which can only be resolved by resolution of the disestablishment debate, there is also a more fundamental issue, having to do with the nature of Christianity itself: how far individual Christians may participate in revolutionary social change.

There are some basic differences between Christian and Marxist principles. One of these is the evident atheism of the latter, which argues that all religion is the invention of a human society unable to cope in any other way with injustice and oppression, and is therefore unnecessary in a classless society. Religion is 'the sigh of the oppressed creature, the heart of a heartless world ... the spirit of spiritless conditions'.[7] And Marx called Christianity 'the special religion of capitalism'.

Difficult to resolve indeed – if one interprets the Gospels as an indication of Jesus' respect for, and submission to, the processes of the state – and a stumbling block for some Christian socialists, who might use Marx's critical method to help them understand the world but would stop short of preaching class struggle and revolution.

Indeed, for most orthodox Christians, God transcends all human institutions. Jesus, tempted in the wilderness, rejected political dominion over the world. Salvation, it is often held, comes through individuals developing their own relationship with God, rather than through the structural social change demanded by Marxists. The concept of all people as individuals, each with potential for good or evil, leads Christians to tolerate all shades of political opinion among their ranks. A coherent political programme for change is therefore not only irrelevant, but also unachievable.

Yet despite all this, there are numerous points of contact. In September 1991 the press reported that 'The new Archbishop of Canterbury, Dr George Carey ... dismissed the Government's explanation for the Newcastle riots and laid the blame squarely on social deprivation. He also attacked many aspects of Conservative education policies ... wrongdoing was "inextricably linked to social deprivation, poor housing and illiteracy".'[8]

More and more Christians are attempting to reinterpret the relevance of the Gospels to today's major social problems. The Cambridge theologian Don Cupitt contrasts the enormous strides made in Christian ethics, under the influence of the positivist thinkers of the nineteenth century and the social commentators of today, with the comparative backwardness of Christian theology, which remains largely medieval and superstitious.[9] What is needed is the rejection of dogmatic theology and its replacement by the practice and philosophy of religion. Cupitt argues that religion is not supernatural but human; he reinterprets the very nature of God, placing him firmly at the centre of human affairs. The aim of Christianity should be to give meaning and purpose to the real world.

David Sheppard, Bishop of Liverpool, faced every day with the contradictions of life in an exploited urban community, has identified[10] numerous potential points of contact between Christians and Marxists: belief in man as a social being; recognition of the formative importance of economic and social structures; scepticism about who controls the means of production; indignation at inequality; belief in a better future; and a longing for a realistic programme to benefit the poor. Though Sheppard also rejects some aspects of Marxism, the most significant thing about his list is its total incompatibility with capitalism. Belief in the perfectability of human beings does not accord with an economic system based on conflict and exploitation.

In the last few years, Christianity and Marxism have come together in the 'liberation theology' of the Latin-American church, especially in the work of Gustavo Gutiérrez in Peru. It identifies the established church with the existing power structure of repressive regimes, and criticizes western Christians for seeing the world through capitalist eyes. We should begin not with theology or even with the Gospels but with people's place in the world. The Gospels become relevant only when they speak on what Gutiérrez calls 'questions derived from the world'. Salvation is not an individual quest but involves 'all men and the whole man' in a 'struggle against misery and exploitation'.

This theme is important to the French Christian Marxist Roger Garaudy.

> Faith is not a promise of power. It is the conviction that it is possible to create a qualitatively new future only if we identify ourselves with those who are the most naked and downtrodden, only if we tie our fate to theirs to the point that it is impossible to conceive any real victory but theirs ... When we are really prepared to make this gift for the least of men, God is in us. He is the power to transform the world.[11]

The transcendent God and the revolution here go together. This is the kind of thinking the church needs to capture if 'Faith in the City' is to become more than just another bourgeois project. At present the church, divided among itself over internal issues like inter-Communion and women's ordination, and generally respectful of conservative points of view, can be expected, in effect, to neutralize its own protest.

There are times, of course, when campaigning and dissent will push the state into a policy of damage limitation. The parliamentary system itself – and I have already quoted Gramsci's comments – is one way of doing this. Governments habitually claim a wider mandate for making environmental decisions – for the development of nuclear power for instance – than is warranted by the simple fact of being elected. They will also change the environmental ground rules – often to achieve narrow class objectives – through their control of the legislative process. I have already mentioned the Conservatives' reforms of the planning system in the interests of private enterprise.

Over many years the policy of successive governments towards public involvement in environmental decisions has been one of containment. During the sixties for instance, the public demanded more say in the planning process. As a result the government set up the Skeffington Committee[12] whose proposals on public consultation and the establishment of 'community fora' were adopted by local authorities. Skeffington was described by John Palmer as 'at best a very minor improvement ... [having] little to do with actual participation in the planning process ... it is unlikely to represent a credible redistribution of power. The middle classes are organized, industry and commerce are organized, the poor are not.'[13]

'Tokenistic' consultation has been a common concept since the sixties, and thrives well in the cynical political climate of today. It was tokenism which motivated much of the 'municipal socialism' of the eighties. In the last chapter I mentioned the decentralization of local services as part of the agenda of leftist planning authorities, an objective desirable in itself, but like all such schemes, capable of cynical misapplication. Soundly rejected by the electorate in the 1983 national elections, the Labour Party decided to retaliate at local level. The decentralization of council services – including architectural and planning services and council-house repairs – from the Town Hall into numerous local offices would, it was thought, emphasize the value of local democracy and would rally local opinion in defence of local-government services, at that time being heavily cut by the government. The working-class electorate was not convinced; it could see that the local Labour administrations, despite their claims, were still carrying out the cuts demanded by the Conservative government; it made no difference to the local people if their increasingly expensive and worsening local services were provided from the Town Halls or from local offices – they were inadequate either way.

Another much bigger experiment in decentralization, displaying similar signs of tokenism, was begun in February 1985 when Mikhail Gorbachev became General Secretary of the Central Committee of the Communist Party of the Soviet Union. The motivating force for the changes he brought about was the Soviet people's increasing dissatisfaction with the country's worsening economic conditions, and led to his policies of *glasnost* and *perestroika*, both intended, like many previous 'top-down' reforms, to stifle social unrest. *Glasnost*, for the government, became the embarrassing victim of its own success, as one group after another sought self-determination, and as opportunist politicians

# reform

**Hillingdon Civic Centre** in London, designed by RMJM Architects –

an accessible architectural style does not necessarily improve the quality or quantity of Local Government services

**new housing in Liverpool** –

again, a populist style does not reflect a change in economic power

Dr George Carey **Archbishop of Canterbury**

**view down Hope Street**, Liverpool – the two cathedrals symbolise the churches' faith in a city which still remains one of the most deprived in Europe

Mikhail Gorbachev

kg per head of population

400
300
200
100
0

meat
dairy products
vegetables
fruit

official norm

actual consumption 1980

**soviet food production,** the gap between the intention and the reality

Source: Prodovol stvennaya Programma SSR, 1981

**glasnost** overtakes **perestroika**

emerged to obscure the issues. *Perestroika* on the other hand has so far proved impossible to achieve, principally because debate at both national and international level has posited western capitalism as the only alternative to Stalinism.

It is clear that neither capitalism nor Stalinism, which after all are two sides of the same coin, offers the better life and the decent environment that more and more people are looking for. If 'dropping out' is ineffectual and 'working within the system' is increasingly difficult, as the state closes off legitimate avenues of protest, the third option, outright opposition to the state, has become a real possibility.

During the eighties many groups, both in the east and the west, have taken matters into their own hands, and environmental issues have been at the very centre of the class struggle. Violence on the streets and housing estates has been seen as a protest at the crude living environment offered to the working class. Women's environmental groups have challenged the way cities are planned and buildings designed in a male-dominated society. As the crisis of capitalism has cut profits and lowered environmental or safety standards, the workers have fought back, on the oil platforms, in the docks, on the building sites, on the London Underground. The rise of Solidarity in Poland forced the closure of many of the regime's most dangerous industrial plants. The British Seafarers' union achieved a ban on nuclear dumping at sea. Ukrainian miners went on strike in 1989 to secure environmental improvements. One of the main issues for the Romanian revolutionaries the same year was Ceauşescu's policy of destroying historic villages and rehousing the people in tower blocks. The rubber tappers of Brazil, in the name of the murdered Chico Mendes, are continuing the fight against the cattle ranchers who are destroying the rain forest, and may yet win where environmentalists and governments alike have so far failed. And recent events in eastern Europe have emphasized that tyrannies can still be overthrown – including the more subtle forms practised in the west.

In Russia an embryo movement is trying to work for an alternative future. The new political freedom has allowed the creation, for the first time since Trotsky's Left Opposition, of real socialist organizations. In Moscow, the New Socialist Committee emerged as a potential political focus. It was based largely on SOTSPROF, a recently-founded federation of socialist trade unions, with branches in St Petersburg, Gorky and elsewhere. On a tour of Europe, one of its founders, Boris Kagarlitsky, said,

> Perestroika has done little to reduce the dead weight of bureaucratic inefficiency, privilege and corruption ... the working class is increasingly being forced into action to defend basic living standards ... In these circumstances, it is vital for socialists to put forward a clear alternative

perspective, emphasising democratic planning rather than market-inspired reforms which offer no solution to the crisis.

During the last few years, politics in both east and west has moved to the right. The increasing authoritarianism of the bourgeoisie, however, does not indicate a strengthening of its power base. World capitalism is in a state of crisis, and it is clear from the increasingly desperate economic measures taken by all the governments that they have no solution.

Capitalism has produced extraordinary technical achievements, from space programmes to biological research, from electronics to nuclear fission. The fantastic form of many of the buildings in the late twentieth-century city are 'wonders far surpassing Egyptian pyramids, Roman aqueducts and Gothic cathedrals'.

Yet there is no escaping the fact that the wealth of the more privileged sectors of modern society, and all their fine buildings, depend on the exploitation of most of the people in the world and of the environment they live in. Even if capitalists wanted to improve the conditions of the poor, they could never do it. In Britain, while the Prime Minister, John Major, talks of a 'classless society', the richest 200 people own assets of almost £50 billion, while over the last decade, state pensions have been reduced by one-fifth, the number of people living under the poverty line has doubled to over 10 million, and unemployment, even by the government's redefined standards, has risen to 2.5 million.

Architects, planners and other professionals, implicated in this process as they are, must consider whether their duty to society outweighs their duty to the state. At the end of *Modern Movements in Architecture*[14], as I have already mentioned, Charles Jencks placed a postscript entitled 'Architecture and Revolution'. He was writing at a time when the successes and failures of 1968 were still vivid enough in the mind to allow revolutionary theory to be incorporated into architectural thought. 'For the first time,' he felt able to say, 'revolutionary theory is beginning to catch up with two hundred years of practice.' He could see popular movements towards autonomy and decentralization beginning to break down the old hierarchies and bureaucracies: a gradual revolution from below. The job of the architect was to 'clarify the situation theoretically, design dissenting buildings within the system, provide alternative models and wait for the propitious moment' in which he or she would, like the constructivists, begin truly to express the nature of the revolution which would have begun to take place all around.

In 1968 many people hoped for a revolution, and the hope created an air of inevitability. All the architect had to do, it seemed, was to help provide the cultural parameters within which the new society would take shape. The mistakenness of this view is perhaps clearer now than it was then. Dissent 'within the system' is a limited conception; real dissent means destroying the system. 'Dissenting buildings' is another illusion; it is people, not buildings, who dissent. And why 'wait for' the propitious moment? Social progress does not arrive of its own accord. It must be worked for – and fought for if necessary.

It is appropriate that one of the greatest and most perceptive British environmental critics should also be our greatest revolutionary theorist. Over a century ago, William Morris wrote:

> The word Revolution, which we socialists are often forced to use, has a terrible sound to most people's ears, even when we have explained to them that it does not necessarily mean a change accompanied by riot and all kinds of violence, and cannot mean a change made mechanically and in the teeth of opinion by a group of men who have somehow managed to seize on the executive power for the moment.[15]

To Morris, the great creative artist, fighting against lies and what he called the 'mumbo-jumbo' of the bourgeois world and its systematic inequalities was a creative act. To him, the word Revolution 'may frighten some people, but it will at least warn them that there is something to be frightened about, which will be no less dangerous for being ignored; and it may encourage some people, and will mean to them not a fear but a hope.'

Effective dissent against the current system is ultimately the only creative act possible. The first step is to recognize that the material conditions, now as never before, are right for a major social change to take place. If at present we are not confident that this is so, it is only because of the hegemony exercised by the ruling class and its delusive ideologies. This dominance can seriously be challenged by the counter-position of an alternative critical theory, one which recognizes the class struggle as a reality.

This depends on defining architecture in terms of the wider environmental struggles within society, involving practitioners and theoreticians alike. The capitalist mode of production has divided labour in the building industry, creating a gulf between the worker in the drawing office and the worker on the site. The struggles of building workers, often admirably militant, against an industry offering perhaps the worst working conditions and the poorest health and safety record of any in Europe, should coincide with those of office workers, exploited by long hours, repetitive tasks, poor conditions of service and sick-building syndrome. A healthy architecture depends on a community of interest between the two.

As manufacturing industry in Britain declines, and its workforce with it, white-collar workers become more influential within the working class. The growing service sector contains large numbers of poorly paid jobs – office staff, railway and dock workers, firefighters, hospital porters, bus, ambulance and lorry drivers, gas, post and water workers, hotel staff and

Divis Tower, containing old people's flats, used as a helicopter pad by the security forces

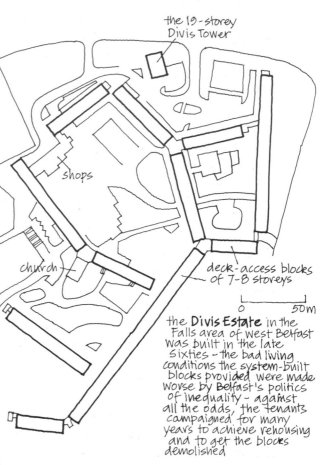

the 19-storey Divis Tower

shops

church

deck-access blocks of 7-8 storeys

0        50m

the **Divis Estate** in the Falls area of west Belfast was built in the late sixties – the bad living conditions the system-built blocks provided were made worse by Belfast's politics of inequality – against all the odds, the tenants campaigned for many years to achieve rehousing and to get the blocks demolished

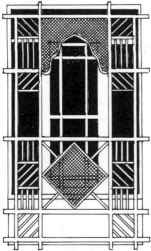

windows with protective grilles at the **Jagonari Centre** in Whitechapel Road, east London – the architectural philosophy of **Matrix** emerges from a class-based as well as a gender-based view of women's oppression

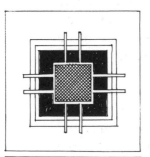

the collapse of **Ronan Point** in Canning Town in east London, in 1968, was the starting-point of a 20-year campaign by the local people to achieve demolition of the remaining system-built towers

**William Morris**, for whom the environment and the class-struggle were 'interdependent'

**Rosa Luxemburg**, who made it clear that social change could not come through the existing power structures

the **Amazon rain-forest**, archetypal example of the conflict between capitalism and a precious eco-system

**Czech demonstrators** celebrate their overthrow of Stalinism in 1989

**the people fight back** - living conditions, employment, and wider environmental issues are often at the centre of civil unrest

● states where there has been recent civil unrest (including overthrow of the state itself)

○ areas where there is an active environmental or peace movement

# future society 1

a humanistic architecture depends on the creation of a fully democratic society – not the other way round

## social control of capital

- ☐ democratic control of the means of production
- ☐ a democratic civil society, valuing humanity and the eco-system
- ☐ democratically controlled economic planning

## social equality

- ☐ fair distribution of the products of labour
- ☐ full value given to the rights of individuals
- ☐ democratically controlled public sector, providing **full social services** and a **system of popular land-use** and transport planning

## useful work

- ☐ full employment
- ☐ greater self-management and autonomy in the workplace
- ☐ democratization of day-to-day decision-making

## useful technology

- ☐ concentration on necessary goods
- ☐ long-life, low-energy products
- ☐ democratic and useful information technology
- ☐ energy deriving from safe, renewable sources

# democratic building process

- ☐ **diversion of skills and resources to where there is the greatest need** — not the greatest profit

- ☐ **building for long life and adaptability** — conserving existing and future building fabric, rather than redeveloping according to the requirements of the property business

- ☐ **taking a critical view of building materials and components** — being aware of the energy needed to manufacture and transport them, and designing to minimize this

- ☐ **designing for energy conservation** — using appropriate rather than high-tech design solutions, and passive rather than active environmental controls, recycling where possible

- ☐ **building for safety**, both for the building's users and for those who build it

- ☐ **using information technology to improve the quality and performance of the built product**, not merely to cut costs or increase marketability

- ☐ **creating a fully democratic design and building process**, in which builders are properly involved in the design decisions, designers in the construction process, and users in both

office cleaners – and white-collar trade unionism has greatly increased, especially among women.

A modern view of the working class should include them, and also the homeless, the unemployed, the women at home, the black and ethnic minority groups, and all others exploited by the system. On an international scale this includes the working classes of Third World countries, doubly oppressed by Western neocolonialism and by their own ruling classes, and also includes the super-exploited urban workers of the newly industrializing countries, fast becoming the new proletariat of the western industrial system. It is with their needs and aspirations that a critical theory must start.

From such an agenda might spring any number of alternatives to what Morris called 'the tyranny of profit-grinding'. Greater social control of capital would lead to higher levels of employment, to more self-management and autonomy among the workforce and to the decentralization of day-to-day decision-making. Social ownership of the means of production would restore the role of the public sector, not as a cynical bureaucracy but as a democratic institution committed to the responsible planning of cities and proper deployment of social services, public transport and community safety. The social control of technology would encourage the production of long-life, necessary goods and buildings, of healthy food, of safely-generated energy and of democratic and useful information technology. Most important of all, society would be mutual rather than exclusive; two-way relationships would replace the one-sided system of exploitation and oppression, and co-operation would replace conflict.

In the task of translating a critical theory into critical practice, the architect's dilemma, like that of most others, is that his or her professional life is bound up with the fortunes of the capitalist economic system and the bourgeois state, and serves only to reinforce them. No wonder so many are led into a sterile utopianism, to the view that it is somehow 'unrealistic' to work for an immediate revolutionary end, and that in any case the gradual reform of capitalism will eventually achieve the same sort of thing.

But Rosa Luxemburg turns this argument around: by itself, it is reformism which is unrealistic.

> Legislative reform and revolution are not different methods of historic development that can be picked out at pleasure ... revolution is the act of political creation, while legislation is the political expression of the life of a society which has already come into being ... people who pronounce themselves in favour of ... reform in place of and in contradistinction to the conquest of political power and social revolution do not really choose a more tranquil, slower road to the same goal, but a different goal. Instead of

... the establishment of a new society they take a stand for surface modifications of the old society.[16]

Most progressive architects, planners and environmental critics of the twentieth century have believed that reforms of the capitalist system would lead to a socialist society. But, as Rosa Luxemburg says, the only way to progress towards a new society, is by opposing the old one. A socialist society can arise 'only on the ruins of the capitalist state'. We must continue to participate in the old society to the best of our ability, but should take up only those positions which offer scope for anti-capitalist struggle. 'Of course, to be effective, Socialism must take all the positions she can in the existing state, and invade everywhere. However, the prerequisite for this is that these positions make it possible to wage the class struggle from them, the struggle against the bourgeoisie and its state.'[17]

The main mistake of all those architects, planners and critics has been their failure to recognize that the real, lasting reforms they have so assiduously sought are impossible without revolution. Critical theory depends on this premise. The task of converting the theory into practice still rests with the mass of the working people, with whom the progressive professional must discover his or her identity and community of interest. 'Practice' does not mean turning one's back, opting out, becoming marginalized. It means widespread, co-ordinated action against state power and capitalist exploitation. The positions occupied and the tasks carried out must contribute to the erosion of the one and the destruction of the other, and to the building of a society which has a genuine 'faith in the city' and in the individuals who comprise it. It is on the success of this that a democratic culture and a humane environment ultimately depend.

# Notes

1. PRODUCTION AND IDEOLOGY

1. Karl Marx, Preface to *A Contribution to the Critique of Political Economy* (1859)
2. *The Faces of Homelessness in London, Interim Report to the Salvation Army* (Department of Psychology, University of Surrey, 1989)
3. Marshall Berman, *All that is solid melts into air* (New York, 1982)
4. Roland Barthes, *Le Degré Zero de l'écricture* [Writing Degree Zero] (Paris, 1953)
5. John Berger, *Art and Revolution: Ernst Neizvestny and the Role of the Artist in the USSR* (London, 1979)
6. Vladimir Mayakovsky, *150 Million*, tr. Anna Bostock (1920)
7. J. M. Richards, *An Introduction to Modern Architecture* (Harmondsworth, 1940)
8. Nikolaus Pevsner, *Pioneers of the Modern Movement* (London, 1936)
9. J. M. Richards, op. cit.
10. Le Corbusier, *Towards a New Architecture*, tr. Frederick Etchells (London, 1927)
11. *Picture Post*, 4 January 1941
12. Ibid.
13. Karl Marx, *Capital*, vol. 1 (1867)
14. Roland Barthes, *Mythologies* (Paris, 1957)
15. *Architectural Design*, August 1962
16. Charles Jencks, *Modern Movements in Architecture* (Harmondsworth, 1973)
17. Ernst Fischer, *Marx in his own Words*, tr. Anna Bostock (Harmondsworth, 1970)
18. Karl Marx, *Captital*, vol. 3 (1894)

2. UNKINDEST CUTS

1. *The Faces of Homelessness in London, Interim Report to the Salvation Army* (Department of Psychology, University of Surrey, 1989)
2. Milner Holland Committee, *Report of the Committee on Housing in Greater London* (London, 1965)
3. Michael Stewart, *Keynes and After* (Harmondsworth, 1967)
4. Milton Friedman quoted in Peter Jenkins, *Mrs Thatcher's Revolution* (London, 1987)
5. J. M. Richards, *An Introduction to Modern Architecture* (Harmondsworth, 1940)

3. DOWN WITH MODERNISM

1. Antonio Gramsci, *Prison Notebooks* (London, 1973)
2. Karl Marx and Friedrich Engels, *Communist Manifesto* (1848)
3. See for example, Paul Gordon and Francesca Klug, *New Right, New Racism* (London, 1986)
4. Roger Scruton in the *Salisbury Review*, Autumn 1982
5. Herbert Butterfield, *The Whig Interpretation of History* (London, 1931)
6. Particularly, Karl Popper, *The Poverty of Historicism* (London, 1942) and Karl Popper, *The Open Society and its Enemies*, vol. 2 (London, 1945)
7. Karl Popper, *The Open Society and its Enemies*, vol. 2 (London, 1945)
8. Roger Scruton, *The Aesthetics of Architecture* (London, 1979)
9. David Watkin, *Morality and Architecture: The Development of a Theme in Architectural History and Theory from the Gothic Revival to the Modern Movement* (Oxford, 1977) and David Watkin, *The Rise of Architectural History* (London, 1980)
10. Roger Scruton, *The Aesthetics of Architecture* (London, 1979)
11. Alan Dobby, *Conservation and Planning* (London, 1978)
12. Gavin Stamp, *The Changing Metropolis* (Harmondsworth, 1984)
13. Quinlan Terry on BBC TV Channel 2, November 1988
14. David Watkin, *The Rise of Architectural History* (London, 1980)
15. BBC TV Channel 2, November 1988

4. THE SURREAL CITY

1. *Architectural Design*, vol. 47, no. 4 (1977)
2. Dennis Sharp, *A Visual History of Twentieth-Century Architecture* (New York, 1972)
3. Robert Venturi, *Complexity and Contradiction in Architecture* (New York, 1966)
4. *Architectural Design*, op. cit.
5. Martin Spring, 'Outré Outram', *Building*, 15 July 1988
6. John Outram in Charles Jencks (ed.), *Free-Style Classicism* (London, 1982)
7. Charles Jencks and William Chaitkin, *Current Architecture* (London, 1982)
8. Bryan Magee, *Guardian*, 22 September 1990
9. Leon Krier reported in Nathan Silver and Jos Boys (eds), *Why is British Architecture so Lousy?* (London, 1980)
10. Nathan Silver in Nathan Silver and Jos Boys (eds), op. cit.

5.  GOING TO THE DOGS
1.  HMSO, *Housing and Construction Statistics* (London, annually)
2.  Grieve Committee, *Inquiry into Housing in Glasgow* (Glasgow, 1987)
3.  Ed Vulliamy, 'We see no ships', *Guardian*, 29 March 1989
4.  Local Government, Planning and Land Act 1980
5.  Ed Vulliamy, op. cit.
6.  Docklands Consultative Committee, *Urban Development Corporations: Six Years in London's Docklands* (London, 1988)
7.  HMSO, *Lifting the Burden* (London, 1985)
8.  Ibid.
9.  HMSO, *Action for Cities* (London, 1988)
10.  *Daily Express*, 8 March 1988
11.  *Guardian*, 8 March 1988
12.  *Guardian*, 9 November 1988
13.  Docklands Consultative Committee, op. cit.
14.  Peter Dickens, 'Corporate Capitalism and the Building Industry' in *Proceedings of the Bartlett International Summer School* (London, 1982)
15.  J. K. Galbraith, *The New Industrial State* (New York, 1967)
16.  Labour Research, *Breaking the Nation* (London, 1985)
17.  HMSO, *Multinational Investment Strategies in the British Isles* (London, 1983)

6.  THE FOUNTAINHEAD SYNDROME
1.  Malcolm MacEwen, *Crisis in Architecture* (London, 1974)
2.  Herbert J. Gans, *People, Plans and Policies* (New York, 1991)
3.  *Architecture and Building* magazine, February 1958
4.  Herbert J. Gans, op. cit.
5.  Peter Buchanan, 'AA Now', *Architectural Review*, October 1983

7.  THEORIES AND HISTORY
1.  Friedrich Schiller, *Letter on the Aesthetic Education of a Man*, tr. Wilkinson and Willoughby (Oxford, 1967)
2.  Friedrich Engels, *Anti-Dühring* (1876–8)
3.  David Watkin, *The Rise of Architectural History* (London, 1980)
4.  William Morris, 'Commercial War', unpublished manuscript (Add. MSS. 45334, ff. 109–131), British Library
5.  Matrix, *Making Space: Women and the Man-made Environment* (London, 1984)
6.  Ciucci, Dal Co, Manieri-Elia and Tafuri, *The American City* (Cambridge, Mass., 1979)
7.  Manfredo Tafuri, *Teorie e Storia dell'Architettura* (Rome and Bari, 1976)
8.  Ibid.
9.  Karl Marx and Friedrich Engels, *The Holy Family* (1845)
10.  Nikolaus Pevsner, *An Outline of European Architecture* (Harmondsworth, 1942)
11.  Matrix, op. cit.

12.  Jean Chesneaux, *Pasts and Futures or What is History for?* (London, 1978)

8.  THE NEW SPIRIT
1.  Bryan Appleyard, *Richard Rogers: a Biography* (London, 1986)
2.  'Geosocial Revolution' (1965) from Buckminster Fuller, *Utopia or Oblivion* (Harmondsworth, 1970)
3.  Paul Goodman, *A Message to the Military Industrial Complex* (London, 1969)
4.  Ibid.
5.  E. M. Farrelly, 'The New Spirit', *Architectural Review*, August 1986
6.  In *De la Grammatologie* (Paris, 1967) and *L'Ecriture et la différence* (Paris, 1967)
7.  Elia Zenghelis, 'The Aesthetics of the Present', in Andreas Papadakis (ed.), *Deconstruction in Architecture* (London, 1988)
8.  *Architectural Review*, August 1986
9.  E. M. Farrelly, op. cit.
10.  Mike Cooley, *Architect or Bee?* (Slough, 1980)

9.  ACCORDING TO PLAN
1.  *Independent on Sunday*, 4 February 1990
2.  *Guardian*, 20 October 1990
3.  Manuel Castells, *City, Class and Power* (Paris, 1972 and London, 1976)

10.  BEYOND PERESTROIKA
1.  Janet Ramage, *Energy; a Guidebook* (Oxford, 1983)
2.  HRH The Prince of Wales, *A Vision of Britain* (London, 1989)
3.  C. Knevitt and N. Wates, *Community Architecture* (Harmondsworth, 1987)
4.  Ibid.
5.  HRH The Prince of Wales, speech at Hampton Court, 1984 quoted in Knevitt and Wates, op. cit.
6.  *Faith in the City*, The Report of the Archbishop of Canterbury's Commission on Urban Priority Areas (London, 1985)
7.  Karl Marx, Introduction to *A Critique of Hegel's Philosophy of Right* (1844)
8.  *Guardian*, 20 September 1991
9.  Don Cupitt, *The Sea of Faith* (London, 1984)
10.  David Sheppard, *Bias to the Poor* (London, 1983)
11.  Roger Garaudy, *L'Alternative* (Paris, 1972)
12.  HMSO, *People and Planning* (London, 1969)
13.  John Palmer, Introduction to British edition of Robert Goodman, *After the Planners* (Harmondsworth, 1972)
14.  Charles Jencks, *Modern Movements in Architecture* (Harmondsworth, 1973)
15.  William Morris, *How we live and how we might live* (1888)
16.  Rosa Luxemburg, *Reform or Revolution* (New York, 1970)
17.  Rosa Luxemburg, *Ausgewählte Reden and Schriften* (Berlin, 1955)

# Index

Figures in italics refer to captions